W9-BWF-114

CAMBRIDGE LATIN AMERICAN STUDIES

49

UNIONS AND POLITICS IN MEXICO

UNIONS AND POLITICS IN MEXICO

THE CASE OF THE AUTOMOBILE INDUSTRY

IAN ROXBOROUGH

*London School of Economics and Political Science and
Institute of Latin American Studies, London*

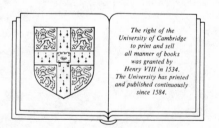

The right of the
University of Cambridge
to print and sell
all manner of books
was granted by
Henry VIII in 1534.
The University has printed
and published continuously
since 1584.

CAMBRIDGE UNIVERSITY PRESS

Cambridge

London   New York   New Rochelle

Melbourne   Sydney

Published by the Press Syndicate of the University of Cambridge
The Pitt Building, Trumpington Street, Cambridge CB2 1RP
32 East 57th Street, New York, NY 10022, USA
296 Beaconsfield Parade, Middle Park, Melbourne 3206, Australia

First published 1984

Printed in Great Britain at the University Press, Cambridge

Library of Congress catalogue card number: 84–4312

British Library cataloguing in publication data
Roxborough, Ian
Unions and politics in Mexico. – (Cambridge
Latin American studies; 49)
1. Trade-unions – Automobile industry workers – Mexico
2. Trade-unions – Mexico – Political activity
I. Title
331.88'1292222'0972   HD6534.A8

ISBN 0 521 25987 8

Contents

Tables

Figures

Acknowledgements

The research which is presented in this book was made possible by a grant from the Social Science Research Council and by grants from the universities of Glasgow and London. I would like to thank the directors of the Institutes of Latin American Studies in those two universities, Peter Flynn and John Lynch, for their assistance and encouragement with this project. Further work on the history of Mexican labour was made possible by a grant from the Nuffield foundation.

While I was collecting the data the cooperation of many people in the Mexican automobile industry was essential, and I would like to thank all those who made space in their crowded schedules to talk to me. On the whole, executives and union leaders were most helpful, with one notable exception. The management of the Volkswagen company refused to give me an interview, and in this they were atypical of the industry as a whole.

The Colegio de México was kind enough to provide infrastructural support during my stay in Mexico, and I would like to thank the then director of the Centro de Estudios Sociológicos, José Luís Reyna, for his help. My colleagues at the Colegio de México were invariably helpful and provided a stimulating and supportive intellectual environment. I would particularly like to thank Francisco Zapata for his help throughout this project.

Many other people in Mexico were also helpful. I will simply list the institutions which responded to my requests for assistance, and by so doing implicitly thank all those in them who facilitated my work: the Junta Federal de Conciliación y Arbitraje; the Departamento de Registro and the Centro de Estadística del Trabajo of the Secretaría del Trabajo y Previsión Social; the Asociación de Manufactureros de la Industria Automotríz; the Junta Local de Conciliación y Abitraje of the States of Mexico, Puebla and Morelos and of the Federal District; the Instituto Nacional de Estudios del Trabajo; the Centro de Estudios Históricos del Movimiento Obrero.

My research assistant, Miguel Zenker, helped greatly in the collection and organization of material for this book. A number of friends and colleagues discussed my work with me and tried to correct some of my errors. They are of course not to blame for those that remain. Mark Thompson, Ken Coleman, Ken Mericle, Richie Kronish, Doug Bennett, Ken Sharpe, Kevin Middlebrook, Javier Aguilar, Ilán Bizberg, Peter Worseley, Bryan Roberts, Alan Angell, John Humphrey, Rhys Jenkins, Danny James, José Luís Reyna and Manuel Camacho are the names that spring immediately to mind.

My secretary, Jenny Law, typed an immaculate first draft and then a series of equally immaculate amended versions.

Finally, it remains to thank my wife, Sharon Witherspoon, who took time off from her own work to help me clarify my ideas and improve the exposition. More importantly, she helped me in a number of non-instrumental ways which were equally essential for the completion of the final product.

FOR SHARON

Preface

I began this study with the object of examining what, in the early 1970s, was a widely held proposition about the role of organized labour in the political system of contemporary Mexico. Briefly, the idea had been developed that the emergence of new forms of 'independent' unionism would challenge the previously dominant forms of corporatist union control. The 'official' unions, tied to the dominant party, had been one of the major pillars of political stability in the post-war period. The development of this new form of 'independent' unionism, then, implied a potential threat to political stability in Mexico.

I decided to examine the behaviour of these independent unions in a single industry, the automobile industry, characterized by the coexistence of both independent and official unions. My aim was to see whether there really were important differences in behaviour between the two types of union.

The results of the empirical research suggested that there were, indeed, important differences between types of union in the auto industry, but that these differences could not be traced solely and exclusively to the dichotomy of independent versus official unionism.

As a result, I was led to explore the implications of my findings in a number of areas. On a fairly concrete level, the research presented in this book seemed to have a number of implications for theories of industrial democracy and militancy, particularly (though not exclusively) in third world countries. These are discussed in chapter 9.

As I moved deeper into the question of exactly how the much-cited but rarely analysed 'mechanisms of control and co-optation' actually operated in Mexican trade unions, I was led to re-examine the prevailing orthodoxy regarding the historical development of the Mexican labour movement and working class.

In my view, the generally accepted versions of Mexican labour history (and perhaps also of labour history in other Latin American and third world countries) place an exaggerated and one-sided emphasis on the fact of *control* over the rank and file, an emphasis which is detrimental to an understanding of the pervasive and persistent movements of worker militancy and insurgency.

Finally, in the concluding chapter of this book, I explicitly take up the original concern of the research project: the likely evolution of the Mexican political system. Here I examine the implications of my findings for certain currently fashionable theories of the relationship between the state and the working class in the third world, namely those theories which are now referred to under the heading of 'bureaucratic authoritarianism'. I then go on to offer some tentative guesses about the possible implications which trends in the Mexican labour movement may have for political stability in that country.

Abbreviations

BUO	Bloque de Unidad Obrera
CGOCM	Confederación General de Obreros y Campesinos de México
CGT	Confederación General de Trabajadores
CNC	Confederación Nacional Campesina
CNOP	Confederación Nacional de Organizaciones Populares
CNT	Central Nacional de Trabajadores
COR	Confederación Obrera Revolucionaria
CROC	Confederación Revolucionaria de Obreros y Campesinos
CROM	Confederación Regional Obrera Mexicana
CSUM	Confederación Sindical Unitaria de México
CTM	Confederación de Trabajadores de México
CUT	Central Unica de Trabajadores
FAT	Frente Auténtico del Trabajo
FITIM	Federación Internacional de Trabajadores de la Industria Metalúrgica
PLM	Partido Liberal Mexicano
PNR	Partido Nacional Revolucionario
PRI	Partido Revolucionario Institucional
PRM	Partido de la Revolución Mexicana
UGCOM	Unión General de Obreros y Campesinos de México
UOI	Unidad Obrera Independiente

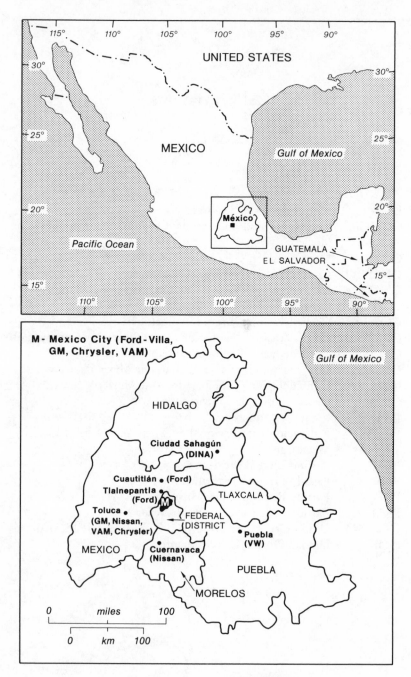

Location of automobile plants

1

Organized labour in Mexico

This book is about car workers in Mexico. Before beginning a detailed analysis of the material, however, it would be as well to situate this study in terms of the larger theoretical debate about Latin American workers and their insertion in the political systems of those countries.

After a brief discussion of these theoretical controversies, this chapter examines what may conveniently be described as the standard account of the historical development of the labour movement in Latin America and, particularly, Mexico. This analysis, which is widely accepted by social scientists, sees Mexican trade unions as more or less passive instruments of an authoritarian state. The corporatist control over labour, it is argued, results in the co-optation or repression of rank-and-file insurgency, and what might otherwise be a potential challenge to the stability of the political system is turned into a bastion of support for the regime. The argument presented in this book is that this 'standard account' is defective in a number of important areas and that, consequently, our understanding of the dynamics of the Mexican political system is in need of substantial modification.

The 'standard account' argues that the subordination of organized labour to the state has deep historical roots, and one of the aims of this chapter will be to provide a brief survey of the history of organized labour in Mexico, indicating on the contrary just how problematic state control over working-class mobilization has been. Whereas the standard account tends to suggest that the imposition of 'top-down' forms of corporatist intermediation has effectively removed any serious possibility of working class insurgency, the view advanced in this book is that rank-and-file insurgency has been a constant feature of Mexican industrial relations and that the control by the state over the organized labour movement is far more fragile and subject to contest than appears at first sight.

Studies of the industrial working class in Latin America have often

1

singled out two features as starting points for analysis: the recency of the formation of the industrial working class, and the heterogeneous structure of industrial employment. Given the fairly low levels of industrial development attained by most Latin American countries, the industrial proletariat is likely to be a minority of the labour force. Although some segments of the working class, such as railway and port workers, may have a long tradition of organization, by and large the bulk of the industrial proletariat, it is sometimes argued, will be composed of recent migrants from the countryside. Such migrants, on their arrival in the city, are faced with a labour market which is sharply divided into a modern, formal sector and an informal sector consisting of small workshops, artisanal enterprises and a wide variety of petty commodity trading and service enterprises. There is disagreement in the literature about the nature of the connections between the two sectors, and about the chances migrants have of passing from the informal to the formal sector.[1]

Nevertheless, it is widely believed that, in these conditions, labour movements in Latin America will differ significantly from their counterparts in the countries of the already industrialized West. Some of these arguments stress the more political orientation of unions in Latin America as compared with the primarily economic orientation of unions in Western Europe and North America. Since organized labour is only a small fraction of the total labour force, and since unemployment is high, the economic bargaining power of labour *vis-à-vis* employers is low. At the same time, because governments in many Latin American countries are relatively fragile, street demonstrations and urban rioting can often topple them or force major concessions. Therefore, the argument goes, instead of striking, unions put pressure on the government (by threatening violence) to intervene in industrial disputes and force employers to raise wages. So long as the real cost of providing foodstuffs to the towns can be kept down (by keeping the incomes of peasants and rural proletarians low), it is possible for the modern, urban sector to form an alliance against the rural poor.[2] This model has been described as one of 'political bargaining', as contrasted with the economic bargaining of trade unions in industrialized countries. Such an analysis is consonant with a description of the organized working class as an 'aristocracy of labour' whose interests are opposed to the unorganized poor. The utility of this description is taken up again in chapter 3. In the meanwhile, it is necessary to consider a second analysis of labour in Latin America which also emphasizes its links with the state. These theories, however, which focus on corporatist control of labour organizations, suggest that labour movements are likely to be weak, to lack autonomy and to be passive instruments of the state.

Theories of corporatism assert that unions are organized by the state and that the conduct of industrial relations is structured through a system of compulsory arbitration. The state oversees elections for union leaders (indeed, it often appoints such leaders), closely controls union finances, fosters a fragmented union structure which prevents the emergence of class-wide action, and effectively regulates industrial conflict and determines the outcomes of bargaining situations. In such corporatist systems, strikes are often restricted and, in any case, are of doubtful value to the workers since decisions concerning wages are made in the labour courts or by political fiat and not in company boardrooms.[3]

Labour in Latin America

Such theories, stressing the corporatist institutions of labour control, frequently locate the origins of these systems in the emergence of populist regimes in the 1930s and 1940s.[4] In this historical version, these theories are frequently referred to under the heading of 'bureaucratic authoritarianism'. Popularized by Guillermo O'Donnell, the notion of bureaucratic authoritarianism postulates a correspondence, or 'elective affinity', between stages of economic growth and the nature of the state, particularly in its relationship to the labour movement.[5] Although many Latin American countries had some industrial base at the end of the nineteenth century, the really dramatic expansion of industrial production began in the period between 1930 and 1950, during the phase of import-substitution industrialization. With the rapid penetration of Latin America by multinational corporations in the late 1950s and the 1960s, there was a further surge in industrial output. The figures for Mexican industrial growth are presented in table 1.1

This dramatic expansion of manufacturing industry involved the incorporation of massive new contingents of workers into the urban proletariat. In some cases, it appeared as if the established cadres of the urban working class were being swamped by these waves of new workers, lacking industrial experience, in many cases fresh from the countryside. According to the standard account, the result was twofold: at the level of the individual worker, it was hypothesized that the new industrial workers would be difficult to win over to specifically pro-

Table 1.1. *The Mexican economy and labour force*

	GNP (millions of 1980 dollars)	Value added by manufacturing (% total GNP)	EAP[a] (000)	% EAP in manufacturing	Unionized workers as % of EAP	
					Total EAP	EAP in manufacturing
1960	31,520	22.6	11,274	13.8	11.5	35.4
1970	62,114	27.1	13,345	16.9	15.0	36.3
1975	81,737	27.7	16,334	17.7	14.2	35.4

[a] Economically Active Population.
Sources: L. Solis, *La realidad económica mexicana* (México, Siglo XXI, 1970).
Nafinsa, *La economía mexicana en cifras* (México, Nafinsa, 1978).
Inter-American Development Bank, *Economic and Social Progress in Latin America 1980–81* (Washington, D.C., Inter–American Development Bank, 1981).

letarian ideologies. They would, instead, be inclined to support charismatic and authoritarian leaders who appealed to certain paternalist sentiments. At the level of the class, it is argued, the incorporation of these new contingents would reduce the urban working class to an amorphous, disarticulated mass. Given this, and the relative weakness of the nascent industrial bourgeoisie as a structured class, the state would be able to exercise considerable autonomy *vis-à-vis* civil society. Taken together, these phenomena set the stage for the emergence of populism in Latin America in the 1930s and 1940s. Charismatic caudillos like Perón in Argentina, Vargas in Brazil and Cárdenas in Mexico provided paternalistic substitutes for autonomous working class organization.[6]

With the arrival of populism in power, the working masses were organized from the top down into state-controlled labour unions. Systems of corporatist industrial relations were set up (the Mexican labour law of 1931 clearly belongs to this genre), and the state assumed the role of arbiter and director in industrial life. The working class remained fragmented by this corporatist structure, and subject to the dictates of the state. The wave of authoritarian military regimes in the sixties and seventies was then able to utilize these corporatist control systems to repress the working class and exclude it from political participation.[7]

This line of analysis then argues that in Mexico there was no abrupt transition from radical, civilian populism to military authoritarianism. There, the shift took place under the aegis of the dominant party, the

PRI (Partido Revolucionario Institucional – Institutional Revolutionary Party.) The trade unions were gradually transformed into passive instruments of the state, to be used to keep wages down in the service of capital accumulation and accelerated economic growth. This phenomenon is commonly known in Mexico as '*charrismo*', and will be discussed below.

This emphasis on the newness of the urban working class, then, led to the development of an analysis which stressed its lack of autonomy, and its passivity and weakness *vis-à-vis* the state. So long as the corporatist control mechanisms operated efficiently, the industrial working class would not engage in sustained militant activity at the industrial level and would be quiescent or pro-regime at the political level.

The second feature of the industrial working class in Latin America, the heterogeneity of employment, also led to the development of arguments which reinforced this image. The structure of industrial production, in terms of its effects on the distribution of the workforce by size of workplace, was highly dualistic in Latin American countries.[8] As table 1.2 indicates, this seems to be the case in Mexico. As a result, it has been argued, the labour force is divided into a small elite of privileged workers, employed in large, modern, multinational corporations, earning good wages and having secure employment, and a large mass of 'marginal' workers with low and irregular earnings, employed in small, technologically backward establishments. In this situation, the elite of the working class, or labour aristocracy, would have a vested interest in the *status quo* and would tend, therefore, to be politically conservative.

Objections to the standard account

Both of these approaches to the study of labour in Latin America call for a number of comments. In the first place, the contrast with the countries of advanced capitalism is overdrawn. The state has always intervened in industrial relations in Western Europe and North America, and union movements in these countries have never been apolitical.[9] Nor is it immediately obvious that the high levels of unemployment in contemporary Latin America serve significantly to differentiate these labour movements from their precursors at early stages of industrial development in the West. This is so for two reasons. First, unions in North America and Western Europe had to deal with the problems of mass unemployment and potential strikebreaking. Secondly, it is not

Table 1.2. *The Mexican industrial labour force, 1970*

Fixed capital (pesos)	No. establishments	%	Total gross production (%)	No. employees	%	Average No. employees/ establishment	Average annual wage (pesos)
0–3m	115,295	96.9	21.5	713,368	45.9	6	11,113
3m–20m	2,712	2.3	25.8	371,837	23.9	137	22,942
20m+	968	0.8	52.7	469,969	30.2	485	32,438
Total	118,975	100	100	1,555,174	100	13	20,383

Sources: Jaime Osorio, 'Superexplotación y clase obrera', *Cuadernos Políticos*, no. 6 (1975).

clear how easily workers in the modern industrial sectors in Latin American countries could be replaced by strikebreakers drawn from the ranks of the unemployed. Quite apart from shortages of experienced and skilled workers, there are often important institutional constraints on employers' ability to dismiss labour, and this makes direct industrial action a more meaningful response by trade unions.

Moreover, to draw the contrast between Latin American countries and the countries of advanced capitalism in terms of the notion of corporatism is rather difficult. The industrial relations systems of advanced capitalist countries are marked by many corporatist features,[10] and it is not clear that there is a significant difference in this respect between the two groups of countries. The criteria for differentiating between different types of industrial relations are seldom explicitly stated in a way that would enable researchers to measure such supposed significant differences in a clear and unambiguous manner. Moreover, corporatism is very much a matter of degree. Industrial relations systems may have a corporatist appearance: the real question is the extent to which the conduct of industrial relations actually fits this model. Here it is important to examine the minutiae of day-to-day shop-floor conflicts as well as the well-publicized national agreements. An excessive attention to the latter may well exaggerate the extent to which corporatist structures accurately reflect the nature of industrial conflict.[11]

These qualifications suggest the need to integrate a concern with the political orientations of organized labour with a detailed account of industrial conflict at the shop-floor level.

This general picture of workers in Latin America commands wide-spread assent. Nevertheless, it has recently been subject to a number of criticisms, some of which are germane to the argument which will be developed in this book. Here I will briefly indicate some of the difficulties involved in this account of Latin American labour history before examining the Mexican case in some detail.

The regimes of Juan Domingo Perón (1945–55) in Argentina and Getulio Vargas in Brazil (1930–45), together with the Cárdenas government in Mexico (1934–40), have frequently been seen as key examples of populist regimes which fit the historical pattern described above. The massive organization of recent migrants from the countryside by these personalist dictators, it is argued, swamped the socialist and Communist unions, and created the basis for a labour movement controlled from above. With the advent of authoritarian regimes, the populist labour movements were either utilized (in the case of Brazil) to implement anti-working-class policies, or (in the case of Argentina) constituted a serious menace to the regime and were, therefore, the object of implacable hostility.

There is, however, evidence to suggest that this picture of populist labour mobilization is not entirely accurate. M. Murmis and J. C. Portantiero,[12] Walter Little[13] and J. C. Torre[14] have all criticized aspects of this model as applied to Argentina. They assert that the mass demonstrations which released Perón from prison and eventually carried him to power were not spontaneous, 'popular' demonstrations, but were the result of a calculated decision to give critical support to Perón by the major trade unions. The established sector of the working class was as supportive of Perón as were the newer contingents. Moreover, the process of turning the unions into passive instruments of state policy was slow, problematic and actively resisted by many groups of workers. Working class support for Perón, moreover, can be explained largely with reference to increasing standards of living in the 1940s and the contrast with the actively anti-labour regimes preceding Perón. There is no need, therefore, to invoke low levels of class consciousness or direct and unstructured ties between a disorganized mass and a charismatic leader to account for working class support for Perón. It can be explained in largely instrumental terms. In all of these ways, the standard account presents a distorted picture, one which downplays the coherence and rationality of trade union responses.

The 1930–45 Vargas government fits the analysis even less. Unlike the Argentine case, there was little working class mobilization during Vargas' dictatorship. The government was hostile to unions and sought to diminish their power.[15] It was only with the return to free elections in the postwar period that unions were able to develop. This period did, indeed, see substantial working class mobilization and the widespread use of populist appeals by a variety of politicians, including Getulio Vargas. But it is crucial that the period of 'populist' politics in Brazil (1945–64) was one of free elections and competitive political mobilization. The unions in this period, quite contrary to the standard account, developed a considerable measure of autonomy and coherence.[16] It was for precisely this reason that the unions had to be radically reorganized after the military coup of 1964.

These and similar arguments suggest that the standard account of labour history in some of the major countries of Latin America is open to question on a number of matters of empirical detail, objections which call into question the utility and validity of the account as such. In this book, it will be argued that this is also the case with Mexico.

As far as Mexico is concerned, the prevailing notions about the development of a corporatist labour movement offer a strikingly one-sided account. As will be argued below, the standard emphasis on the corporatist control of the labour movement by the state needs to be balanced by an analysis of the forces making for continued rank-and-file insurgency.

The standard account of the historical development and political behaviour of the urban working class in Mexico and in the rest of Latin America is based on a broad generalization from what was believed to be an accurate description of historical reality. In fact, until recently, there have been very few detailed monograph studies of workers in Latin America. Only in the second half of the 1970s did a substantial number of research publications begin to appear. In the light of this new body of literature, it is increasingly clear that the standard account of Latin American labour history presents an over-homogenized picture. The differences in the historical experiences of labour movements vary markedly between one Latin American country and another. It is more and more difficult to discern some 'modal pattern' of which particular countries are simply variants.

It has also become increasingly clear that, for each Latin American country taken on its own, the received notion of the historical development of the labour movement is subject to historiographical debate. The historical contours and defining features are by no means as clear as some theorists believe. Although this argument could be made for the majority of Latin American countries, our present concern is with Mexico.

The history of Mexican labour

The second half of the nineteenth century saw a number of attempts at union organization in Mexico. The mutualist associations which grew up under the modernizing dictatorship of Porfirio Díaz (1876–1911) were frequently formed by urban artisans. Towards the end of the century, they were joined by unions of textile workers and of miners.[17] The nascent industrial proletariat was regionally dispersed, and had considerable difficulty in establishing permanent and meaningful organizations. Although anarchist and utopian socialist ideologies were widespread among the workers, there was also a sizeable section of the working class which believed that its best chance lay in support for the

Díaz regime; it hoped thereby to win concessions and benefits from the government. This division of the labour movement into apolitical anarchism and a pro-government wing continued through the revolution of 1910 and until the 1930s. Porfirian economic growth had created the beginnings of a modern proletariat, and the later years of the dictatorship were marked by major strikes at the Cananea copper mine in 1906 and at the Río Blanco textile mill in the following year, strikes which threatened the political stability of Mexico and which were put down with force by the government.[18]

Some authors have seen these strikes as precursors of the revolution of 1910. Certainly, some part had been played by the Partido Liberal Mexicano, which had made efforts to organize workers in the mining and textile centres. Led by the Flores Magón brothers, the PLM subscribed to an eclectic ideology with strong anarchist overtones. The PLM was active in the northern part of the country when the revolution broke out in 1910, but after ephemeral successes in Baja California, it was rapidly eclipsed by other revolutionary movements. Ricardo Flores Magón was imprisoned by the United States authorities. In any case, there is some doubt as to whether the PLM had any profound or lasting influence among Mexican workers. Moreover, although the strikes of 1906 and 1907 were taken seriously by the government and were put down with considerable violence, it is by no means clear that they were a major factor in bringing about the revolution of 1910.[19]

Like most major events, the Mexican revolution was the result of a complex concatenation of causes.[20] On the one hand, the rapid modernization of the country under the Paz Porfiriana had brought in its wake a number of social tensions. The expansion and consolidation of large landed property had brought with it the expulsion from the land of a number of peasant communities, particularly in the central highlands, and had led to the rapid proletarianization of large numbers of rural labourers. Elsewhere in the country, the picture was somewhat different, with the development of medium-sized ranchos oriented toward commercial production occurring in some regions in the north and in parts of the Huasteca. In the north-west, the expansion of the latifundios had exacerbated the endemic conflicts with the Yaqui Indians, and the attempt by the Porfirian state to resolve this problem by the forcible transplanting of indians to Oaxaca and the Yucatán had merely aggravated the situation. On top of these structural changes in the agrarian sphere, a series of bad harvests and economic recession in 1907 raised tensions in the countryside to a dangerous degree.

To this agrarian crisis was added an intractable political crisis concerning the presidential succession of 1910. Without the political crisis, the agrarian tensions of the first decade of the twentieth century would merely have been yet another in a long series of rural uprisings which marked nineteenth-century Mexico. This political crisis had been engendered by the very nature of the Porfirian political system. Díaz had surrounded himself with a select coterie of political advisers and henchmen, the so-called *científicos*, embued with a positivist ideology which justified an elitist approach to government. By the systematic use of machine politics and patronage, coupled with the persecution of political opponents, Díaz and the *científicos* were able to maintain themselves in power during thirty years of profound social change. But the cost was an increasing distance between the Porfirian ruling elite and large sectors of the economically dominant classes, particularly the commercial agrarian bourgeoisie of the north.

Díaz, possibly in an attempt to cut the ground from under his critics' feet, in an interview with an American newspaperman let it be known that the upcoming elections of 1910 would be relatively fair and open.

However, as the date for the elections approached, Díaz, having made the fatal mistake of raising the expectations of his opponents, retracted his promises of free elections and began to take steps to get himself re-elected yet again. This was too much, and Francisco Madero and others took up arms against the dictator.

The Mexican revolution of 1910 shattered the political stability of the Porfirian dictatorship. Although the moving forces of the revolution were the peasants and certain sections of the northern bourgeoisie, rather than the urban working class, the revolution represented a major opportunity for working class organization. In 1911 an anarcho-syndicalist organization, the Casa del Obrero Mundial, was formed around a nucleus of printing workers in Mexico City. The early revolutionary government of Francisco Madero was weak, and the Casa adopted an aggressive and militant posture, called a number of successful strikes and rapidly expanded its membership. When Madero was overthrown by the reactionary forces of Victoriano Huerta in 1913, the Casa initially refrained from attacks on the government. By the end of the year, however, it had moved into opposition and, by the time Huerta was defeated by the revolutionary army of Venustiano Carranza in 1914, enjoyed widespread support among the working class of Mexico City.[21]

By now the revolutionary forces had split into two wings: the peasant armies of Francisco Villa and Emiliano Zapata, the 'Conventionalist' forces; and the 'Constitutionalist' armies under the bourgeois leadership of Carranza. The latter moved rapidly to enlist organized labour in its cause.

In 1915, one of the leading Carranza generals, Alvaro Obregón, negotiated with the Casa del Obrero Mundial for them to supply the Carranza armies with six army battalions, drawn from the ranks of the workers, in exchange for government support for the organization of the working class in Constitutionalist territory. It is unclear how important these 'Red Battalions' were in the military conflict with the peasant armies of Zapata and Villa.[22] Nevertheless, some historians have tended to see this action of organized labour as a betrayal of the possibility of a worker–peasant alliance and as subserviance to the bourgeois forces represented by Carranza and Obregón.[23]

Whatever the merits of the case, some sections of organized labour did well under the victorious revolutionary governments of Adolfo de la Huerta and Obregón. For a while the Casa prospered under the Carranza government. Nevertheless, continued inflation, unemployment and food shortages created urban unrest and, in 1915 and 1916, the Casa led a number of bitter strikes. The reaction of the government was clear. First, the Red Battalions were disarmed and demobilized. Then, when the Casa announced a general strike, martial law was declared, the strike broken and the Casa suppressed.

Attempts by the workers at resistance failed. After some sporadic street-fighting, it became clear that the government forces had the upper hand. The defeat of the Casa was a severe blow to anarcho-syndicalist aspirations. However, the revolutionary governments needed labour support. Within the ranks of labour, the anarchist debacle had cleared the way for the ascendancy of a new breed of reformist leaders who were willing and eager to work together with the government. The alliance was cemented with the formation in 1919 of the Confederación Regional Obrera Mexicana (CROM), under the leadership of Luís Morones.[24]

The initiative to form the CROM came when the governor of the northern state of Coahuila sponsored a meeting of labour organizers at Saltillo in 1918. Leadership of the new organization was rapidly assumed by Morones and his political camarilla, the Grupo Acción. Explicitly opposed to the now largely discredited anarchist strategy of placing emphasis in the general strike as the principal method of political action, the Grupo Acción sought to use their links with the state as a way of obtaining concessions. They formed the Partido Laborista Mexicano as the political wing of the CROM and set out to increase their access to government office. In addition to important posts in both federal and state governments, the CROM sought to place its representatives on the Juntas de Conciliación y Arbitraje which were being set up in a number of states and which often proved to be the key arbiters of industrial conflict.

This organization supported the new *caudillo*, Alvaro Obregón, in the overthrow and assassination of Carranza in 1920 and, when Obregón was challenged by the de la Huerta uprising of 1923, moved to his aid. In return, the CROM received official support in its unionization efforts. This government patronage was necessary in the CROM's struggle against the still powerful anarchist enclaves in textiles, urban transport, railways and elsewhere.

— In 1921 an anarcho-syndicalist confederation was formed, the Confederación General de Trabajadores (CGT), and the 1920s were a period of intense and bloody internecine strife between the 'red' CGT and the pro-government CROM.[25] It is no small tribute to the combativeness of the workers of the CGT that they survived many of the attacks against them. The textile zones of Atlixco and Metepec, close to the city of Puebla, were the scene of intense fighting between the CROM and the CGT. In some cases, the workers on the day shift would belong to one confederation and the workers in the same mill on the night shift might belong to the rival confederation. During periods of tension, many workers would take pistols to work with them, and there were several incidents when rival groups clashed, or when workers from one mill attacked workers from a mill belonging to a rival confederation. The army garrison was constantly called upon to control the disorders.[26]

A similar situation prevailed on the railways. The majority of workers were enrolled in CGT-affiliated unions. But a substantial minority of workers in the *departamento de vías* were organized into a CROM union. The presence of CROM members within the railways meant that strikes against the government were always extremely bitter, and often violent.[27] The fact that large parts of the countryside were still only marginally under government control meant that there were powerful pressures by the military to keep the trains running, and that strikes could easily be seen as acts of treason. This was particularly so during the war of the Cristeros, 1926–9, when large parts of central and western Mexico were the scene of prolonged conflict between Catholic insurgents and government forces.[28]

Elsewhere, the CROM was able to use its position of strength to defeat its rivals in the union movement.[29] Strikes declared by non-CROM unions were declared illegal or non-existent by the CROM-controlled *juntas de conciliación* or by the CROM-controlled Ministry of Labour, Industry and Commerce. Not surprisingly, official strike statistics for this period fell to dramatically low levels. Rather than an indication of a state of industrial harmony, these strike statistics merely emphasize the extent to which the CROM was able to use its influence in the state apparatus to further its own ends.

The years of defensive struggle against the CROM had a high cost for the 'red' CGT. Its energies expended in a series of rearguard actions, the political practice of the CGT became increasingly divorced from its radical anarcho-syndicalist ideology. By the end of the decade the CGT was eager to curry government favour and had, *de facto*, abandoned its revolutionary pretensions in exchange for the feeble hope of government patronage. Indeed, given the political situation in Mexico, this was by no means an unrealistic posture on the part of the CGT.

Given the level of official support for the CROM, it is by no means easy to assess the relative strengths of the various tendencies in the Mexican union movement in the 1920s, particularly in a rapidly changing situation. There is little doubt that the CROM greatly increased in strength and influence during the Calles regime, and was able to actively repress its competitors. From the point of view of both Obregón and Calles, the CROM was able to provide an important base of support. The events of the de la Huerta uprising of 1923 give some indication of this.

When, in 1923, Adolfo de la Huerta decided to challenge Obregón over the question of the Bucareli agreements which effectively gave American oil companies a number of important concessions, important sections of the organized labour movement actively supported him. This revolt was a major challenge to the government and, after some months of fighting, left a total of some 20,000 dead. Against the insurrectionary forces, which included two-thirds of the regular army, Obregón called upon peasant and worker militias. The Partido Nacional Agrarista armed 6000 men. The CROM and the PLM in Puebla alone put some 10,000 men into arms under the command of General Celestino Gasca.[30]

In 1924 Obregón handed power over to Plutarco Elías Calles. The relationship between organized labour and the revolutionary regime became even closer. Morones was given a cabinet post as Minister for

Industry, Commerce and Labour. Nevertheless, by the time of new presidential elections in 1928, Morones' aggressive self-serving and political ambitions had led to a major split with Calles.[31]

Already by 1927 Morones' name had been put forward as a possible presidential candidate by a substantial group of his supporters. The CROM was divided over this issue, with substantial minority groups within the organization supporting other candidates or arguing for an apolitical stance. Internal dissent began to develop in the CROM and some unions began to disaffiliate. A substantial section of the labour movement refused to support Morones' bid for the presidency and switched support to Obregón, who appeared to be the likely winner. But before Obregón could assume the presidency he was shot dead outside a restaurant in Mexico City by a Catholic activist, outraged at the anticlerical policies of the Sonoran jacobins. Tension rose, and the CROM was accused of being the 'intellectual author' of the assassination. It was widely rumoured at the time that the CROM was responsible for the deed, and Calles moved immediately to distance himself further from the CROM. With its protection by the state removed, the CROM began to disintegrate. Starting in 1928, and gathering momentum in the next few years, union after union began to disaffiliate from the CROM. Once again Mexican labour organizations were divided and engaged in a bitter struggle for control of the working class movement. The CROM was struck a further blow when Portes Gil became President in that year. Portes Gil was actively opposed to the CROM, and sought to weaken it at every available opportunity.

The first important section to disaffiliate from the CROM was the powerful Federación Sindical de Trabajadores del Distrito Federal in 1929, led by Fidel Velázquez and Fernando Amilpa. Together with Jesús Yurén, Alfonso Sánchez Madariaga and Luís Quintero, they became known as the '*cinco lobitos*', the 'five little wolves'. In the early twenties, Fidel Velázquez and Alfonso Sánchez Madariaga had founded the Unión de Trabajadores de la Industria Lechera and had organized the dairy farms which at that time surrounded the city. With this as their base, they extended their operations to urban transport and municipal workers, linking up with the other three '*lobitos*'. The next step was to organize hotel workers and workers in the multitudinous small industries in the capital. By the time they left the CROM, the '*cinco lobitos*' controlled an extensive network of unions in the capital city. Based predominantly in small enterprises, such unions depended heavily on support from the state rather than on any inherent industrial

muscle. This was rapidly forthcoming; control of the Juntas de Conciliación y Arbitraje was handed over to the '*cinco lobitos*' by the
incoming – and strongly anti-CROM – President, Emilio Portes Gil.[32]

Then in 1932 the few unions which remained to the CROM in the
Federal District were lost as Alfredo Pérez Medina led another breakaway movement and founded the Cámara del Trabajo. This new
organization rapidly secured the allegiance of the CGT, the Federación
Sindical de Trabajadores del DF (controlled by the '*cinco lobitos*'), and a
number of important unions such as the electricians, the railway
workers and the tramway operatives. In 1933 Pérez Medina was
instrumental in securing the affiliation of the Cámara del Trabajo to the
official party, the PNR (Partido Nacional Revolucionario, forerunner
of the PRI). This provoked considerable internal dissension, and the
Cámara collapsed into its constituent parts. Both the CGT and the '*cinco
lobitos*', together with many of the other unions, attacked Pérez Medina
for getting them involved in politics, and left the organization.

Paradoxically, the collapse of the Cámara came as yet another body
blow to the CROM. The CROM had not collapsed overnight, when it
fell from official favour in 1928. Certainly, Morones' hold over the
organization had been broken and he himself soon ceased to exert any
appreciable influence in the CROM. Since 1928, a reform wing within
the CROM, led by Vincente Lombardo Toledano, had tried to separate
the CROM from the Partido Laborista, but their efforts had been
consistently frustrated by the Grupo Acción. In 1933, with the first
attempt at unification under the aegis of the Cámara in ruins, Lombardo
Toledano seized his opportunity. In a celebrated speech entitled 'El
Camino está a la Izquierda', he effectively split from the CROM,
claiming that his supporters constituted the real CROM, the 'CROM
depurada', the 'purified CROM'. With this new excision, all that
remained to the CROM of Morones and the Grupo Acción were a
number of unions, primarily in the textile industry in Veracruz, Puebla,
Tlaxcala, Jalisco, Durango, Baja California and Zacatecas. The CROM
depurada, on the other hand, had enough strength to serve as the magnet
for another attempt at unification, and in October 1933 the majority of
Mexican union organizations formed the Confederación General de
Obreros y Campesinos Mexicanos.

Thus, by the beginning of the 1930s, four major organizations were
locked in conflict for control of the Mexican working class: the CROM,
fallen from grace but still powerful; the once militant CGT, now eager
to step into the place of honour vacated by the CROM; the unions

which had broken away from the CROM, headed by Vicente Lombardo Toledano, and now mainly grouped into the CROM *depurada*; and the unions organized by the Communist Party, the Confederación Sindical Unitaria de México (CSUM). It is difficult to measure the strength of Communist influence in the Mexican labour movement during the thirties, but it was much more widespread than the simple numerical strength of the CSUM might indicate. In the revolutionary climate of Mexico, and particularly after the Comintern's adoption of the Popular Front line in 1935, the Mexican Communists were able to command considerable support in many parts of the Mexican union movement.[33] In practice, Communist union tactics in the early thirties were oriented toward building up cells within existing unions, though they did manage to create or take over a number of smallish unions. The Communists were particularly successful in building up support in the railway unions and, to a lesser extent, in the electricians' union.

The final steps in the unification process were triggered off by events in national politics. As Cárdenas assumed power, the bulk of organized labour was hostile to or at least suspicious of him, viewing the Cárdenas government simply as another continuation of the Callista Maximato. The labour movement was only now recovering from the disastrous years of the late twenties and the early thirties. Together with the disintegration of the CROM and the bitter infighting of the period, Mexican trade unions had been severely weakened by the economic recession. Many unions, including such important sectors as the railways, had been faced with massive layoffs and wage cuts. However, by the mid-thirties, a general recovery was apparent, and the number of strikes began to rise sharply in 1933, in the last year of Abelardo Rodríguez' presidency. Cárdenas was to inherit this strike wave.

With the disastrous experience of the CROM fresh in their minds, the Lombardista unions and the bulk of the industrial unions were reluctant to get involved in political alliances with the state. The Communist Party, for its part, was still following the extremist policies of the 'Third Period', and had adopted the policy of 'Ní con Calles, ní Cárdenas' ('Neither Calles nor Cárdenas').

Such was the situation in the union ranks when the Calles–Cárdenas conflict became the major issue of Mexican politics. This conflict had been in the making for some months, and Cárdenas had been preparing for a split with the 'Jefe Máximo' by reorganizing key posts in the army so as to prevent a Callista military uprising. The rupture itself was sparked off by Calles' criticism in June 1935 of the strike wave, his accusation that Cárdenas was doing nothing to stop it, and his demand for a toughening of the law on strikes. Calles' remarks brought forth a wave of protest from the unions. The Electricians summoned a meeting at which was formed the Comité Nacional de Defensa Proletaria.[34] In the same year the Communist International had changed its line and now advocated a policy of Popular Fronts.

Cárdenas thus found himself with the bulk of the organized labour movement as an unexpected ally in his fight to liberate himself from Calles' tutelage. As for organized labour, the political crisis and mass mobilization provided the final impetus for the formation of the Confederación de Trabajadores de México (CTM) in 1936.

Instead of continuing the Maximato, a system whereby the incumbent President was largely a figurehead, with real power being wielded behind the throne by Calles, the new President moved to establish his independence of his former mentor. Calles challenged Cárdenas; a political crisis ensued, in which the bulk of organized labour demonstrated its support for the new President; and Calles, together with his now faithful crony, Luís Morones, was banished from the country.

With this major threat to his power removed, Cárdenas embarked on a series of major reforms, including the nationalization of the railways and the oil industry. He also moved to reorganize the political system. The dominant party was reorganized. From being an agglomerate of local clienteles, it was transformed into a corporate structure. The new party, the Partido de la Revolución Mexicana (PRM), was composed of four sectors: labour, comprising the recently formed CTM, the CGT, the CROM and some individual unions; the peasant sector, represented by the Confederación Nacional Campesina (CNC); the military; and the popular sector, brought together in an umbrella organization, the Confederación Nacional de Organizaciones Populares (CNOP), created to unify diverse groups of state employees, middle class supporters of the government, housewives and tenants' associations, etc. Perhaps more important than the corporatist reorganization of the official party were the moves by Cárdenas to complete the institutionalization of the army and to destroy the last of the regional caudillos. Cárdenas initiated a major reorganization of the army, placing his own supporters in key positions and demoting or retiring many Callistas and Obregonistas. He did the same with the state governorships, and by 1938 had established his control firmly at all levels. In Veracruz the disarming of the peasant leagues was completed.[35]

At the founding convention of the CTM, Lombardo Toledano was elected General Secretary of the organization. The other posts in the new organization, however, were bitterly contested by the *'cinco lobitos'* on the one hand and the Communists and the industrial unions on the other. Miguel Velasco, a Communist union organizer, was elected organizational secretary of the CTM. The ex-CROMistas, led by Fernando Amilpa and Blas Chumacero, immediately proposed that Fidel Velázquez be given the post or they would leave the CTM. The Communist Party – anxious to preserve the unity of the new organization – withdrew Velasco's candidature. With this key post in their hands, the *'cinco lobitos'* began to stack the cards in their favour, granting official recognition to union leaderships which were loyal to them, and supporting parallel unions and oppositional caucuses.

These organizational manoeuvres were not to the liking of the industrial unions. In June 1936 the mining and metallurgical union left the CTM, and at the Fourth National Council of the CTM in 1937 the conflict between the Communists and the supporters of Fidel Velázquez split the organization down the middle. The three Communist secretaries in the CTM operated from the headquarters of the railwaymen's union, while the four secretaries who supported the Lombardo–Velázquez line remained where they were. Each group claimed to represent the CTM. Although there are major discrepancies in the figures offered by the two sides in the dispute, there is little doubt that the decision by the industrial unions (together with a number of other groupings) to leave the CTM had seriously weakened the organization.[36]

Faced with this situation, Lombardo Toledano persuaded the Communist International to intervene. Earl Browder, leader of the Communist Party of the USA, was ordered to Mexico to enforce compliance with the International's line.[37] This he succeeded in doing, and with a statement supporting 'Unity at all costs' the Mexican Communist Party returned to the fold. It used its influence in many of the industrial unions to persuade them also to return to the ranks of the CTM. This sudden switch in tactics greatly strained the relations between the Communist Party and the leaders of the industrial unions, and was a clear signal to the *'cinco lobitos'* that they could more or less do as they liked without fear of major repercussions. During these conflicts between the left and the *'cinco lobitos'*, Vicente Lombardo Toledano sought to maintain a posture of neutrality, although in practice he generally decided in favour of the Velazquista faction.

By 1938 the epoch of major reforms had come to an end. The official party had been reorganized, the army brought completely under control, a massive agrarian reform carried out, the conflict with the church ended, petroleum nationalized, and the labour and peasant organizations organized as more or less unconditional supporters of the government. There were, however, still threats to the regime from the right. Juan Andreu Almazán had considerable support from the middle classes, and from sections of society which had not benefited directly from the Cardenista reforms (and which had suffered the effects of escalating inflation in 1938 and 1939). The Sinarquista movement constituted a potential base of rightist mass mobilization.

In this situation the question of who would be designated as the official candidate for the 1940 election became vital. Despite considerable leftist support for Múgica, Cárdenas clearly preferred a candidate of conciliation, Manuel Avila Camacho. Worried by fear of a possible civil war or a fascist putsch, Lombardo Toledano, with the examples of Spain and Germany vividly in mind, pronounced, on behalf of the CTM, in favour of Avila Camacho. Such was the dominance of the pro-government forces within the CTM that the left could do nothing to promote Múgica's candidacy and had to content itself with verbal protests. In November 1939, the Sindicato Mexicano de Electricistas, never very happy with the situation in the CTM, broke away and declared itself apolitical. With the Second World War, the Mexican government put pressure on the unions to aid the Allied war effort by accepting wage restraint. (It should be noted that the Communist Party did, of course, support this line and therefore offered no serious opposition to the CTM leadership.)[38]

In March 1941, President Avila Camacho modified the labour law so that workers could be fired for participating in 'illegal' strikes. The law of social dissolution was used against strikers, and in 1942 the main labour organizations signed a 'workers' solidarity pact' in which they agreed not to strike for the duration of the war. This posture was reaffirmed in April 1945 with the signing of the Pacto Obrero Industrial between the CTM and one of the employers' confederations, CANA-CINTRA. Once again the CTM pledged itself to work for harmony in labour relations. But if there had perhaps been some reason in signing a no-strike pledge in the early days of the war, there could be little justification for a similar agreement at the very end of the war except, of course, under the banner of national unity and economic growth.[39]

But while the CTM bureaucracy was moving to the right, real wages had dropped dramatically during the war. The result was an explosion of strike activity in 1943 and 1944, and the emergence of internal conflicts in the CTM. Not only did the number of strikes increase to an all-time high, but the number of strikers shot up to 165,000. Strike activity was higher than during the heady days of Cárdenas.

The years immediately following the end of the Second World War were troubled ones for Mexican labour. The final years of the war had witnessed an upsurge in union militancy, despite – or because of – the no-strike pledges of the CTM. The rapid inflation and the tremendous demand for industrial production acted together to produce a climate of restiveness amongst organized labour. As a result, the period between 1946 and 1949 witnessed a series of dramatic challenges by the forces of the left, challenges which were soundly defeated and which set the basis for the economic miracle of the fifties and sixties. The events of this period are complicated and are only now beginning to receive the attention they deserve from historians. These events include a struggle for the leadership of the CTM; an attempt to establish a rival confederation; the establishment of an opposition mass party; the expulsion of Lombardo Toledano (and later the Communists) from the CTM; and a series of internal conflicts in the major industrial unions which are referred to as the '*charrazo*'. The ideological context for these struggles was given by the onset of the Cold War and by a general shift to the right by the ruling party.

By 1946 the CTM had become heavily dependent on government support and was in many ways an extremely weak and fragile organization. In the elections for the General Secretary of the CTM in that year, the left put forward the leader of the railway workers' union, Luís Gómez Z, against the candidate of the '*cinco lobitos*', Fernando Amilpa. When the result was declared in favour of Amilpa, Gómez Z and the railway union withdrew from the CTM in protest. At the same time, there was considerable dissatisfaction within the CTM over the decision to affiliate with the PRI. At the beginning of 1947 Gómez Z established the Central Unica de Trabajadores (CUT).[40]

While the railway union was in the process of distancing itself from the CTM, the opposite appeared to be happening in the petroleum workers' union. The nationalization of the petroleum industry in 1938 had brought with it the unification of numerous small unions into a single national union. It also meant that the diverse contracts hitherto prevailing in the industry had to be unified, and this was necessarily a process of high conflict, with the union insisting that wages be levelled upwards. In the last two years of his presidency, Cárdenas and the petroleum workers' unions were continually at loggerheads, and the period up to 1946 was marked by considerable tension between PEMEX and the union. In April 1946 the union went on strike and, in so doing, incurred the hostility of the CTM. Fidel Velázquez, the incumbent General Secretary, publicly denounced the strike as unnecessary, and, in retaliation, in July the petroleum workers' union refused to recognize the national committee of the CTM. In January 1947, PEMEX took the unusual step of initiating a legal proceeding against the union. The response by the union was confused and divided. An oppositional group, led by Abrego, was elected to replace the existing executive committee, reaffiliated with the CTM, and strove to harmonize relations with the enterprise.

There were, however, protests from a number of sections, and by December 1947 there was a successful move to remove Abrego from the union, and elect Ibáñez as General Secretary. With the petroleum workers' union back in the militant camp, the three major industrial unions – railway workers, petroleum workers and miners – formed, in January 1948, a triple alliance, pledging themselves to come to each other's aid in the event of a strike.

Meanwhile, back in the CTM, events had gone from bad to worse. In November 1947, Amilpa engineered the expulsion of Lombardo Toledano from the CTM, and led a witch hunt against the Communists, resulting in a purge of Communists in the following year. Indeed, the heavy-handed actions of Amilpa had become so counterproductive that Fidel Velázquez apparently felt obliged to unseat him late in 1947, and take control of the CTM once more.

Outside the CTM, the alliance of the industrial unions posed a major threat to the confederation's claim to speak for the Mexican working class. At the same time, the project which Lombardo Toledano had initiated in 1946 of creating a new leftist party had got under way with the formation in 1948 of the Partido Popular. Although this party was later to become a factor of very minor importance in Mexican politics, in the period between 1948 and 1952 it had many of the characteristics of a mass party, and appeared to many to have considerable political potential.[41] It brought together many sections of the Mexican left, particularly a number of independent Marxists.

With the expulsion of Lombardo Toledano from the CTM, the situation appeared ripe for a new regrouping of the forces of the left. Moves began to constitute a new union confederation in opposition to the CTM. Before they could prosper, however, events in the railway workers' union signalled the beginning of a government counteroffensive.

The events surrounding the change of leadership in the railway workers' union which is popularly known as the '*charrazo*' are still by no means entirely clear. In elections for the executive committee of that union in January 1948, one of Gómez Z' supporters, Jesús Díaz de León, nicknamed 'the Charro' for his passion for dressing in the traditional cowboy, '*charro*' style, complete with silver-buckled tight trousers and wide-brimmed hat, was elected General Secretary. However, according to Luís Medina,[42] Díaz de León was, compared with Gómez Z, a relatively unknown and minor figure, and Gómez Z continued to exert considerable influence in the running of the union. In September 1948, in order to break free of Gómez Z' power, Díaz de León accused the former Secretary-General and the previous Treasurer of misuse and theft of union funds. This was a risky move on the part of Díaz de León, since only a minority of the sections supported him. He turned, therefore, to the government for assistance. Instead of taking the case up with the union's internal vigilance committee (staffed by supporters of Gómez Z), Díaz de León took the case to the public courts, to the Procurador General de Justicia.

While this was happening, the internal vigilance committee (on 12 October) removed Díaz de León from his post as union head and replaced him with Francisco Quintana. Díaz de León replied by forcibly seizing the union headquarters, and, in the face of a resolution by the Ministry of Labour that Díaz de León was the legitimate head of the union, there was little that the opposition could do. With clear support from the government, Díaz de León began a mass purge of his opponents.[44]

The significance of the *charrazo* lay in the fact of deliberate government intervention to support one union faction against another. By so doing, the government was essentially able to control the major unions directly. The *charrazo* in the railway workers' union was followed by a similar intervention the following year in the petroleum workers' union, and by a *charrazo* in the important mining and metalworkers' union in 1950. (Some historians argue that the 1947 change of leadership in the petroleum workers' union also constituted an example of a *charrazo*, though there is little evidence of direct government intervention. In any case, pro-government leadership in the petroleum union lasted only a few months before being thrown out by rank-and-file protest.)[45]

By the time the Lombardista unions called for the formation of a new union confederation, the Unión General de Obreros y Campesinos de México (UGOCM), in 1949 the tide had already turned. The railway workers were now under the tutelage of pro-government leaders; the electricians, always suspicious of inter-union alliances, had returned to their preferred tactic of remaining independent; and only the miners and the deeply divided petroleum workers supported the formation of a new confederation. The petroleum workers were to return to the CTM in 1950, following the *charrazo* of 1949. In the face of government hostility, the UGOCM gradually fell apart, losing the major industrial unions as these fell victim, one by one, to *charrazos*. By 1952 the UGOCM was clearly a force of minor importance, Lombardo Toledano's hopes for a mass leftist party had been dashed, and he himself had lost nearly all his former standing in the ranks of Mexican labour.

The Mexican labour movement had undergone a massive reorientation in the late forties. Perhaps most symbolic of the nature of this change were the switch in the slogan of the CTM in 1947 from 'For a society without classes' to 'For the independence of Mexico', and the designation of President Miguel Alemán as 'obrero número uno de la patria' (worker number one of the Fatherland) – strange title for someone who was to preside over the *charrazos* of 1948 and 1949. Perhaps equally symbolic of the prevailing Cold War climate was the initiative taken by Chief Justice Corona in February 1948 to restrict the right to strike, an initiative which failed, but which clearly revealed the discomfiture of the industrialists and sections of the government with worker militancy.[46]

Finally, the economic context of the defeat of industrial militancy must be noted. July 1948 saw a major devaluation of the peso. The breaking of a possible union offensive to regain higher wages was to prove, in years to come, to have been a major foundation stone for the new phase of the Mexican miracle; the phase of 'stabilized development'.

Throughout the 1950s dissident sections of Mexican unionism initiated a number of attempts to wrest the CTM's dominant position away from it. These attempts at unification outside the CTM were supported by the state, following the corporatist logic of unification–organization–control. In 1952 several of the non-CTM forces were unified in the slightly left-of-centre Confederación Revolucionaria de Obreros y Campesinos (CROC), which affiliated to the PRI.

The CTM, the CGT, the CROM and several national industrial unions (Telephone, Electricity, Mining, Railways, etc.), partly in response to the formation of the CROC, formed an umbrella organization – the Bloque de Unidad Obrera (BUO) in 1955. This remained a purely paper organization. The CROC never affiliated, and the BUO was dissolved in 1966 to give way to what is now the Congreso del Trabajo, Mexico's latest umbrella organization.

Despite the devaluation and inflation of 1954, the economy continued to grow in the post-war period and – depending on the industry – real wages generally rose in the 1950s. Nevertheless, the period saw major wage conflicts, culminating in the railway strikes of 1958–9.

The importance of the railwaymen's strikes of 1958–9 (strikes mainly over wages) was that the incumbent *charro* leadership was ousted by a relatively unknown militant group, led by Dimitrio Vallejo. The strike was conducted as a series of regional strikes, and the government conceded many of the demands of the strikers until March 1959, when it moved against the strikers with massive repression. The leadership was imprisoned, many workers were arrested and some 20,000 workers lost their jobs. The reason for the display of force seems fairly evident: 'During the second half of 1958, and the first quarter of 1959, Mexico was very close to political instability. It had been demonstrated that the working class, with a purely relative and in some measure autonomous organization, was capable of placing the system in check.'[47]

Nor were the railway workers alone in demonstrating the essentially fragile base of the *charro* union bureaucracy. A similar movement had developed in the national teachers' union, and the immediate aftermath of the railwaymen's defeat witnessed massive purges in the teachers' union and in the telephone and petroleum workers' unions.

But despite these repressive measures, the militant sectors of Mexican unionism continued to be a force to be reckoned with. The electrical industry continued its tradition of being a stronghold for industrial militants, and these workers, together with the CROC, brought together a rival to the BUO in the form of the Central Nacional de Trabajadores (CNT) in 1960. However, the oppositional nature of the CNT and these sectors of militant unionism must not be overstated. The CNT has always been an opposition within the terms of the Mexican political system, and it should come as no surprise to discover that the CNT and the BUO merged in 1966 to form the Congreso del Trabajo.

With the Congreso del Trabajo we come to the recent period. Like the BUO, the Congreso is largely a paper organization, and its constituent parts retain their autonomy. Thus, the old conflicts between the CTM and its rival confederations, and the uneasy relationships between the confederations (composed mainly of small unions in traditional sectors) and the national industrial unions, continue, as does the constant conflict between the rank and file of the labour movement and the union leadership.

Charrismo

The persistence of this opposition to the union bureaucracies, and its occasional, though often short-lived successes, suggest a re-evaluation of the concept of *charrismo*. Rather than a monolithic and all-powerful system of control (which is an image widely diffused in the Mexican left) I would argue that union bureaucracies are often in relatively weak positions and that their methods for controlling their membership vary considerably from one union to another. Only in key national disputes, such as the railway strikes of 1958–9, is the full weight of state repression used. Although the state frequently intervenes in the internal affairs of industrial unions (such as the electricians) in an attempt to impose its own preferred leaderships, there are definite limits to its ability to do so with any degree of success and maintain a certain degree of legitimacy.

But this sort of direct government interference has not been used as frequently as some interpretations of Mexican labour might suggest. Contrary to much current thinking on the subject, the Mexican state appears to allow considerable autonomy to many unions, intervening only in major national conflicts. This has meant that, in the post-war period, a considerable degree of complexity has characterized the union structure of Mexico. Like union officials in many countries, the established leaderships of many Mexican unions have sought to retain their power and to influence their rank and file in the direction of moderate policies. In some unions incumbents have been challenged by insurgent tendencies, sometimes successfully, often unsuccessfully. It is this rather than the direct intervention of the state which accounts for much of the conservatism of large parts of the Mexican labour movement.

A weak labour movement?

The prevailing picture of Mexican working class organization emphasizes the weakness of trade unions as bargaining agents acting to enhance the interests of organized labour. The unions are generally held to have a restricted coverage and to be ineffectual in raising wages for all but a few privileged workers. Paradoxically, the reason for the weakness of trade unions *vis-à-vis* employers is seen to stem from the strength of the union bureaucracy *vis-à-vis* its membership. There is no contradiction here. The state supports the union leaderships against possible insurgent movements within their unions and, in return, union leaders act in a 'statesman-like' manner to secure 'responsible', moderate wage increases.

As evidence for this interpretation it is frequently pointed out that the distribution of income in Mexico has become increasingly unequal in the post-war period. This is indeed so.[48] However, with a growing GNP *per capita*, a regressive redistribution of income is not necessarily incompatible with rising real wages. Indeed, throughout most of the post-war period, real wages for industrial workers have risen. The analysis by M. Everett suggests that 'there was a considerable fall in real earnings during the beginning of the 1940s, stagnation during the period 1945–55, and a strong upwards movement during 1955–63'.[49] A slightly different conclusion is reached by J. Bortz. His data indicate a decline between 1939 and 1946, followed by an almost uninterrupted rise between that date and the recession of 1975.[50]

These data are susceptible to differing interpretations, depending on whether emphasis is placed on the war-time decline in wages or on the post-war growth. Clearly, the experience of the war years, particularly as it followed on the heels of the pro-labour Cárdenas administration, was a traumatic shock for many workers. The rapid inflation, coupled with the no-strike pledges of the CTM, had a devastating effect on real wages. A major outbreak of strike activity at the end of the war testifies to the massive discontent which had accumulated. It is hardly surprising that for many years workers felt that they were bearing the cost of industrial growth. (Indeed, Bortz' data indicate that the purchasing power of wages did not return to its 1939 level until 1969.)

On the other hand, particularly for workers entering the labour force after the war, the period up to the mid-seventies was one of constantly rising incomes. For those workers whose reference point was the post-war period, they had reasons to believe that their unions were, indeed, delivering the goods. Whether the unions could have done more, and secured higher rates of wage increases, must remain an open question. Nevertheless, it is difficult to argue an *a priori* case that the unions were weak or that they clearly acted against their members' interests. Such arguments depend entirely on counterfactual assumptions about what *might* have been possible, rather than on what actually occurred. The data on wages do not necessarily lead to the conclusion that Mexican unions are weak. Nor do the data on levels of unionization, if we now return to that issue.

The Mexican economy as a whole, and manufacturing in particular, expanded rapidly in the period after 1940. The labour force also grew, particularly in manufacturing, and by 1975 some 18 per cent of the economically active population was employed in manufacturing (table 1.1). As table 1.2 indicates, nearly half of Mexico's industrial labour force worked in small establishments. Nevertheless, some 30 per cent of the industrial workforce, nearly half a million workers, were employed by a small number of large enterprises. Their average wages were nearly three times those earned by workers in small-scale industry. This difference in wages rates is also reflected in table 1.3. Clearly the industries which tended to be characterized by large-scale modern establishments paid higher wages than other industries. There can be no doubt that car workers are among the highest-paid sections of the Mexican working class.

Not surprisingly, levels of unionization mirror this general picture. Both table 1.1 and table 1.4 indicate that, despite the fairly low level of unionization in the economy as a whole,[51] over a third of the industrial labour force is unionized. Because Mexican labour law has a closed-shop provision, this means that nearly all modern, large-scale industrial enterprises are 100 per cent unionized. This is the situation, for example, in the automobile industry, at least for manual workers.

It could reasonably be argued, however, that the data on strike activity in Mexico indicate the weakness of the union movement. Strike frequency is not high, and this is often attributed either to the weakness of unions (which do not wish to risk losing a strike) or to the pro-government (and hence anti-strike) attitude of union leaders. In general, both these arguments have some force, though it should also be borne in mind that the industrial relations system encourages settlements in the labour courts and the Ministry of Labour without recourse to strike action.

The question is, however, bedevilled by the usual problems with Mexican official data. As Francisco Zapata notes in his review of Mexican official statistics on labour, 'their reliability is deficient, and they must be used with extreme caution'.[52] In the first place, data on the number of workers involved in strikes and the number of days lost are

Table 1.3. *Wages in Mexico City, by industry, 1975*

Industry	Weekly take-home pay (1975 pesos)	Hourly rate (1975 pesos)
Automobiles	1203	27.6
Tyres	1749	41.3
Cement	807	23.5
Furniture	704	17.4
Beer	777	17.0
Shoes	688	14.9
Printing	730	15.2
Minimum wage	444	7.9

Source: Secretaría de Programación y Presupuesto, *Trabajo y salarios industriales 1975* (México, SPP, 1977), pp. 6–8

not always available for every year. For most purposes, therefore, the *number* of strikes must be used as the sole measure of strike propensity. Unfortunately, a simple index of strike frequency fails to tell us either how long the strikes were or how many workers were involved. It therefore represents only one of the three dimensions of strike activity which are of interest. Secondly, the government only publishes data on *legal* strikes. A sizeable, but unknown, number of strikes are declared illegal, or fail to meet the requirements that they be declared legal, and are not counted in the official statistics.

A third difficulty stems from the division of the Mexican labour force into two parts, one subject to federal jurisdiction and the other falling under local jurisdiction. Many statistics, including strike frequency, are published separately for federal and local jurisdiction. This is not, in principle, a problem, since the two sources can be summed. Nevertheless, not all investigators appear to be aware of this division of strike statistics into two parts, and often publish analyses based on only one set of statistics.[53]

I have been unable to obtain a complete time series of strikes in industries under federal jurisdiction. However, the data for the period 1972–6 appear to be as shown in table 1.5. In this period, the number of workers in each jurisdiction was approximately equal, though there were about four times as many unions registered under local jurisdiction. There appears to be little or no relation between the strike trends in the two parts of the labour force and, hence, any study based on only

Table 1.4. Unionization in Mexico, 1971

Sector	EAP (000)	% of total	No. unions	% of total	Workers unionized	% of total	Average no. workers/union	% unionized per sector
Total	13,697	—	16,332	—	2,122,533	—	130	15.5
Primary	5,306	38.7	1,786	10.9	156,248	7.4	87.5	2.9
Industry	3,182	23.2	7,482	45.8	1,168,367	55.0	156	36.7
Services	5,209	38.0	7,064	43.3	797,918	37.6	113	15.3

Source: Nafinsa, *La economía mexicana en cifras,* p. 413.

Table 1.5. *Strikes and unionization in federal and local jurisdiction, 1972–6*

	Local jurisdiction			Federal jurisdiction		
	No. unions	Membership	Strikes	No. unions	Membership	Strikes
1972	13,871	1,161,908	207	3,081	986,581	33
1973	14,291	1,183,454	136	3,175	994,999	92
1974	14,822	1,211,531	337	3,267	1,013,812	400
1975	15,339	1,233,918	236	3,421	1,061,218	121
1976	15,799	1,254,993	547	3,740	1,180,000	107

Sources: Anuario estadístico de los Estados Unidos Mexicanos 1975–6 (México, Secretaría de Programación y Presupuesto, 1979); *Memoria de Labores 1975–6* (México, Secretaría de Trabajo y Previsión Social, 1976).

one section may well be misleading. Fortunately, since the purpose here is merely to provide illustrative background for the study of industrial relations in the automobile industry, these methodological headaches may be left to other researchers.

On the whole, the arguments about the weakness of the Mexican labour movement, whether based on its relationship to government, on coverage or on strike frequency, are not conclusive. Before asserting that the Mexican labour movement is weak, more detailed analyses of union behaviour are necessary. Perhaps, in comparison with labour movements in Chile and Argentina (during periods of civilian government), the Mexican labour movement may be regarded as relatively weak. But the degree to which one can speak, in absolute terms, of the strength or weakness of Mexico's trade unions is still an open question, and the standard account is, once again, open to serious challenge. The apparent surface tranquillity of Mexican industrial relations cannot be attributed to the existence of weak unions and a strong state without a number of important qualifications.

Within a panorama which appears on the surface to be one of complete domination of the union structure by a corporatist state apparatus, acting to further the rate of capital accumulation by restraining wages and discouraging strikes, there is a hidden complexity. While the central role of the Mexican state in the conduct of industrial relations must not be lost sight of, a realistic assessment of the Mexican union movement must give due weight to the continuing and widespread combativeness of large sections of the industrial labour force, and to the problematic nature of the control exercised by union bureaucracies over their rank and file.

In the 1970s yet another element was added to further complicate the picture. Throughout the post-war period, rank-and-file militancy had taken the form of oppositional caucuses within the unions affiliated with the official party. These movements were particularly strong in the national industrial unions,[54] with the smaller unions being largely exempt from internal challenges. The new factor was the creation, in the 1970s, of a number of 'independent' unions. Mexican labour law allows for the formation of a variety of types of union, including company or plant-wide unions. During the government of Luís Echeverría (1970–6), some of these smaller unions broke away from the CTM to form a new union confederation which was not affiliated to the PRI.

Independent unions

The account of Mexican labour history presented above indicates that the control of the labour movement by the trade union bureaucracy has not gone unchallenged. Insurgent movements have always been a feature of Mexican unionism. In the 1970s, however, they took on a new form. Previous union reform movements had generally been attempts by factional groups, or rank-and-file movements, to wrest control of the union from incumbents. Now these were joined by a wave of breakaway movements. The general pattern was for individual factories to secede from the official union and set up their own 'independent' union, independent in the sense that it was not affiliated with the official party or with the official union structure.[55]

This movement was given the tacit support of President Echeverría, in a bid to distance himself from the CTM, as part of a more general 'opening' of the political system. The authoritarian governments of the 1950s and 1960s had largely managed to repress, but not to release, the tensions generated by rapid economic growth, urbanization and social change. A particularly dramatic incident occurred in 1968 when protesting students were massacred by police and army units at the Tlatelolco housing estate in Mexico City.[56] Echeverría clearly felt that the political system had suffered a serious erosion of legitimacy, and moved to present himself as a reforming President, free from binding ties to the more conservative elements of the *ancien régime*, such as the CTM. Without the tolerance of the President, it is unlikely that the wave of independent unionization which marks the 1970s would have taken place. (The breach between Echeverría and the CTM was rapidly healed. Nevertheless, a certain political space was indeed opened, and the independent unions emerged to fill it.)

By the late seventies, over a hundred independent unions had been .formed. These were located in a variety of industrial sectors including textiles, the metal and rubber industries, and food processing. Most of these unions joined a new independent federation, the Unidad Obrera Independiente (UOI). Among these independent unions were three in the automobile industry. The state-owned DINA plant in Ciudad Sahagún, the VW plant in Puebla, and the Nissan plant in Cuernavaca all split away from the CTM and formed independent unions, affiliated with the UOI. Other plants in the automobile industry remained under the control of the CTM.

The emergence of these independent unions on a wide scale in the 1970s, together with increasing militancy of oppositional movements in the national industrial unions, raised a number of questions about the possible future of industrial relations in Mexico. Did the independent unions represent a new phenomenon in Mexican labour conflict? Would they behave differently, particularly in pressing wage claims more strongly and in striking more frequently than the official unions? Would there be a realignment in the union movement, with the leftist forces gaining strength; and would such a change imperil the basis of political stability in Mexico?

Mexican authoritarianism

Many political scientists had argued that the political stability of post-war Mexico, and the impressive rates of economic growth of that period, rested on the corporate control of subordinate classes by the Mexican state.[57] In so far as control over urban labour was concerned, it was argued that the corporatist provisions of the Federal Labour Law of 1931, together with the control of the union bureaucracy by the 'charros', meant that rank-and-file militancy was restrained, strikes were few and predictable, wages rose less than productivity, and organized labour could be counted on as a fundamental pillar of support for the policies of the regime. By not pressing wage claims and by abstaining from the use of the strike weapon, organized labour simplified the government's task of macroeconomic management and helped create a propitious climate for foreign investment. The emergence of labour insurgency in the form of the growth of independent unions might mean the erosion of this system of political control and, perforce, a radical restructuring of the system of political alliances in Mexico.

Although, as will be argued in chapter 10, the authoritarian features of the Mexican political system may have been somewhat exaggerated, there is a considerable element of truth to the descriptions. It is difficult to deny that political stability and control over labour are not conducive to economic growth.[58] However, to argue this is not to assert any necessary connection between economic growth and control over labour. Control of the labour movement may facilitate economic growth; it is difficult to argue that it is a prerequisite. Nor is it necessary to argue that there is an 'elective affinity' between certain stages of economic growth and certain state forms, as some theorists of 'bureaucratic authoritarianism' appear to suggest.[59] The utility of authoritarian control is not confined to any specific situation. Rather, authoritarianism is a tendency inherent in all capitalist states. To conflate the notion of authoritarianism with that of corporatism is a mistake. The Mexican political system exhibits both authoritarian and corporatist features. The link between them is, however, by no means as clear as the standard account would have it. In the standard account, the success of Mexican authoritarian government is due, in part, to the functioning of corporatist structures of control over labour. The argument of this book is that corporatist control over labour in Mexico is both weaker and more uncertain than the standard account implies, and that the long-run trend is to further weaken corporatist mechanisms.

There is also always a tension between authoritarian control and the need for legitimacy. The ways in which a balance is struck between legitimacy and authoritarianism vary widely, of course, and it is likely that certain forms of development will tend to produce highly authoritarian state forms. The point, however, is that the need for legitimacy on the part of the Mexican state ought not to be de-emphasized, as many analyses of the authoritarian features of the Mexican political system do. It is precisely the need for legitimacy and the relative openness of the political system that permit independent union movements to develop, even though such developments bring with them the risk of political instability. The question revolves around the ability of the Mexican state to resolve the conflicting goals of the maximization of capital accumulation and the minimization of the use of political violence. The response to the development of a variety of potential challenges, including labour insurgency, may possibly entail major changes in the nature of the Mexican political system.

2

The Mexican automobile industry

Research design

In chapter 1, I argued that the history of labour in Mexico illustrated a continual conflict between militant initiatives on the part of the rank and file and the desire by conservative union leaders and government officials to avoid strikes and 'excessive' wage increases. Control by the state over the union movement was, I argued, much more problematic than might be inferred from the 'standard account' of the history of Mexican labour. In the 1970s rank-and-file militancy increasingly took the form of breakaway movements from the official union confederations and the establishment of 'independent' unions. This development raised the question of whether such unions would be more radical than the official unions, and whether growth in the independent union sector would alter the existing role played by Mexican unionism in supporting political stability and economic growth. It was in the light of these general questions that the research presented in this book was designed. The most general aim of the research was to see whether there were, indeed, important differences in union behaviour between the independent and the official union sectors, and to consider further whether such difference might have implications for political realignments in Mexico.

With this in mind, a decision was taken to focus on the automobile industry. Given the presence of both types of union in that industry, and given the relatively homogeneous structure of the industry (this will be qualified later), it was felt that a study of the automobile industry would yield results which might, with certain qualifications, be generalized to other sectors of industry. This is taken up in the final chapter. This chapter outlines the historical development of the Mexican automobile industry up to the late 1970s. Following this, intra-industry differences in strike propensity are discussed. This is the principal measure of the

35

degree of conflict-proneness of each union in the industry. It is demonstrated that the nine unions clearly fall into two discrete categories: the 'militant' and the 'conservative'. This division into militant and conservative unions, together with the distinction between independent and official unions, provides a starting point for the analysis of the correlates of these differences which occupies chapters 5 through 8. Chapter 3 of this book presents an overview of wages and conditions of work in the Mexican industry and some data on the social origins of workers in that industry, and addresses itself to the question of whether militancy is correlated with a more rapid growth of wages. Chapter 4 offers an overall view of the development of industrial relations in the industry, on a company-by-company basis.

Chapters 5 through 8 proceed to examine systematically the hypotheses about differences in union behaviour which are set out below. Chapter 9 summarizes the conclusions of the research and speculates on the possible causes of the patterns of industrial militancy identified. (Readers may wish to begin with this chapter, before reviewing the evidence which is presented in detail in chapters 5 through 8.) Finally, in chapter 10, some speculations about the possible implications of the research results for our understanding of contemporary Mexican politics are presented. At the risk of repetition, it should be emphasized at this point that the aim of this book is to examine the impact on political processes in Mexico of the specific forms which class conflict takes at the level of the factory, at the level of trade union organization, and at the level of political alliances.

The hypotheses

The principal questions are set out below in the form of a list of hypotheses. This is largely an expositional device to clarify the issues. There is no intention of making any claim that this work meets all the criteria of a strictly scientific enquiry. Nevertheless, I have done what I can to examine the various propositions as critically as possible and to examine the evidence with a view to invalidating the hypotheses presented. The principal hypothesis examined in this book is that the behaviour of the independent unions in the automobile industry differs from that of the official unions in that industry. Specifically, it is hypothesized that

(1) independent unions will have a greater strike propensity than official unions;

(2) independent unions will be more likely to engage in conflicts over conditions of work than official unions;

(3) independent unions will be more likely to attempt to control the internal labour market than official unions;

(4) the number of shop-floor union officials, their range of power and discretion, will be greater in independent unions than in official unions;

(5) there will be a greater measure of internal union democracy in independent unions than in official unions;

(6) independent unions will secure higher wage increases and fringe benefits than official unions;

(7) a greater percentage of the work force will have job security in the independent unions than in the official unions;

(8) within the ambit of the system of labour courts, the official unions are more likely to be involved in conflicts with their own members than are the independent unions; conversely, the independent unions are more likely to support members' grievances against employers than are the official unions.

These hypotheses have their counterpart null hypotheses. Against the hypothesis that the independent unions are more militant and democratic, there is the counter hypothesis that there are no discernible differences between the two groups of unions. This alternative hypothesis suggests that, far from being a radical innovation, the independent unions are independent in name only. In all other respects, they behave exactly as do the official unions. This might be called the '*neo-charro*' hypothesis.

The following chapters will discuss the evidence for and against these hypotheses in some detail. At this point, before discussing some of the methodological issues raised by the study, it may be useful briefly to anticipate some of the research findings.

It will be argued throughout the book that the evidence strongly supports the notion that the independent unions are, in many respects, quite different in behaviour from most of the official unions in the Mexican car industry: they strike more frequently, are more democratic, have stronger shop-floor representation, are more likely to engage in conflicts over work processes and job security. But within the six official unions two unions stand out as anomalies: the Ford union and the union in GM's Mexico City plant. Both of these unions closely resemble the independent unions in their behaviour. It must be concluded, therefore, that the simple distinction between independent and official unions fails to capture the variation in styles of union behaviour in the Mexican automobile industry.

However, it cannot be said that the null, or neo-*charro* hypothesis is a better predictor of union behaviour. It seems better to reformulate the original hypothesis, rather than abandon it completely. It will be argued in this book that there are, indeed, two styles of unionism in the Mexican automobile industry, one militant and the other conservative. It will be further argued that the cause of this difference lies in the establishment of an institutionalized form of internal union democracy at some point in the history of the union concerned. Those unions in which democratic procedures become institutionalized for some reason or other (at a later point in the book the possible reasons for the emergence and consolidation of union democracy will be explored in more detail) will, it is here argued, be more militant. This is so because, where union democracy prevails, the rank and file will pressure the union leadership to bargain more aggressively. Of course it is by no means the intent here to counterpose an 'iron law of democracy' to Michels' famous iron law of oligarchy.[1] Nevertheless, it does not seem unreasonable to argue that the forms of internal union government have some influence on union policies.

These issues will be discussed at various points below. In the meanwhile, some methodological issues need to be clarified.

Methodological issues

The hypotheses outlined above are presented as a static comparison. They might usefully be reformulated in dynamic terms, since it is of interest to know the likely direction of future trends. Concretely, are the militant and democratic unions becoming less militant and democratic, or are they likely to retain their democratic structures and continue to be more combative than their official counterparts? Are the official unions likely to remain as conservative as they are at present, or are they likely to become either (a) more repressive of their rank-and-file membership or (b) more militant as they respond to competition from the other unions?

The data gathered for this study cover a ten-year period. While this is adequate for a static comparison, it is too short a time period to do more than offer a very rough answer to the dynamic questions. Nevertheless, some projections are possible, even on the basis of such a short time period, providing the reader accepts the cautious and provisional nature of the extrapolations.

The unit of analysis in this study is the individual union. The research is a comparison among nine separate and distinct unions in the Mexican automobile industry. The hypotheses all refer to aspects of union behaviour. This means that the research problem is approached from a specific starting point and that a number of interesting alternative approaches to the study of industrial conflict in the Mexican auto industry are not considered in any detail.

For example, this study does not use the kind of data on the attitudes and opinions of individual workers which might be obtained by sample surveys or by participant observation. This does not imply that such data are of no relevance or interest. Rather, both the theoretical formulation of the research problem and the time and resources available pointed in the direction of different sorts of data. The principal concern of this book is with differences in types of union behaviour. Of course, such an analysis has implications for more general questions about the industrial and political militancy of the Mexican working class, and some indirect evidence can be derived from the data generated in this study. This is done in chapters 9 and 10. Nevertheless, it is perhaps worth emphasizing that the interest in questions about comparative union behaviour pointed in the direction of certain types of data and not others.

The nine unions considered in this book are all relatively small; the biggest has about ten thousand members. They are all basically similar in structure as well as in size, and present few problems of comparability.

The data in this study are drawn basically from three types of sources: from interviews with trade union leaders, industrial relations executives and a variety of other key participants in the industry; from union contracts; and from a variety of archives. These included the archives of the Secretaría del Trabajo, a sample of one hundred cases of individual grievances in the federal labour courts, union and company archives, and newspaper and periodical sources. With the exception of Volkswagen (a result of non-cooperation on the part of management), all the union leaders and industrial relations executives in the industry were interviewed. Often more than one union official or executive from a given union or company was interviewed, and some informants were interviewed several times. The interviews were semi-structured, and generally lasted about an hour.

The universe for this study was defined as all the unions in plants or enterprises which produced passenger cars in Mexico in 1978. There were seven companies producing cars in a total of thirteen plants. These companies were unionized either on a plant-wide basis or on a company-wide basis, with a total of nine unions in the industry. Each union held exclusive jurisdiction of the blue collar workforce in its plant or company. Some companies had multiple plants which were organized into a single union (Ford, Chrysler and VAM), others had multiple plants which were organized by different unions (GM, Nissan), and the rest (VW and DINA) each had one plant with one union. The situation in the industry is set out in table 2.1

Clearly, the unit of analysis for this study could have been the enterprise, the plant or the union. Since the aim was to explain differences in union behaviour, rather than differences in strike-proneness among different plants or enterprises, the choice of the union as the unit of analysis was obvious. Nevertheless, these factors have not been neglected entirely in the discussion which follows.

The fieldwork was carried out mainly in 1978. Some data were also gathered during shorter visits in 1976, 1977 and 1981. The research, then, basically refers to the situation in the decade of the 1970s. Whether patterns and trends observed will also hold for the next decade or so is discussed in chapter 10.

Validity and reliability

As the data are gradually introduced in chapters 5 through 8, specific problems of validity, reliability and interpretation will be discussed in the context of the various hypotheses. At this point some general comments may perhaps be in order.

Many researchers have noted the very considerable difficulties involved in the collection of valid and reliable data in Mexico. Evelyn Stevens devotes nearly one-third of her book *Protest and Response in Mexico* to a discussion of the problems involved in research in Mexico. She says that in Mexico there is a

generalized attitude toward information as a potentially dangerous weapon . . . Data are both scarce and unreliable . . . interpersonal communication by Mexico's Spanish-speaking population is characterized by a high degree of indirectness, evasiveness, cryptic remarks, and deliberate falsification.[2]

Mexicans delight in misleading each other, but they enjoy even more the opportunity of misleading foreign researchers.[3]

The problem is particularly acute in the field of industrial relations. There have been very few empirical studies of industrial relations in

Table 2.1. *The Mexican automobile industry*

Enterprise	Started production	Ownership in 1977	Principal plants	Units produced (000)		No. workers	
				1974	1978	1974	1978
Nissan	1966	Japanese	Cuernavaca; Toluca	19.8	26.6	2452	3284
DINA	1954	Mexican govt (Renault licence)	Ciudad Sahagún	17.4	13.6	6539	7000[a]
VW	1966	German	Puebla	104.1	86.3	11,067	8845
Ford	1926	US	Mexico City (3 plants)	33.5	31.5	4721	6486
GM	1935	US	Mexico City; Toluca	18.0	21.8	5610	6221
Chrysler	1938	US	Mexico City; Toluca	35.6	43.0	5000[a]	7313
VAM	1953	60% Mexican govt; 40% American Motors (US)	Mexico City; Toluca	20.2	19.8	1673	1013

[a] Estimate.

Sources: Secretaría de Programación y Presupuesto, *La industria automotriz en México* (México, SPP, 1981); Secretaría de Industria y Comercio, archives.

Mexico until recently. Those that have been published have frequently relied almost exclusively on newspaper and other documentary sources. At the time that this research was carried out, there were only a limited number of studies on the Mexican automobile industry published or in process, many with an anthropological focus on the individual case study and none which used a variety of data sources and/or research techniques to compare the different forms of union behaviour systematically. The most comparable study was one by Francisco Javier Aguilar, though his research was based almost entirely on newspaper sources.[4] As a result, the study presented in this book was conducted in largely unexplored terrain. The various studies in progress or completed by other researchers were often of considerable help in specific areas, and they have been drawn on throughout this book, but very little systematic comparative work seemed to have been done, either in the automobile industry, or elsewhere for that matter. (The situation, it should be added, is now rapidly changing, and more and more researchers are now turning their attention to the empirical study of industrial relations in Mexico.)[5]

This meant that much effort had to be expended to obtain even the most elementary information about wages and strikes in the industry. Even the collection of a series of union contracts proved to be a major undertaking, and it was not always possible to get a complete series for each union. Like much of Mexican political life, industrial relations have, at least until very recently, been shrouded in a certain degree of secrecy and obfuscation. It was only in 1977, for example, that workers in the Ford Motor Company in Mexico were given copies of the union contract. Until 1965 only the union head had a copy of the contract. The general obfuscation and lack of information were, of course, a useful weapon for conservative union leaders as well as for company management since they made rank-and-file opposition harder to organize. In this general climate even elementary pieces of information, such as the seniority structure of a given company, were often unavailable or could only be obtained with considerable effort. (It must be said that some companies, such as the Ford Motor Company, VAM and Nissan were extremely cooperative and open. But this was by no means a general attitude in the industry.) Despite these difficulties, much could be done, and the bulk of the data employed in this book have been taken from sources which indicate a very high degree of validity and reliability. More important than such problems is the matter of missing information. In some parts of this study, complete sets of comparative data simply were not available. Although this necessarily restricts some of the conclusions which can be drawn, by and large such gaps in the data as do exist are relatively minor. More specific methodological issues are discussed at relevant points throughout this book.

The Mexican automobile industry

The definition of the automobile industry used in this study is a somewhat restrictive one: it includes all enterprises which manufacture passenger cars, but excludes parts manufacturers and enterprises which produce only tractors or trucks. Of course, the manufacturers of passenger cars also produce other things. Some also produce trucks or tractors; some produce auto parts for sale to other subsidiaries of the same corporation. This heterogeneous production structure, of course, makes certain comparisons (of productivity, for example) very complicated. Moreover, even in terms of passenger car output, there are considerable differences in the products sold by each company, VW, for example, specializing in the production of smaller and cheaper vehicles.

In the period up to the late 1960s, the Mexican automobile industry was essentially an assembly industry, based on completely knocked-down (CKD) kits imported from the USA. There were a large number of producers, selling a wide range of models. In 1958, the Mexican auto industry consisted of eleven firms producing 44 makes and 117 models.[6] In the 1960s the Mexican government decided to rationalize the industry by reducing the number of auto producers and restricting the range of models produced, and by encouraging manufacturing in Mexico.[7] In 1962, after protracted bargaining between various multinationals and the Mexican state, a decree was passed restricting the number of automobile producers to seven, and requiring that 60 per cent of the value of the cars be produced in Mexico.[8] This was the situation when the data were gathered for this study in 1977 and 1978. Since then there have been some changes in the legal situation and in the structure of the industry, but these do not affect the results of this study in any way.

After the 1962 integration decree, seven enterprises produced passenger cars in Mexico: Ford, General Motors, Nissan, Diesel Nacional (DINA), Vehículos Automotores Mexicanos (VAM), Chrysler and Volkswagen. The majority were wholly owned subsidiaries of foreign multinationals. Two enterprises, VAM and DINA, had substantial amounts of Mexican state capital. The former produced American Motors vehicles, with a 40 per cent share of capital held by American

Motors and 60 per cent held by SOMEX, a Mexican financial development corporation. DINA was a wholly state-owned enterprise producing Renault cars under licence to the French company.

It is with the unions which represent the workers in these seven firms that this study is concerned. But before examining unions in detail, let us look more closely at the firms themselves. The most established firms were the big three US corporations, Ford, GM and Chrysler, which had begun assembly operations in the inter-war period. Of the firms which were operating in the 1970s, the two with state capital, VAM and DINA, had begun to produce cars in 1953 and 1954, respectively. Finally, both Nissan and VW were newcomers to the market and were established in the wake of the 1962 integration decree.

With the expansion of the Mexican auto industry in the 1960s and 1970s, the already established companies set up new plants. Ford built two new plants in the northern industrial zone of Mexico City, in Tlalnepantla and Cuautitlán. These were located outside the boundary of the Federal District, in the State of México. Thus, although they were in the same city as Ford's original La Villa plant, the new plants were actually located in a different federal entity. The other three American corporations, VAM, GM and Chrysler, each supplemented its Mexico City plant with a new factory in the booming industrial town of Toluca, in the State of México, some forty miles west of Mexico City.

The DINA plant had, for political reasons, been set up as part of an industrial complex in the impoverished agricultural region of Ciudad Sahagún, Hidalgo, some thirty miles to the north of Mexico City. The new corporations, VW and Nissan, set up their plants in Puebla and Cuernavaca, respectively. (Nissan later added another plant in Toluca.) Puebla is a medium-sized state capital, some fifty miles south-east of Mexico. Its industrial base was the declining textile industry, and the VW plant rapidly became the major industrial employer. Cuernavaca is a small state capital some twenty miles south of Mexico City, with a small, and new, industrial park, in a state characterized primarily by the cultivation of sugar cane.

The location of the industry was, therefore, concentric. Six plants in Mexico City were surrounded by another seven plants in the small and medium-sized cities of Toluca, Cuernavaca, Cuidad Sahagún and Puebla. Of these, only Toluca was a really modern industrial city. Some firms opted to set up operations in more than one location; others, to stay in one place.

The automobile industry as a whole has experienced steady growth,

Table 2.2. *Production of
automobiles, 1950–79*

Year	Passenger cars
1950	10,384
1955	17,255
1960	31,003
1965	70,242
1970	133,218
1975	237,118
1979	280,051

Sources: 1950–60: Gudger, 'Regulation of
Multinational Corporations', p. 127.
1965–75: Asociación Mexicana de la
Industria Automotríz, *La industria
automotríz de México en cifras* (México
AMIA, 1976), pp. 62–3.
1979: Secretaría de Programación y
Presupuesto, *La industria automotríz en
México* (1981), p. 67.

interrupted by a recession in 1975–7. The late sixties and early seventies, in particular, witnessed rapid growth (see table 2.2). By 1979, the value of production in the automobile industry amounted to some 7.6 per cent of total manufacturing production in Mexico.[9] The aggregated annual figures mask, however, two important phenomena. The first is the high degree of monthly variation of car production. The second is the changing market position of the companies.

Some of the monthly variation can be accounted for by annual vacations. Chrysler is a clear example of this. The monthly production data for 1974–7 show a fairly regular output with the exception of the September vacations. On the other hand, the data for some other firms are less susceptible to easy interpretation. Production of GM cars seems, for example, to be quite erratic. In part this pattern can be accounted for by the impact of strikes. The Ford data illustrate a third phenomenon: the decrease in production as a response to the recession of the 1975–7 period. The effects of the recession on output and sales were such that the clear seasonal patterns began to disintegrate and give way to a much more unstable situation.

Market shares (as measured in number of autos sold) also changed. (This measure of market share is very crude, and inflates the importance

Table 2.3. *Mexican auto market shares*

	% of units			% of sales		
	1974	1976	1978	1974	1976	1978
Chrysler	15.3	16.7	19.3	18.6	21.7	28.2
DINA	8.3	12.0	6.4	13.4	16.8	ND
Ford	14.2	11.0	14.7	21.1	19.1	25.5
GM	7.7	9.4	10.1	13.3	12.8	17.4
Nissan	8.5	11.8	12.5	5.3	6.9	8.3
VW	37.6	29.1	28.4	23.1	16.6	20.7
VAM	8.4	ND	ND	5.2	6.0	ND

Source: Secretaría de Programación y Presupuesto, *La industria automotríz en México* (1981), pp. 122, 153.

of companies which mainly produce cheap vehicles.) As will be apparent from table 2.3, although VW remained the largest producer in terms of units sold, it faced increasingly tough competition. The second part of table 2.3, which expresses market share in terms of percentage of total sales, brings this out even more clearly. In these terms, VW loses its lead and is overtaken by both Chrysler and Ford by 1978.

As will be evident, the apparent homogeneity of the automobile industry begins to dissolve once considerations of product, ownership, technology, etc. are considered. The effects of such factors will be discussed in the ensuing chapters, in so far as they bear on the principal hypothesis of this book. It may, however, be as well to anticipate the conclusion by stating that the principal argument of this book tends to minimize the effect of variables such as the nationality of the corporation, its product mix, etc. This may seem surprising, given the importance of such theories in industrial sociology. The point is not that these theories are incorrect but simply that they are not relevant to the explanation of the phenomena described in this book. For example, differences in technology may explain why the pattern of industrial relations in one industry differs from that in another, or why industrial relations alter over time as the technology employed in a particular industry undergoes changes. In dealing with questions of this nature variables like technology, organizational structure and factor proportions are likely to be important factors in the explanation. But it must be borne in mind that this book is concerned with a single industry, in a single country, during a brief historical period. There are no major differences in technology, organizational structure, factor mix, etc. among the seven companies studied. Such differences as do exist are relatively minor and hence it is unlikely that they account for the marked variations in union behaviour which form the subject of this book.

There is an additional, more powerful, argument for minimizing the impact of variables related either to the nature of the industry or to characteristics of the firms involved. It is that great variations in union behaviour can be found within the same company. Both GM and Nissan have two plants, each in separate locations, each controlled by a different union. In both GM and Nissan, management must confront one militant union and one conservative union. What seems to have happened in these two companies is that, for various reasons, the union which controlled the principal plant became militant and this failed to occur in the second plant set up by these companies. The simple fact of such wide variation of union behaviour within a single company suggests that factors other than technology, managerial style, product mix, etc. are at work. It is true that management attempted to learn from previous experience and hence it is possible to argue that managerial strategy was different in the newer plants. It might also be argued that the newer plants had slightly different technology. Such a line of reasoning, however, is flatly contradicted by the developments in Chrysler and Ford. In these companies also, there was an expansion which took the form of building new plants in new locations. However, in Ford and Chrysler it was in the new plants that militant movements erupted, whereas the sites of militancy in the GM and Nissan cases were in the plants which were established first.

In the final analysis the argument is inconclusive. The research was not set up to examine the importance of such variables and hence cannot confidently pronounce upon them.

Strikes

The incidence and duration of strikes, together with the number of workers involved, make up the most widely used indicator of industrial conflict. As an indicator, it has the advantage for the outside investigator of being relatively easy to record. For want of a better measure it will be used in this book. There are, however, relatively few strikes in the Mexican automobile industry, reflecting the very low strike propensity of Mexican industry as a whole. According to available evidence, in the

Table 2.4. *Strikes and duration (in days), 1970–80*

	1970	1971	1972	1973	1974	1975	1976	1977	1978	1979	1980	Total no. strikes
Nissan–Cuernavaca	—	—	1	1	21	—	46	1	1	—	—	6
DINA	—	—	—	—	14	—	1	6	3	1	—	5
VW	—	—	—	—	7	—	8	1	15	—	—	4
Ford	—	—	—	—	—	—	30	—	1	—	12	3
GM–DF	—	—	—	1 + 6[a]	—	30	—	62	—	22	106	6
GM–Toluca	—	—	—	—	—	—	—	—	—	—	—	0
Chrysler	—	—	—	—	—	2[b]	—	—	—	—	—	0
VAM	32[b]	—	—	—	—	—	—	—	—	—	—	0
Nissan–Toluca	—	—	—	—	—	—	—	—	—	6[b]	—	0

[a] There were two strikes that year in GM–DF, one of 1 day and one of 6 days.
[b] Unofficial strikes against union leaderships.

eleven-year period 1970–80, there were twenty-three official strikes and three unofficial stoppages in the seven companies producing automobiles (table 2.4).

The three unofficial stoppages were wildcat strikes by the rank and file directed against the union leadership. Two occurred in Chrysler and one in Nissan–Toluca. These stoppages will henceforth be excluded from consideration (though they are dealt with in chapter 4).

The most noticeable thing about strike frequency in the Mexican automobile industry is that it is possible to divide the unions neatly into two groups. On the one hand, there are five unions (Nissan–Cuernavaca, DINA, VW, Ford and GM–DF) which have high strike propensities; on the other, four unions (Nissan–Toluca, Chrysler, VAM and GM–Toluca) which have never struck at all during this eleven-year period.

As I shall attempt to demonstrate in subsequent chapters, this division of the union ranks is highly correlated with other variables, such as internal union democracy and control by the union over work processes. It is this division into unions with a high level of strike activity (henceforth, 'militant' unions) and those with a low propensity to strike ('conservative' unions) which is the central dividing line within Mexican auto unions, rather than the division between the three independent unions (Nissan–Cuernavaca, VW and DINA) and the remaining official unions. Why this should be so will be dealt with later in the book.

3

Wages and workers in the Mexican automobile industry

This chapter looks in detail at wages in the Mexican auto industry, and examines the hypothesis that rates of increase in wages are correlated with union militancy. There then follows a description of the social background of workers in the auto industry and a discussion of the utility or otherwise of describing these workers as an 'aristocracy of labour'.

Wages

The principal interest in examining differences in wages among the various auto companies is to see if there is any relationship between union militancy and wage gains. The hypothesis is that there is a positive relationship, and it is argued that such wage gains are a direct result of union militancy. For a variety of methodological reasons the argument is somewhat complex. There are three principal sources of difficulty. The first is incomplete data. It was exceedingly difficult to obtain complete and comparable time series for all the companies. As a result, a number of partial comparisons have had to be made, and inferences drawn therefrom. Secondly, and relatedly, we are not interested primarily in comparisons at one point in time. Wages do differ between companies, and this reflects, among other things, the different local labour markets. It is not surprising that money wages are lower in the towns outside Mexico City. What is of more interest is the *rate of growth* of wages over time: i.e. do the more militant unions obtain higher percentage wage hikes, irrespective of the varying starting points? Finally, we need to clarify what exactly it is that is being compared. Money wages are not earnings, and the relationship between wages and earnings may vary from firm to firm. Also, since the cost of living varies from city to city, money wages are only an imperfect measure of real incomes. Moreover, fringe benefits need to be taken into

50

account, and this in itself involves a number of methodological problems. And how should we take into account the varying skill and seniority mixes of the various workforces?

The measure adopted here has been the rate of increase of money wages during the period 1975–80. This has its drawbacks, and these are discussed below. An attempt has been made to discuss other measures and to consider the index selected in the light of such other evidence as is available. Briefly to anticipate the methodological discussion, most of the evidence on wages points in the same direction and lends support to the hypothesis of a positive relationship between rates of wage increase and union militancy.

Reliable data on wages in the Mexican automobile industry, are
difficult to come by. Ideally, for the purposes of this book, yearly wage costs and number of employees for each company would give a reasonable measure of relatives wages in the various companies. Alternatively, yearly wage rates in the various companies for specified job categories would also be a reasonable measure. Unfortunately, neither measure is easily available.

Yearly wage costs were not generally available for all the companies included in the study. Nevertheless, another author has published data on wage costs for 1976, and these are discussed below and reproduced as table 3.1. Comparison of wages for specified job categories is difficult owing to differing job definitions between firms and changes in job classifications over time within firms. This kind of comparison, has, however been attempted by the Ford Motor Company for the privately owned enterprises (i.e. DINA is excluded) and the results are reproduced as table 3.2.

In addition to problems derived primarily from unreliability of data,
there is a substantive issue which affects the choice of measure. As mentioned below, the various auto companies have workforces which differ considerably in composition. Long established firms like GM tend to have a high percentage of their workers in the upper ranges of skill and seniority, with a consequent distribution of workers among wage categories which favours the upper end of the distribution. In contrast, newer firms like Nissan tend to have a wage distribution which is loaded toward the bottom end of the scale. The question therefore arises of whether we should compare wage costs to the firm (and thereby ignore differing labour force compositions) or compare wages paid for the same job. Unavailability or unreliability of data on labour force composition once again exacerbate the problem. Fortunately,

Table 3.1. Wages and fringe benefits, 1976

	Wages (mill. pesos)	Salaries (mill. pesos)	Fringe benefits (mill. pesos)	Workers	Total labour costs (mill. pesos)	Total cost per worker (pesos)	Wages & salaries per worker (pesos)	Fringe benefits/ worker (pesos)	Fringe benefits as % of wages and salaries
Ford	222	193	436	4944	851	172,127	83,940	88,188	105.06
GM	155	311	209	5043	675	133,849	92,405	41,444	44.85
VW	137	362	280	9379	779	83,058	53,204	29,854	56.11
DINA	406	536	ND	7911	—	119,075	—	—	—
Chrysler	206	218	221	5018	645	128,537	84,496	44,041	52.12
Nissan	91	143	54	2959	288	97,330	79,081	18,249	23.08
VAM	78	58	22	1964	158	80,448	69,246	11,202	16.18

Source: J. O. Quiroz Trejo, Proceso de trabajo en la industria automotriz terminal, 1980, Cuaderno 40 (México, Centro de Estudios Latinoamericanos, Universidad Nacional Autónoma de México, 1980). p. 31.

Table 3.2. *Wages for selected jobs, 1980 (pesos/day)*

	General assembler	Maintenance mechanic	Solderer	Driver	Inspector	Storeman
Nissan–Cuernavaca	392	638	578	320	524	347
VW	261	606	413	316	606	288
Ford	468	689	569	569	629	524
GM–DF	614	809	614	519	809	443
GM–Toluca	449	835	601	516	742	374
Chrysler–DF	353	854	634	455	815	456
Chrysler–Toluca	237	738	432	355	626	357
VAM–DF	230	506	369	272	401	265
VAM–Toluca	223	494	304	263	429	256
Nissan–Toluca	274	482	343	307	431	274

Source: Ford Motor Company, 'Perspectivas de la industria automotríz', *Proyección*, vol. 2, no. 14 (May 1981), pp. 1–4.

wage spreads in the Mexican auto industry, as discussed below, are small, and this diminishes the magnitude of the problem. A related difficulty of comparing money wages is that it neglects fringe benefits. The value of fringe benefits to the workers (as distinct from the cost to the company) is difficult to estimate with any degree of reliability. In table 3.1, the cost of fringe benefits as a percentage of wage costs is presented in the final column, based on data presented by Quiroz. According to these data, the cost of fringe benefits varies from 16 per cent of wages to 105 per cent of wages, with a weighted average of 56 per cent. Data for a wider range of industries gathered by Mike Everett suggest that fringe benefits add about 12 per cent to take-home pay.[1]

Data published by the Ford Motor Company offer a slightly different picture (table 3.3). Ford's calculations refer to the fringe benefits accruing to all workers which are received as cash additions to wages. (These do not include fringe benefits which only some workers receive, such as scholarships for children, or non-monetary fringe benefits such as subsidized lunches at work.) The data of table 3.3, therefore, do not represent the cost to the company, but rather the direct monetary benefit to the average worker of certain fringe benefits. These also vary considerably, from 10.2 per cent in the case of Chrysler's Toluca workers, to 28.6 per cent in the case of GM's Mexico City workers. These data correspond more closely to Everett's results and suggest that Quiroz' figures should be treated with caution.

Table 3.3. *Wages and fringe benefits for an average worker*

	Yearly salary (pesos)	Yearly fringe benefits (pesos)	Fringe benefits as % of salary
Nissan–Cuernavaca	155,161.50	34,433.10	22.2
VW	127,552.90	27,956.80	21.9
GM–DF	256,803.95	73,551.23	28.6
GM–Toluca	168,830.75	31,453.40	18.6
Ford	205,896.50	38,922.90	18.9
Chrysler–DF	178,897.45	29,752.24	16.6
Chrysler–Toluca	127,844.90	13,064.70	10.2
VAM–DF	119,796.65	16,771.53	8.5
VAM–Toluca	94,670.05	13,124.12	13.9
Nissan–Toluca	120,669.00	17,521.80	14.5

Note: According to *Proyección*, average wages and seniority for each company or plant have been used to calculate these figures.
Source: As table 3.2, p. 3.

A considerable part of the difference between companies is due to seniority-related benefits, as there are considerable variations in the seniority structures of the various plants and firms. This, however, is unlikely to be the case with Nissan–Cuernavaca and VW. The hypothesis that the more militant unions have higher monetary fringe benefits is borne out by the data, with the partial exception of GM's Toluca workers. These workers – with an 18.6 per cent increase of monetary fringe benefits over average workers – are well below the other GM workers in Mexico City (28.6 per cent), but come close to the figures for other militant unions.

Once again, although the differences are not large, they are in the right direction. Although other factors are clearly at work, militancy does seem to have a pay-off in terms of material benefits for the workers involved.

Not only do the data on fringe benefits published by the Ford Motor Company seem more useful than those presented by Quiroz, they are also probably more reliable. Quiroz' data on total direct and indirect labour costs are at odds with the data I obtained directly from Nissan and VAM. The total cost to the company of fringe benefits, expressed as a percentage of direct wage costs, was as follows: in Nissan fringe benefits were 38.5 per cent of wages in 1970 and 51.7 per cent in 1980; in VAM the figure for 1974 was 36 per cent and for 1980 was 44.4 per cent. These are quite different from Quiroz' 1976 data.

The VAM and Nissan data also indicate a trend of increasing fringe benefit costs as a percentage of total labour costs. Lack of systematic comparative data, unfortunately, prevents us from knowing whether this was true for the industry as a whole, and whether different firms had different experiences in this area.

The data provided by Quiroz (summarized in table 3.1) provide some indication of relative wage costs. Unfortunately, he does not provide separate data for fringe benefits in the case of DINA, including them in with wages and salaries. As might be expected, wage costs per worker are highest for the three established American corporations, GM, Chrysler and Ford. The relative ranking is similar whether wage costs are expressed as wages plus salaries or as wages plus salaries plus fringe benefits. Only in Ford is there a change of position of more than one step in the range, thanks to the unusually large fringe benefits there.

According to these data, there is a considerable range of relative labour costs in the industry, due no doubt to substantial differences in capital equipment and product mix and local labour markets. GM workers, on average, received 74 per cent more in wages in 1976 than VW workers. Including fringe benefits, Ford workers in the same year received 113 per cent more than VAM workers.

Wage trends

Unfortunately, the kinds of data presented in table 3.1 are only available for one year, 1976. If we assume that each company continues to pay the same proportion of its total wage bill on fringe benefits, then we can take the percentage wage increases as an indicator of trends in earnings over time. However, this assumption may not be justified. Particularly in a period of government incomes policy, companies with official unions may be more likely to compensate for low wage increases by greater increases in fringe benefits. This may not be equally true for the companies with independent unions.

We have long time-series data for two firms: GM and Chrysler. The comparison is useful, since (as we shall see later) the GM plant in Mexico City has a militant union and the Chrysler plant has always had a relatively passive union. If union characteristics affect wage levels, this should show up over a twenty-year period. In order not to complicate the issue by looking at the varying distribution of workers in the different job categories, I will here examine only two of these categories.

The two selected are those which contain a large number of workers. Taking 1954 as a base, and looking at workers in categories 1 and 3 in each company, we have the time series of table 3.4, unadjusted for inflation. The overall impression is one of very little difference in the evolution of wages in the two companies. Category 1 workers differ very little. Category 3 workers in GM appear to have a slight edge over their counterparts in Chrysler. This evidence is in the expected direction, but hardly indicates major differences in wage increases over the 1955–77 period.

A further index of nominal wages was constructed for General Motors. The distribution of the workforce among job categories was available for 1954, 1963 and 1972. The wages for each category of job were weighted as follows: the years 1954–8 were weighted according to the distribution of job categories in 1954; the years 1959–67, according to the distribution for 1963; and the years 1968–77, by the distribution for 1972. The results of this procedure are shown in the last column of table 3.4. They are not dissimilar to the evolution of nominal wages of category 3. Given the high degree of wage compression, this is hardly surprising.

Of course, the critical period for comparisons is the 1972–8 period, when the differences between militant and non-militant unions should be at their greatest. In addition to the familiar problem of missing and/or unreliable data, there are three other problems. First, there is no common base year for comparison. Some companies negotiated contracts in odd-numbered years, others in even-numbered years. Secondly, we have to make the assumption that the ratio of cash wages to fringe benefits remained constant for each company over this period. Lastly, the time period is very short, and comparisons are therefore somewhat risky.

To make these comparisons, two sources were used: union contracts and a table published by Ford. The Ford Motor Company published a comparison of wage increases for the privately owned firms for the period 1975–80. This is reproduced as table 3.5. Two comments are in order: first, the differences are not very large; secondly, with the exception of the GM union in Mexico City, the differences are in the expected direction. Ford, Nissan and VW obtained wage increases in the range of 274 to 293, taking 1975 as a base, while VAM, Chrysler and the Toluca GM union obtained increases in the range 248 to 255.

The second source for comparisons of wage rate increases was the union contracts. Indices were constructed for a selected job category in

Table 3.4. *Wages in GM and Chrysler*

	Chrysler		GM		GM
	Category 1	Category 3	Category 1	Category 3	Weighted average[a]
1954	100	100	100	100	100
1955	115.13	114.93	115.11	115.27	113.9
1957	132.89	131.73	132.34	132.51	131.5
1958	142.54	142.40	145.53	145.57	144.7
1959	164.47	165.07	168.72	168.97	166.0
1961	189.25	190.13	192.77	197.78	193.1
1963	213.82	215.73	213.83	229.31	221.1
1965	—	—	241.70	259.36	249.9
1967	278.95	279.20	263.40	284.73	274.4
1969	309.87	310.93	289.57	313.55	312.4
1971	—	—	330.21	357.39	356.1
1973	398.90	400.53	379.57	411.08	409.4
1975	—	—	623.62	67.98	675.7
1977	967.76	976.80	961.91	1048.77	1042.2

[a] See text for explanation.
Source: Junta Local de Conciliación y Arbitraje, DF, archive.

each firm. (These were chosen to include an unskilled assembly-line worker and were representative of the vast majority of the workforce.) There were two principal difficulties with this comparison. First, some unions renewed contracts in odd-numbered years, others in even-numbered years. Secondly, complete time series were unobtainable.

Without adjusting for differences in time periods it is impossible to compare all the unions as a single group. Nevertheless, certain comparisons are possible. Two sets of wage data have the same starting and end points for eight-year periods. The wage indices for Ford, Chrysler and GM–DF over the period 1969–77 show Ford and GM–DF slightly ahead of Chrysler. From a base of 100 in 1969, average wages in Ford had risen to 337 by 1977, and those in Chrysler and GM to 314 and 334 respectively. The comparison of VAM, Nissan–Cuernavaca, VW, GM–Toluca and DINA for 1972–80 show DINA, VW and Nissan considerably ahead of GM–Toluca and VAM. During this period, wages in VW, DINA and Nissan rose from a base of 100 to 538, 470 and 493 respectively, while the indices for GM's Toluca workers and VAM's workers rose to 433 and 407 respectively. The differences are very slight and the time periods are short; nevertheless, all the differences are in the

Table 3.5. *Increases in wage rates, 1975–80*

	1975	1976	1977	1978	1979	1980
Ford	100	118	167	194	229	293
GM–DF	100	114	154	174	204	251
GM–Toluca	100	115	156	178	208	255
VW	100	120	165	192	226	281
Chrysler	100	115	156	176	207	253
Nissan–Cuernavaca	100	120	165	188	222	274
VAM	100	112	152	173	199	248

Source: Ford Motor Company, *Proyección*, vol. 2, no. 14 (May 1981).

expected direction. Companies with militant unions give slightly higher money wage increases. (N.B. small differences in fringe benefits could easily alter this picture.)

The results from the comparisons of union contracts are quite similar to the data published by the Ford Motor Company. Ford, Nissan, VW and DINA clearly obtain larger wage increases than VAM, Chrysler or GM–Toluca. The GM–Mexico City union, unfortunately, can be compared with Ford and Chrysler only for the 1969–77 period. Its performance in this period is closer to that of Ford than to Chrysler, and this tends to support the hypothesis that the Mexico City GM union belongs to the high-strike, high-wage-increase category.

This result contradicts the findings of the Ford Motor Company comparison which were presented in table 3.5 and which suggest a poor performance on the part of GM's Mexico City union. There is, however, a way of attempting to reconcile these conflicting data, since they refer to two distinct time periods. According to the union contracts, the wage increases obtained by GM's Mexico City union were quite good in the period 1969–75, and fell off slightly in 1977. According to the Ford Motor Company survey, the decline which began in 1975 continued throughout the next five years, so that by 1980 this union's performance had come closer to that of the conservative unions. It is tempting to speculate that this poor performance was due to determined opposition by GM management, as they dug in their heels to weather a series of lengthy strikes (see table 2.4).

The figures which appear in the summary table in chapter 9 are the 1975–80 indices of money wage increases which appear in table 3.5.

Wage distribution within firms

The best data are for the GM plant in Mexico City. I have detailed data on wages over a fifteen-year period at four points in time, 1954, 1963, 1970 and 1972[2] (table 3.6).

The wage distributions for GM are quite compressed. The bulk of the labour force falls into categories 1, 2 and 3. These three categories account for between 73 and 78 per cent of the manual labour force in the years considered. Expressed as a percentage of the wages for category 3, workers in category 1 earned between 16 and 7 per cent more. There is a consistently declining trend over time. If all positions listed in the collective contract are included in the analysis, then top wages are approximately double the lowest. This holds true throughout the period 1952–73. If actual wages paid to all workers (excluding apprentices) are considered for the four years where we have detailed information, then the wage spread (top wage as per cent of bottom wage) declines from 324 per cent (in 1954) to 252 per cent (in 1972). Since wages are, in fact, concentrated in categories 1, 2 and 3, these measures overstate the amount of dispersion.

Accordingly, in table 3.7, which summarizes available data on wage spreads in the Mexican automobile industry, those job categories which together contain between 70 and 80 per cent of the workforce have been selected for comparison. Naturally, the use of this measure provides a lower index of wage dispersion than the use of the total range of wages. Since the distribution of wages is unimodal, the measure used here is probably a reasonable descriptive tool.

The data in table 3.7 are for wages, not earnings. Luckily, more precise information was available for earnings in the Ford truck assembly plant of Cuautitlán, employing some 877 workers. This provides some notion of the relationship between nominal hourly wages and actual earnings.

The Ford Motor Company frequently moves workers from one job to another. Where this involves the worker performing a job which has a higher rate attached, the worker is paid at the higher rate. This means that some workers may be earning more than their base rate. In June 1978, 319 workers out of 883 increased their earnings in this way. This involved a 4 per cent increase in cost to the company over and above basic salaries. (Base salaries for the 883 workers for that month totalled 32,629 pesos. Compensations for work in higher categories amounted

Table 3.6. GM–DF *wages*

Category	1954 Wage	1954 No. workers	1954 %	1963 Wage	1963 No. workers	1963 %	1970 Wage	1970 No. workers	1970 %	1972 Wage	1972 No. workers	1972 %
—	48.75	52	5.9	95.25	23	1.7	129.10	17	1.0	147.15	14	0.8
—	38.60	35	4.0	82.25	66	5.0	111.45	177	10.7	127.05	213	11.4
1	37.60	58	6.7	80.40	70	5.3	108.90	317	19.1	124.15	394	21.1
1	36.40	11	1.3	78.40	3	0.2	106.20	2	0.1	—	—	—
2	34.25	91	10.3	76.40	217	16.3	104.50	225	13.6	119.15	300	16.1
3	32.50	522	59.3	74.50	749	56.2	101.85	713	43.0	116.10	764	41.0
3	—	—	—	69.25	1	0.1	—	—	—	—	—	—
4	28.00	11	1.3	63.00	19	1.4	86.15	16	1.0	98.20	25	1.3
5	24.45	14	1.6	53.25	58	4.4	72.75	1	0.1	82.95	1	0.1
5	23.00	1	0.1	49.75	1	0.1	68.00	4	0.2	77.50	2	0.1
5	—	—	—	45.50	1	0.1	60.90	2	0.1	69.45	2	0.1
5	20.10	27	3.1	42.50	36	2.7	58.10	107	6.9	66.25	90	4.8
5	19.05	1	0.1	40.70	11	0.8	54.35	45	2.7	61.95	45	2.4
5	18.75	10	1.1	39.75	35	2.6	51.15	21	1.3	—	—	—
—	17.50	5	0.6	37.40	4	0.3	43.70	1	0.1	58.30	13	0.7
—	15.05	14	1.6	32.00	10	0.8	36.75	9	0.5	—	—	—
—	14.00	2	0.2	27.00	11	0.8	28.35	1	0.1	—	—	—
—	12.00	8	0.9	23.50	6	0.5	24.65	1	0.1	—	—	—
—	10.00	9	1.0	16.50	11	0.8	—	—	—	—	—	—
—	8.00	9	1.0	—	—	—	—	—	—	—	—	—

Table 3.7. *Comparative wage distributions*

Company	Year	Categories in comparison	% of workforce in categories	Wage of highest category as % of lowest
GM–DF	1954	1–3	77.5	115.7
	1963	1–3	77.8	107.9
	1970	1–3	73.1	106.9
	1972	1–3	78.3	106.9
Chrysler–DF	1976	1–4	70.0	124.0
Ford	1977	3–11	76.7	134.2
VAM–DF	1978	1–4	77.2	190.9
DINA	1976	7–9	76.2	120.7

to 1306 pesos.) For those workers involved in temporary promotions, this was equivalent to an 11 per cent increase in pay.

Overtime was normal, and consisted of an extra four-hour shift on Saturday mornings. Paid at double time, this was equivalent to another 17 per cent on top of the weekly wage.

Regrettably, we have no way of knowing to what extent it is safe to generalize from this illustrative example, or whether there are systematic variations in the wages–earnings ratio in the industry. Since our principal interest, however, lies in comparing rates of increase of wages among companies, it is unlikely that the absence of systematic data on actual earnings will materially affect the results of this research. In the absence of comprehensive data on earnings, I have used money wage increases as a proxy for earnings.

Job tenure

Mexican labour law provides for two basic types of employment contract. In the *planta* contract, a worker is hired for an indefinite period and can be fired only with due cause. If the worker is laid off, he or she is entitled to financial compensation amounting to three months' salary plus twenty days' salary for every year in the job.

The second type of contract provides for a variety of short-term employments of less than one year. These may be for a fixed, specified piece of work, or for a time period of less than one year. These are known as *eventual* contracts. Workers on this type of contract, *eventuales*, have less job security and lay-off compensation than *planta* workers. From the point of view of the worker, *planta* status is highly desirable.

From the company's point of view, the purpose of *eventuales*, over and above a reduction in direct labour costs, is to meet fluctuations in demand for labour without making long-term commitments to keep a permanent workforce. There is, therefore, some conflict of interest between employer and employee over the type of work contract.

The Mexican auto industry uses a labour force comprising a mix of *planta* workers and *eventuales*. In 1974, the percentage of the labour force with *planta* status in some of the car factories was as shown in table 3.8.

Incomplete as these data are, they tell us something. The two independent unions in this table have more *planta*-status workers than the other unions. Interviews with management confirmed this general picture. Chrysler, which has one of the least combative unions, is an enterprise which is notorious for its preference for *eventuales*. Moreover, longitudinal data further support the hypothesis that independent unions tend to have higher percentages of their workforces on *planta* status. The comparison of DINA and VAM in chapter 6 illustrates this point.

A typical pattern is for *eventuales* to be hired for eleven months, fired, and then rehired one month later for another eleven-month period. After several years, an *eventual* worker may be upgraded to *planta* status. (The implications of this for union organization are considered in chapter 6.) However, if there is a contraction in the labour force, then the *eventuales* will be the first to be laid off. This is illustrated in figure 1. When the Ford truck plant in Cuautitlán reduced its workforce in late 1975, nearly all the *eventuales* were laid off, and the percentage of workers on *planta* status jumped from 57.8 per cent in August to 98 per cent in September. While there were, indeed, some layoffs of *planta* workers, these were minor compared to the drop in the number of *eventuales*.

The data, such as they are, on *planta* status must be interpreted with caution. The comparison among VAM–DF, Nissan and DINA in table 6.1 certainly suggests that more combative unions tend to increase the proportion of their workforce on *planta* contracts more rapidly than the less combative unions. However, data from Ford and GM remind us that the original purpose of *eventuales* is to enable companies to adjust their workforces rapidly to changing demand. The GM data indicate that the percentage of the labour force with *planta* status can vary

Table 3.8. *Percentage of workers on* planta *contracts, 1974*

Nissan	85
DINA	75
Ford[a]	50
GM–DF	50
VAM–DF	65
VAM–Toluca	58

[a] Figures refer to the Cuautitlán truck plant.
Source: Interviews, contracts and archives of Registro de Asociaciones.

Table 3.9. *Workers with* planta *contracts, GM–DF, 1949–74*

Year	Workers with *planta* contracts	Total no. workers	% *planta*
1949	370	751	49.3
1950	350	902	38.8
1951	365	1361	26.8
1952	407	1302	31.3
1960	583	1296	45.0
1970	1228	1648	74.5
1974	1316	2596	50.7

Source: Archives of Registro de Asociaciones.

greatly over a twenty-five-year period (table 3.9). The graph of monthly variations in one of the Ford plants during the period April 1973 to May 1978 indicates how the percentage of workers on *planta* contracts can fluctuate in response to changing demand.

The interpretation of these data depends on the wording of the relevant clause in the collective contract agreement (if any) and the economic situation in the industry. If a company is committed to keeping, say, 90 per cent of its workforce on *planta* status (as in Nissan), then its hands are tied. If it expands its workforce then many of these new workers must be given *planta* status. It will thereafter be costly to reduce the workforce. If, on the other hand, as is the case in VAM, the

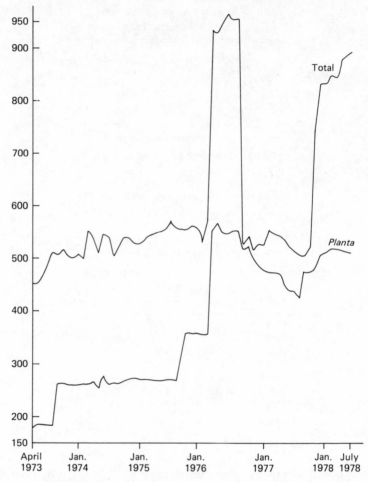

Fig. 1. Total number of workers in the Ford Cuautitlán plant and number of workers on *planta* contracts, 1973–8

contract merely stipulates an absolute number of *planta* jobs, then expansions and contractions can take place using *eventuales*.

Recruitment

Who are the auto workers? Where do they come from? Common sense would suggest that in newly industrializing countries like Mexico, factory workers would tend to come from peasant families and perhaps even have been peasants themselves. Moreover, recent studies suggest that the dynamism of industrial growth in recent decades has meant that many migrants have been absorbed into heavy industry.[3] Not all of these migrants come directly from agricultural occupations. Even in the case of the Las Truchas steel complex, situated in the midst of a large zone of rural poverty in Michoacán and Guerrero, only one-fifth of workers had come directly from agriculture, though many more had rural origins.[4] However, because both industrialization and urbanization have been proceeding apace in Mexico for over forty years, by the 1970s there must have been many new entrants to the labour market who came from working class families, and whose fathers had urban, industrial employment. In the industrial zone to the north of Mexico City, one study found that only 26 per cent of the labour force had been born in the countryside, and that 60 per cent had been born in the Federal District.[5] This compares with a study of Cuernavaca, which indicated that 48 per cent of the labour force in the industrial park in that city had been born in the countryside.[6]

Two factors, job inheritance and credentialism, would tend to reinforce the latter trend in the auto industry. Because job aspirants have to be recommended by the union, because some auto companies have a policy of preferring sons and relatives of existing workers, and because some union contracts stipulate that sons of existing workers have preference in hiring (see chapter 6), there will be a trend towards job inheritance. This will be most visible in companies which have been operating in Mexico for some time. In newly established companies, or in plants which have recently expanded their workforce, this will be less visible.

Credentialism, the tendency for employers to demand high educational qualifications of job aspirants in situations of excess labour supply, will discriminate against people from rural backgrounds. Consequently, sons of fathers with reasonable incomes in urban areas will be favoured in the job market for the auto industry. This phenomenon should operate to increase job inheritance among the industrial working class of Mexico City *vis-à-vis* all other categories.

However, these are simply plausible hypotheses. What do the data indicate? Once again, our information is woefully inadequate for the task at hand. There have been a number of anthropological studies of the DINA and Nissan plants, located in new industrial centres. I was able to supplement the information contained in these studies with impressionistic comments made in interviews and with some data gathered from a sample of job application forms at one of the Ford plants.

The general impression is of a marked contrast between the labour force in Mexico City and elsewhere. Workers in plants located in Mexico City (which is where Ford, Chrysler and GM began their operations before the Second World War) retain a core of older and experienced workers. Although the rapid expansion of the late 1960s and early 1970s diluted these with massive contingents of young workers, these were predominantly from urban working class families. In contrast, the newer plants in Cuernavaca and Ciudad Sahagún hired peasants or sons of peasants. Toluca appears to be an intermediate case. The situation in Puebla is unknown. Other studies have also suggested that trends in industrial employment are leading to an increasing differentiation of the Mexican working class. The study by Jorge Balán *et al.* in Monterrey argues that the different rates of labour absorption by the dynamic and traditional sectors of industry leads to an internally differentiated working class,[7] and Orlandina de Oliveira's research on Mexico City suggests a similar phenomenon, with the development of an increased differentiation between entry and non-entry occupations in the labour market.[8]

Thus, while workers in industries located outside Mexico may experience considerable occupational mobility as they move from agricultural to industrial employment, this may be less true for sons of industrial workers in Mexico.[9] Just as the pattern of development in Mexico as a whole has created an industrial working class which is considerably fragmented, with vast differences in occupational experience and expectations, so also is this the case for the auto industry, split as it is between a core of older plants in Mexico City and a periphery of newer plants in the smaller industrial towns around it.

Father's occupation

A study by Guillermo Campero and Giovana Valenti gives data for the present (1976) occupation of respondents' fathers[10] (table 3.10).

It is interesting to compare these data with a sample of 250 workers in one of the Ford plants in Mexico City. Because data on fathers' occupation in this sample (taken by the author) were based on job application forms, there is a high percentage of cases without information. Although the fact that only one-third of the cases had information on father's occupation must counsel extreme caution in interpreting

Table 3.10. *Father's occupation:*
Nissan workers

	%
Services	34.6
Peasant	47.1
Worker	11.0
Construction	3.7
Unknown	2.2
Other	1.4

Table 3.11. *Job applicants with*
friends or relatives in Ford

	%
Yes, not specified	20.4
Yes, relative	24.8
Yes, friend	14.8
No	5.2
NA	34.8

these data, it is interesting that very few Ford workers (4.8 per cent) had fathers who were peasants. The remainder (27.6 per cent) came from urban working class families. This is consonant both with the location of the plant (Mexico City rather than a new industrial park in a basically rural zone) and with the length of time Ford has been operating. Here the different recruitment processes of Ford and Nissan need to be considered.

As mentioned elsewhere, Ford tends to hire sons of existing workers. The job application forms usually (though not invariably) contain the question 'Do you have friends or relatives in Ford?' Answers to this question from the sample of 250 are shown in table 3.11.

Since Nissan is a new company in the industry, recruitment in the initial years was not based on connections in quite the same way. This does not, of course, prevent relatives being hired in the same plant. Indeed, in DINA, Victoria Novelo and Augusto Urteaga argue that many aspects of the internal politics of the union can best be explained in terms of ties of kinship and residential location.[11]

Place of birth

The majority of respondents in a survey of Nissan workers carried out by Francisco Zapata and Ken Coleman had been born in Cuernavaca (31 per cent) and the industrial zone of Juitepec (26 per cent).[12] Another 13 per cent had been born elsewhere in Morelos. A study of automobile workers in Cuernavaca's industrial park by Patricia Arias and Lucia Bazán (which includes other factories besides Nissan) produced similar results, with 58 per cent coming from Morelos and another 22 per cent from neighbouring Guerrero.[13] In the Coleman–Zapata study, half of the respondents stated that they had been born in rural areas, 14 per cent in medium-sized towns, and 37 per cent in towns of over 100,000 population. The Campero–Valenti study gives somewhat different figures. In this sample, 29 per cent of respondents were born in urban areas and 71 per cent in rural.[14]

The Novelo–Urteaga data for DINA, based on a 10 per cent sample, indicate that 69.9 per cent of the workers were born in Hidalgo and 10 per cent in neighbouring Tlaxcala.[15] My sample of Ford workers indicates that 54 per cent were born in Mexico City. Many of the rest were born in the towns and villages just to the north of the city. These data suggest that at least a substantial part of the labour force of each plant was born locally.

Prior job experience

Some job applicants come to the auto industry straight from school and hence have no previous job experience. Others come from peasant backgrounds, and yet others have had previous occupational experience in modern industry. At one time it was hypothesized that new workers with rural backgrounds would experience difficulties in adjusting to the rhythms and demands of modern factories. Specifically, they would be low in commitment. The general conclusions of empirical studies of labour commitment, however, indicate that this is not a serious problem.

Nevertheless, the effect of occupational background on industrial and political militancy remains an open issue. Data for Ford and Nissan are presented in table 3.12. These data have a high margin of error, and should be regarded as merely indicative. They suggest that the prior occupational experience of auto workers, if any, is rather diversified and not particularly drawn from the modern industrial sector. Of course,

Table 3.12. *Previous job experience*

Ford–Villa[a]		Ford–Cuautitlán[b]		Nissan[c]		
Industry	%	Industry	%	Industry	Previous job %	First job %
Automotive	17.3	Other automotive	13.6	Peasant	8.8	30.1
Mechanic's shop	15.4	Other large-scale industry	28.0	Services	44.3	47.0
Plastic, paper, printing	11.5	Mechanical workshop	10.4	Worker (*obrero*)	33.0	7.4
Personal services	9.6	Agriculture	1.2	Construction	5.8	2.2
Metal products	7.7	Other	22.4	None	7.4	7.4
Family business	6.7	NA	22.4	Other	0.7	5.9
Construction	6.7					
Business	5.8					
Electronics	4.8					
Clothing	3.8					
Agricultural	[d]					

Sources: [a] Miller *et al.*, 'Modern Sector Internal Labor Market Structure', p. 15 (N = 104).
[b] My sample (N = 250).
[c] Campero *et al.*, *La incorporación obrera*, p. 91 (N = 136).
[d] Under 1%.

these results may be due to the fact that samples were drawn from relatively new plants with a relatively young labour force. These data may be compared with a sample of workers drawn in 1965 by Richard Miller from Ford's La Villa plant, which has been in operation for a long time. Miller *et al.* found that most workers had some prior industrial experience, and that 33 per cent of La Villa workers had previously worked either in automobiles or in a mechanic's shop.[16] The contrast with the Cuautitlán sample is striking, and is a useful caution against generalization from particular plants to the industry as a whole.

Age of labour force

One factor which may perhaps help account for the relative militancy of certain unions in the Mexican automobile industry is the age of the workforce. It might be hypothesized that young workers would be more militant. Table 3.13, which gives data for some of the car plants, does not entirely support this hypothesis. It is true that the Nissan workers are quite young (and this is probably also true for VW), but the workers in Ford and GM–DF, both of which are militant unions, are, on average, quite old. There appears, therefore, to be no systematic and direct connection between the age of the workforce and militancy.

Standard of living

What does it mean to be a Mexican car worker in terms of a standard of living? We have already seen in chapter 1 that wages in the auto industry are good compared to wages elsewhere. But in a country where there is so much poverty, what does this tell us about absolute living standards? The Coleman–Zapata survey of Nissan workers provides some data on type of housing and ownership of consumer durables. These are presented in table 3.14.

Although no comparable data are available for workers in other car firms, a few comments can be made. First, Nissan wages are not the highest in the industry. There is, therefore, every reason to suppose that other workers in the auto industry also have adequate housing and neighbourhood services, and many consumer durables. Of course, the cost of living is lower in Cuernavaca than in Mexico City. An indication of the magnitude of the difference is given by the government-stipulated minimum salaries for the different areas. These explicitly take into account regional variations in the cost of living.

Table 3.13. *Age of workforce*

Company	Date	Average age	Source	Total no. workers
Nissan	1971	24.6	Bazán	547
Nissan	1978	27.0	STPS	2075
Ford	1977	42.4	Roxborough	4658[a]
GM–DF	1945	33.1	STPS	146
GM–DF	1954	32.5	STPS	912
VAM–DF	1956	25.8	STPS	141
VAM–DF	1974	36.8	STPS	640
VAM–Toluca	1974	30.7	STPS	205
Chrysler–Toluca	1976	33.0	STPS	5134[b]

[a] Estimate based on sample of 250 workers.
[b] Estimate based on sample of 103 workers.
Sources: L. Bazán, 'Sindicalismo independiente: el caso de Nissan Mexicana' mimeographed, 1977; STPS: Archive of Registro de Asociaciones; Roxborough: sample of 250 workers.

Table 3.14. *Nissan workers: housing and consumer durables*

Housing	%	Consumer durables	%
Rented accommodation	25	Refrigerator	95
Own accommodation	76	Gas stove	99
Electricity supply	99	Blender	97
Water	99	TV	97
Drainage	96	Stereo or record player	94
Paved streets	61	Telephone	10
Brick or cement housing	86	Washing machine	59
Two-bedroomed residence	62	Car	32
Three-bedroomed residence	34		

Source: Coleman–Zapata survey.

In 1980, the minimum salary in Cuernavaca was 100 pesos a day. In Toluca and Puebla it was about the same, 106 and 105 pesos a day respectively. The minimum salary was lower in Ciudad Sahagún (80 pesos) and higher in Mexico City (120 pesos). If this is a reasonable index of working class cost of living, then it would be necessary to deflate money wages by a factor of 25-50 per cent (taking Ciudad Sahagún as the base line), depending on location.

Perhaps the most variable factor in workers' standard of living is whether they have to rent accommodation. In the Nissan sample, only one-quarter of the workers had to rent accommodation, but this was a substantial drain on their resources. We may surmise that a higher proportion of workers in Mexico City have to rent accommodation, and this may also be true of Ciudad Sahagún, which is notorious for its housing shortage.

However, even taking these factors into account, there can be little doubt that Mexican car workers can live comfortably. This does not imply, by any means, that they will therefore be politically and industrially conservative. In this book, the question of the political attitudes and behaviour of individual workers is not considered. Industrial behaviour, such as strike action, is largely a collective phenomenon. As such, the unit of analysis is the union and not the individual. The argument developed in this book is that wages, whether absolute or relative, explain less about union militancy than other factors having to do with trade union organization as such. Indeed, the argument of this book is the reverse: industrial militancy is rewarded by higher than average rates of wage increase.

An aristocracy of labour

Given their relatively high wages and job security, it might be thought useful to analyse these Mexican car workers as a labour aristocracy. Clearly no working class is ever homogeneous; some sections are always better paid than others. The implications of this are, however, by no means obvious. Moreover, the notion of an aristocracy of labour is something which requires a more precise specification. The term is widely used in a variety of ways, and its empirical referent is sometimes an entire social class, sometimes the skilled, well-paid or unionized section of the working class, or sometimes a historically specific and culturally defined stratum of workers with certain value orientations.

In one usage, the notion of a labour aristocracy has been used to account for the conservatism of the British working class by adducing the claim that the fruits of empire enabled the British bourgeoisie to buy off the working class with high wages.[17] Such an argument is implausible for Britain and, in any case, inapplicable in Mexico. Most usages of the term, however, refer to a stratum of the working class which is economically advantaged. It is argued that this stratum is disposed toward accommodation with employers and that its subsequent failure to adopt a revolutionary political position consigns the working class as a whole to accommodationist politics. This happens because the labour aristocracy monopolizes leadership positions in the labour movement and/or establishes a pattern of industrial and political behaviour which other sections of the working class perforce accept.

In order to be acceptable, such arguments need to demonstrate the existence of such a stratum and show how it influenced the rest of the working class. The criteria proposed for identifying a stratum of labour aristocrats are various. John Foster suggests that the labour aristocracy should be identified as a privileged grade within the labour force – those skilled workers who exercised positions of authority in the productive process.[18] It is their position of authority at work, rather than skill or high wages *per se*, which is the key feature in Foster's account. Whatever the merits of Foster's argument,[19] it is inapplicable to auto workers in contemporary Mexico. The entire labour force lacks control and authority *vis-à-vis* management.[20]

Other writers, such as Gray and Crossick, have focussed on the ways in which certain skilled tradesmen developed a specific culture, centred on the values of thrift, providence and industry.[21] While this set them apart in their style of life from the mass of unskilled workers, it also never completely integrated them into bourgeois culture. Respectability was not incompatible with industrial and political militancy.

While these studies of British labour history convincingly demonstrate the existence of a stratum of skilled workers with a specific culture, they do not provide reasons why the influence of this stratum on the rest of the working class should be important and conservative, nor do they suggest that the labour aristocracy in Victorian Britain was uniquely accommodationist. Indeed, the thrust of the argument about the culture of this stratum is that labour aristocratic values and beliefs exist in an uneasy tension with the dominant bourgeois ideology.

It is still an open question whether Mexican factory workers constitute such a cohesive and distinct cultural elite within the working class as a whole. In any event, no inference about political or industrial conservatism can be adduced from such arguments. This is even more applicable to claims that there is an inverse correlation between radicalism and income or skill level. The empirical studies in this area do not, on the whole, support such a proposition.[22] Moreover, as John Humphrey has argued in the case of Brazilian car workers, in terms of either income or skill it is not easy to identify car workers as a whole as particularly privileged.[23] As the previous discussion of wage differentials in the Mexican auto industry indicates, wage spreads are small. There are, of course, a small number of workers who are more highly paid than the average. Whether these form an aristocracy of labour remains, at this stage of our knowledge, an open question. It is also possible that certain skilled groups within the auto industry could, perhaps, be described as a labour aristocracy, though this is unlikely since there is little evidence that they enjoy a special position *vis-à-vis* the rest of the workforce when it comes to industrial bargaining.

In arguing that the notion of a labour aristocracy is not useful for this research, there is no intention of suggesting the opposite: that the entire Mexican working class, or the auto workers, are imbued with revolutionary ideology. It has been suggested that working classes may lack class consciousness in the sense that their actions are circumscribed within the limits of the existing society, and that they do not visualize any concrete alternative, without necessarily implying any positive acceptance of the *status quo* or of bourgeois ideology.[24] The factors underlying working class consciousness are, no doubt, complex and, in any event, beyond the scope of this book. However, differences in levels of union militancy may often be explained without direct reference to the attitudes and beliefs of individual workers. Without denying the importance of studies of the consciousness of Mexican workers, studies of variations in industrial militancy need not start with such individual-level data. Indeed, it seems more plausible to argue that variations in degrees of union militancy are most parsimoniously explained with reference to variations in union structure and organization.

The argument of this book is that variations in union behaviour have, independently of the professed beliefs of the individuals involved, consequences for political stability. As a result, the state needs to control labour militancy. It does so in a variety of ways, one of which is an attempt to establish legitimacy by direct appeals to the working class. It is at this juncture that the questions of the values and beliefs of individual workers become relevant. The main part of this book concerns the structural factors leading up to a crisis of legitimation for the state. The final chapter then goes on to discuss the possible implications of such a crisis for future political developments in Mexico.

4

The unions: a historical analysis

This chapter provides a historical account of the development of the unions in the Mexican automobile industry. Each union is treated separately, and systematic comparisons among them are postponed until chapters 5–8.

As indicated in chapter 1, Mexican labour law allows for the formation of a variety of types of union: plant unions, enterprise unions, national industrial unions, craft unions and general unions. There is, therefore, no reason in principle why the Mexican automobile industry should not have been organized into a single national industrial union, like the United Auto Workers of America or, indeed, into a series of craft unions and general unions, as in the United Kingdom.[1] The automobile industry could, also, have been incorporated into the large mining–metallurgical union. As it happened, the automobile industry in Mexico was basically organized on a plant-by-plant or enterprise-by-enterprise level.

The situation in 1978 is outlined in table 2.1. With the exception of the GM plant in Toluca, where the union was organized as a section of a state-wide metallurgical union (and the Ford plants prior to 1977, which were organized in a similar manner), all the unions in the industry were autonomous entities, affiliated to various union confederations but in principle enjoying autonomy in bargaining and union government.

The organization of this chapter follows the chronological establishment of the automobile plants in Mexico. The oldest firms are discussed first. A considerable amount of detail has been provided in this chapter in order to illustrate the richness and complexity of shop-floor conflicts within the industry. It is to be hoped that this will counterbalance any notion that the only important events in Latin American labour history are those that involve national bargaining between the state and politicized labour leaderships.

Ford

The early history of union organization in the Ford plant is somewhat unclear. The Unión de Obreros y Empleados de la Industria Auto-movilística y Similares del DF was formed in December 1932, and affiliated with the CROM.[2] Although seriously weakened by this date, the CROM was still a force to be reckoned with, and it is not altogether surprising that it should have been able to gain adherents in the auto industry.[3]

This was obviously a purely paper organization. Although there had apparently been an unsuccessful strike in 1929, the Ford workers appear to have experienced considerable difficulty in forming an effective plant organization. According to Richard Miller, 'in 1934 a committee of fifteen workers from Ford presented various complaints personally to President Cardenas, declaring that the company had thwarted at least five attempts to form a union within the plant'.[4]

By 1935, there were moves to break away from the CROM. At least some of the Ford workers wished to join the Sindicato Unitario de Trabajadores Metalúrgicos, affiliated with the Communist-led CSUM. The confederation to which the Ford workers finally agreed to affiliate in June of 1936 was the anarcho-syndicalist CGT. As argued in chapter 1, the CGT was anarcho-syndicalist in name rather than in action. As Córdova has said, 'Its anarchism was purely rhetorical . . . Anarchism served those opportunistic, ignorant and treacherous "leaders" simply to disguise their irresponsibility with respect to every obligation which integrally concerned the workers' organizations'.[5] In those early years there were a number of fierce fights for leadership posts in the union, with Enrique Rendón and Vicente Rendón prevailing over the other factions in 1936. Their reign lasted less than a year, when they were pushed out of office by a rank-and-file revolt. There seems to have been widespread disgust with the arbitrary way in which the leadership was using the *cláusula de exclusión*, and an attempt was made by a group of insurgents to overthrow the union leadership and replace it. Mexican labour law provides for a closed shop in which one union has exclusive jurisdiction over a place of work. Workers who do not belong to the union must, therefore, be dismissed. By expelling someone from union membership, the incumbent leadership can effectively bring about his or her dismissal from the company. It seems that the Rendón brothers were using the *cláusula de exclusión* in this manner to stifle opposition to their leadership. As chronicled by union minutes, 'Brother Fuentes proposes, in view of the fact that we have practically been without an executive committee since this gives no sign of life other than to apply the *cláusula de exclusión* against us for any and every reason, that in this meeting the above-mentioned Executive Committee be removed'.[6]

The two leadership groups now battled it out in the labour courts, each claiming that the other Executive Committee was illegitimate. Lying behind these conflicts and mutual accusations was a jurisdictional struggle between the CGT and the CTM for control of the union. In February 1938 the Junta Local de Conciliación y Arbitraje apparently ruled in favour of the CTM group, and the union settled down to a period of relative tranquillity which was to last for some thirty-five years.

By 1940 Vicente Rendón was back in the saddle as General Secretary. Apart from a short-lived internal challenge in early 1943, Rendón continued unchallenged until 1948, when he passed on the mantle of office in an uncontested election to the next in line in the union hierarchy, the Interior Secretary. This regular succession of leadership posts within the same self-renewing group continued down to the mid-seventies.

Although there had apparently been brief stoppages in 1929, 1938 and 1939, the first mention of a serious strike at Ford is in 1948. There appears to have been some discontent simmering among the rank and file at this time. The following year, 1949, saw an attempt to call a strike at the Ford plant by the UGOCM. This union confederation had recently been formed by a number of left-leaning national industrial unions which had broken away from the CTM. In what appears to have been an attempt to bring the Ford workers out of the CTM and into the UGOCM, the latter set in motion the legal process to call a strike at the car factory. The Junta Federal de Conciliación y Arbitraje declared the strike non-existent, and the Ford workers thereafter remained in the ranks of the CTM.[7] Apart from this, there appear to be no written records of strikes in Ford until the 1970s.

Ford had begun operations in Mexico in 1924, and bought its La Villa plant in the eastern section of Mexico City in 1931. With the expansion of the industry following the 1962 integration decree, Ford set up two new plants in the northern industrial suburbs of Mexico City, Tlalnepantla and Cuautitlán. (The Cuautitlán operation was, in turn, subdivided into three separate plants: motors, assembly and trucks.)

With the change in the organization of production came a series of changes in the union. Large numbers of new workers were hired, and a substantial number of experienced workers were moved from the Villa plant to the new plants to get production moving. Certain start-up problems arose, but were rapidly solved. While the workers transferred from the Villa plant provided a core of experience, the large number of new workers substantially offset this, even though many of the new workers were themselves from urban working class backgrounds.[8] Insurgent movements developed in the early and mid-seventies, and these seem to have been concentrated in the new Cuautitlán and Tlalnepantla plants.[9]

The Ford workers initially were part of the Unión de Obreros y Empleados de la Industria Automovilística y Similares de DF, affiliated to the CTM. When they were started up, the Tlalnepantla and Cuautitlán plants, which were located outside the boundaries of the Federal District, were organized by the Unión Sindical de Trabajadores de la Industria Metálica y Similares del Estado de México, also a CTM union. These seem to have been highly bureaucratized unions, with the union leaderships being drawn from professional CTM leadership and having no connection with the Ford factories.

The bureaucratic features of these unions were probably strengthened, at least from the point of view of the Ford workers, by the fact that they were unions in which the various sections had little autonomy. Liaison with the workforce was maintained through a full-time committee man, who was not himself a member of the Executive Committee of either of the unions. The distance between the union and the membership was such that when, in 1960, a group of students carried out a survey of workers' attitudes in the Ford factory, 80 per cent of the workers stated that the plant did not have a union.[10] At the time, Ford management felt that this was a desirable state of affairs, since they were committed to a paternalistic and manipulative policy toward the union.[11] (This management policy was later to change, as will be seen.)

Shortly after the Cuautitlán and Tlalnepantla plants had begun operations, industrial relations at Ford were complicated by a power struggle within the CTM leadership. The professional union leader who had been given control of the Villa union was expelled from the CTM in 1974, along with other leaders. The following year, these ex-CTM leaders founded the COR (Confederación Obrera Revolucionaria – Revolutionary Workers' Confederation).[12]

This situation was particularly inconvenient for Ford management since they had previously negotiated identical contracts with the two CTM unions. Now that the two unions were affiliated with different confederations, there would obviously be difficulties in negotiating similar contracts, and if differing contracts were negotiated, this in itself would doubtless be the cause of discontent sooner or later.

In addition, the rank-and-file insurgency posed a potential threat of the take-over of one or both of these official unions. The full-time committee man was increasingly less able to control the actions of the *delegados departmentales* (the shop-floor departmental representatives) and wished to retire. He was persuaded by management to stay on for another year, and talks between management and workers over the question of independent unionism were initiated. In a bid to recoup legitimacy, the union in the Villa plant presented an aggressive set of demands.[13] Unfortunately for management, the committee man died at this juncture, and, in the words of the head of industrial relations, 'there was chaos'. For their part, the union leadership was deeply split. There was considerable sentiment in favour of forming an independent union, though whether it should be the FAT (Frente Auténtico del Trabajo) or the UOI or should be unaffiliated with any confederation was a matter of considerable dispute. An attempt was made to bring the International Metalworkers' Federation, FITIM, into the dispute as an arbitrator. At the same time, Fidel Velázquez' assistance was sought. He appointed one of his close collaborators as adviser to the union, and this man took over the contract negotiations. At this time the other plants had not as yet presented their demands for contract revision, and the CTM was able to capitalize on the opportunity to bring the errant union back into the fold. This was done by the formation of a single union with national jurisdiction which encompassed all three plants.[14] The union delegates were changed. Through another coincidence, the CTM leader appointed by Fidel Velázquez to advise the union also died at this time, giving the insurgents greater scope once again for renewed activity.

The following year, 1976, there were new union leaders and a new set of demands was presented to the company. The union elections of February 1976 were fought, apparently for the first time, by a number of organized slates. There was a three-way line-up, among the insurgents, the old-guard union *delegados* and a very conservative group. The voting was 769, 397 and 28 respectively.[15] The new leadership was under some pressure to demonstrate that it could deliver the goods,[16] and they called a strike which lasted three weeks. They won an 18 per cent wage increase. (The company was apparently prepared to offer 20 per cent, according to a *post hoc* interview with management.)[17] The union continued its tough bargaining stance, and in 1977 the negotiations over the contract revision lasted nine weeks, with daily meetings and the items being discussed point by point.

While these negotiations were in progress, the insurgents moved against the incumbent leadership. The CTM leader was recalled, and a new set of demands was presented. The leader agreed to step down, though at this time the insurgents did not have enough force, apparently, to break completely with the CTM. Once again the union was formally reorganized, with the new name of Sindicato de Trabajadores de Ford Motor Company – CTM. While formally remaining within the CTM, the new structure effectively devolved power to the leaders elected by the workers themselves, and ended the domination of the union by professional CTM bureaucrats.[18]

This arrangement suited the new leadership of the Ford union. By remaining within the CTM they would have access to a number of important benefits, such as housing, without being hampered by the CTM's moderation.[19] When the CTM and the government were implementing an unofficial incomes policy in 1978, the Ford union went ahead and, after a brief strike in August, negotiated a wage increase substantially above the norm. As the General Secretary said, 'It doesn't matter to us what the CTM thinks'.[20]

In April of that same year, the union had also threatened the company with a strike for violation of the contract, claiming that widespread attempts at speed-up had occurred. Ford management interpreted this as yet another move to head off internal opposition within the union and give the company a nasty surprise.[21] They nevertheless agreed to reduce the speed of the assembly line.[22] All indications are that future industrial relations at Ford will continue to exhibit high levels of conflict as union leaderships strive to retain their legitimacy in the eyes of a militant workforce. And despite the relative independence of the Ford union within the CTM, there are indications that some sections of the rank and file wish the union to break away completely from the CTM.

General Motors

General Motors began operations in Mexico in 1935. The union was formed in 1937, and affiliated with the Federación Local del DF. This federation appears to have been a relatively militant anarcho-syndicalist organization, distinct from the CGT, having as its General Secretary Luís Araiza. According to Araiza's account, the Federación Local was one of the constituent organizations which called for a unification congress in 1933, giving rise to the CGOCM (Confederación General de Obreros y Campesinos de México).[23]

In 1947 the GM workers, now some 860 strong, decided to affiliate with the CUT.[24] When the CUT was absorbed in the CROC in 1952, the GM union joined the CROC.[25]

Seemingly, the first strike by GM workers took place in 1965, and was followed by a second in 1973, and by a lengthy strike in 1975. Another lengthy strike followed in 1977. All these took place in the Mexico City plant. Meanwhile, GM had set up a second plant in Toluca. This was organized separately, as a section of the metallurgical workers' union of the State of México, and was affiliated to the CTM.

One issue in the 1975 strike was a fear on the part of the GM workers that the company was intending to move its operations entirely to the new plant in Toluca.[26] The union struck for twenty-eight days, and received some support from the UAW and the International Metalworkers' Federation.[27] The union won a 13 per cent wage increase and a number of fringe benefits. The 1977 strike lasted a full sixty-two days, and was clearly a trial of strength between company and union. The outcome of this strike appears to have been ambiguous.[28]

After another strike in 1979, there was once again, in 1980, a full-scale test of strength between GM and the union. The principal issue here was a demand by the union that they be given the bargaining rights for the new plant which GM was about to establish in Ramos Arizpe, Coahuila, in the northern part of the country. After more than three months on strike, the union gave in.

The Toluca plant provides an interesting contrast with the Mexico City plant. It has not experienced any strikes, and, in contrast to the situation in Chrysler (see below), the union leadership has not faced a serious challenge to its authority. The reasons why a separate union was established in the Toluca plant after it began operations in 1965 are not entirely clear. The union leadership of the Mexico City plant apparently made no effort to prevent this happening. One suggestion[29] was made that the union leadership exchange the right to unionize the workers in Toluca for an increase in the number of workers with *planta* status in Mexico City. At any rate, the Toluca plant was unionized by a CTM union, the Sindicato de Trabajadores de la Industria Metalúrgica del Estado de México, which was a state-wide metalworking union.

The Toluca plant was established entirely with locally recruited workers.[30] It may perhaps be surmised that this was a factor differentiating GM's experience from that of strife-torn Chrysler. However, in

the opinion of GM management, Chrysler's problems did not stem
from their labour recruitment policies, but rather from the way in which
they attempted to control the union. Whatever the factors operating in
the Chrysler case, it is certainly the case that the GM set-up in Toluca
illustrates very well one of the classical ways in which the CTM controls
its apparatus.

The CTM in Toluca is essentially a family concern. Four brothers
from a working class family began union careers with the CTM in the
1930s, and worked their way up the hierarchy. When the research for
this book was carried out in 1978 they all held important posts in the
CTM apparatus. One was the legal adviser to the CTM in the State of
Mexico. A second was General Secretary of a number of unions,
including the metalworkers' union. A third was the section leader for
the GM section of the metalworkers' union, and was also a *regidor* (local
municipal councillor). The fourth was a deputy in the state Chamber of
Deputies. The CTM offices were staffed with relatives of theirs; at least
one cousin and one niece were working in the offices at the time. All this
is, of course, highly impressionistic evidence. But precisely because of
this, it must surely understate the web of power and influence which
these four brothers have woven in Toluca.

The fact that it is a family concern is not really the most important
point. What is important is the way in which a small group of union
leaders (a) hold multiple union offices, (b) simultaneously hold political
offices and (c) operate a pyramidal structure of union power which
makes any rank-and-file challenge difficult to organize. Similar
pyramidal structures existed in Ford before the 1977 reorganization. (It
would be interesting to explore the hypothesis that the CTM
bureaucracy has controlled the rank and file through organizational
techniques of this kind, rather than through direct repression and
manipulation, as is suggested by certain commentators. The small size of
CTM unions[31] would seem to be *a priori* support for such a hypothesis.)
Both unions have gone their own way, and there are no contacts
between their respective leaderships.

It may be symptomatic of the connections between local union
structure and political power that the leaders of the Toluca union prefer
to deal with the state-level labour court, the Junta Local de Conciliación
y Arbitraje rather than with the federal labour court, the Junta Federal
de Conciliación y Arbitraje.[32]

While the GM union in Toluca has never experienced a strike or a
rank-and-file challenge to the incumbent leadership, the history of the

union in GM's Mexico City plant has been a turbulent one. When the union was formed in 1937 the original constitution specified that meetings were to be held every two weeks and the Executive Committee was to be elected every six months. An elaborate procedure was set up whereby candidates for union office would have their qualifications discussed by speakers for and against. Then the number of candidates would be reduced to two by acclamation, followed by a secret ballot. Each post was considered in turn, and unsuccessful candidates could, and did, run for other positions. In the 1930s the total membership was about 300, so this sort of informal democracy was perhaps feasible. Elections soon became yearly, rather than six-monthly affairs, however, and meetings were held monthly instead of every two weeks.

By the mid-1940s, although union membership had dropped to about 150, the electoral process had become more formal, with slates being organized for elections. In 1945 the statutes were once more reformed to give the Executive Committee a two-year period of office, with half the officers being elected each year. The slates, however, still bore traces of the kind of informal and personality oriented democracy that prevailed. For example, in the election of 1947, four officers were up for election and five slates were presented. There were, however, only fourteen candidates in all, since some candidates appeared on more than one slate.

There existed the real possibility of a lapse into anarchy. This is illustrated in the election of 1950. Again, four offices were to be filled. Nine slates were presented, with a total of only eighteen candidates. However, there were also a number of independent candidates: two for one post, four for another and five for a third post.

This chaotic situation lasted until 1955, when the slates became more organized and stable, and began to have names. By now union membership had reached 800–1000. (The figures fluctuate considerably since *obreros eventuales* were unionized and had the right to vote.) Throughout this period the union's life went on without major problems, with high turnouts to the monthly meetings and frequent rotation of union officers.[33] The meetings appear to have been somewhat boisterous and there were occasional difficulties in obtaining a hall to meet in, since the owners frequently complained about the damage caused by the GM workers.[34]

The first real internal conflict occurred in 1963. A quotation from a labour inspector gives the flavour of events: 'The meeting began with the attendance of the majority of workers, approximately 1200 of them; said meeting from the very beginning was run in complete disorder,

Table 4.1. *Principal slates contesting elections in GM union*

Year	Names of principal slates	Total no. of slates
1955	Blanca Verde	2
1957	Blanca Azul	6
1958	Circulo–Verde Azul	2
1959	Circulo–Verde Azul	4
1960	Circulo–Verde Azul	2
1961	Circulo–Verde Unificación	2
1962	Circulo–Verde Unificación	2
1963	Unificación Democrático	4
1964	Circulo–Verde Azul Unificación	4
1965	Circulo–Verde Azul Unificación	6
1966	Coalición[a] Unificación	2
1967	Coalición Unificación	3
1968	Coalición Unificación	2
1969	Acción Coalición Unificación	5
1970	Acción Coalición Unificación FUT[b]	2
1971[c]	Acción Unificación FUT	4
1972	Acción Renovación-sindical[d] Unificación FUT	6
1973	Acción Renovación-sindical Unificación FUT	9
1974[c]	Acción Unificación FUT	5
1975[c]	Acción Renovación-sindical Unificación	13
1976[c]	Acción Renovación-sindical Unificación	9
1977[c]	Acción Renovación-sindical Unificación	13

[a] Circulo–Verde and Azul joined to form Coalición.
[b] Frente Único de Trabajadores.
[c] No single slate won.
[d] Coalición changed its name to Renovación-sindical.
Winners are underlined.
Source: Union minutes.

resulting in approximately 300 people leaving the hall . . . rather than a meeting it was a complete carnival'.[35] The cause of the uproar was a proposal to vote by slates instead of voting individually for each secretary. The Secretaría del Trabajo ordered a recount, which confirmed the results of the election which had ended with the walk-out.

By this time, Michels' iron law of oligarchy seemed to be producing its usual unpleasant side effects. In 1964 the first serious accusations were made against one of the union leaders: 'nothing has been done . . . he has transformed the union office into a den of iniquity where affairs of all kinds are dealt with . . . rather than a union office it seems like a police station' (General Secretary, referring to the Secretary of Labour).[36]

Before the matter went further, the Secretary of Labour was fired for having stopped the assembly line. The union voted to continue to pay his salary until he could find other work.

The elections in 1965 were the cause of some dispute. The absence of the incumbent General Secretary was used as a reason for not accepting his candidature in the election. The Secretary of Labour ordered a recount, and the results of the election were reconfirmed. The new office-holders were then accused by the deposed General Secretary some months later of abusing their authority in applying the *cláusula de exclusión* to a worker for posting notices in the workshops. A period of incessant sniping and recrimination had set in. By June 1967 the deposed General Secretary was using his position as chairman of meetings to bring about changes in the membership of the union's internal control commissions. The incumbent Executive Committee was outraged. Each side wrote its own version of the minutes of the meetings of 26 August 1967.

The elections of that day resulted in a victory for the Coalición slate, supporting the ex-General Secretary – but only after a skirmish between the two groups for control of the ballot box and the abandoning of the meeting by the supporters of the incumbent General Secretary, organized around the Unificación slate. The elections were held again a few days later. The Coalición group again received a majority, but a greatly reduced one. For the next three or four years Coalición and Unificación fought each election, with Coalición retaining the upper hand, despite occasional reverses.

The state of mutual animosity may be gauged from the following comments of the incumbent General Secretary (Coalición) about his opponents: 'Brother X (Unificación) was sanctioned with one day's pay for having insulted the present Executive Committee, and Y for having directly insulted the General Secretary; these gentlemen, unhappy with the sanction applied, took the Executive Committee to the Junta de Conciliación y Arbitraje, accusing us of abuse of authority.'[37]

In turn, the General Secretary was accused of enriching himself at the expense of union funds, and a group of workers wrote to the Junta expressing their 'unhappiness with the undemocratic and illegal form in which the electoral meeting was conducted'. And another group wrote demanding the cancellation of the 1969 elections by the Junta stating:

The meeting was characterized by a complete disorder in which intoxicating drinks were allowed . . . permitting the blatant manoeuvre of cutting off the electric current for several minutes in the hall . . . the Labour Inspector left the hall and returned some minutes later accompanied by certain elements belonging to one of the groups contesting the elections, to whom he assuredly promised to give legal endorsement to the acts committed.[38]

Similar accusations were made about the 1970 elections. The discontent surfaced again in the 1971 wage negotiations; one worker claimed that 'in the last strike a venal "leader" sold us out and today some venal and bandit "leaders" have done the same with this strike'.

The 1973 elections again saw complaints about procedure.[39] By this time the more or less formal two- or three-party democracy had once again degenerated into a motley collection of short-lived alliances. The 1977 elections were fought among no fewer than twelve slates, often with overlapping candidates.

With all the reservations which must necessarily be made as a result of the incompleteness of the data, what conclusions can be drawn from GM's long and tortuous history? First, the GM union in Mexico City has never fallen into a really solidified oligarchy. The tendency, in fact, has been towards the opposite extreme, towards an undisciplined libertarianism. The tendencies towards oligarchy have always been present, but each time a particular group appeared to be gathering the reins of power for its own private uses a storm of protest from the rank and file forced it to desist or overthrew it. The successful operation of this veto power seems to be a result of the continuing existence of permanent factions within the union.

The degree to which these factions represent political alignments is unclear. They appear to be quite stable, and seem to be organized primarily in terms of the parochial politics of the GM plant. Whatever their base, the existence of these factions has produced a history of open, if turbulent, government in GM.[40]

Chrysler

The origins of the Chrysler plant go back to 1938, when the Azcárraga family started Fábricas Auto-mex, assembling Chryslers. Fábricas Auto-mex was wholly owned by the Azcárraga family until 1959, when one-third of the equity was sold to Chrysler.[41] In 1971 Chrysler bought out most of the remaining shares, and the name of the enterprise was changed in 1972 to Chrysler de México.[42] The plant was located just to the north of Chapultepec Park in Mexico City. With the changed situation following the 1962 integration decree, Chrysler established a second plant in Toluca. This plant mainly produced engine blocks, and began operation in 1964.

The original union constitution was altered and a Sindicato Nacional was formed in March 1964. Both this and the previous union were affiliated with the CTM.[43]

When the union was formed in 1964 a single slate was presented for the five principal union offices and approved unanimously. Two years later the General Secretary died and was replaced by the Secretary of the Interior. In the elections held the following year there was a substantial reshuffle. Only one of the four previous incumbents was re-elected, but he moved from Treasurer to General Secretary. The new committee was elected at a meeting of 1680 workers, the General Secretary being elected unanimously, and the Secretary of the Interior by a mere 63 votes. The Secretary of the Exterior was elected by 902 votes, and the other offices were not contested.[44]

There were complaints over the next couple of years that the General Secretary was hardly to be seen in Toluca, and that he received his information from a confederate in that city.

In July of 1968, at a well-attended union meeting, the incumbent leadership was vociferously challenged by one of the more established workers. (He had worked for the company for seventeen years.) After the meeting he was threatened and told to keep his mouth shut. Some days later, he was fired. The incipient insurgent movement was stopped in its tracks.[45]

Nevertheless, discontent continued to simmer under the surface and erupted in a wildcat strike two years later. Meanwhile, the confederate of the General Secretary, who did not hold an official union post, had begun to carve out an informal empire for himself in Toluca. He began to build up a clientelistic network by effectively choosing which applicants would be given jobs in the factory. He apparently hoped to be elected to union office in the forthcoming elections in 1970. (The company, seemingly, contemplated this possibility with some concern, particularly in view of the background of unrest in Toluca.)

The operations at the Toluca plant had expanded rapidly, and by the end of 1969 the company employed over 5000 workers, compared with 1500 in 1963. This rapid expansion in the workforce was likely, in and of itself, to create problems. In addition, the change in ownership in 1970–1 brought with it an extensive reorganization of the company which was not always immediately accepted by the workforce.[46]

There was, however, a more direct cause of the discontent which finally manifested itself in a strike in November 1970. Apparently, the company had experienced some difficulties in recruiting sufficient workers in Toluca itself and, partly because of this and partly because of the need to use experienced workers during the start-up period, had brought workers by bus from Mexico City, a journey of about an hour. There were complaints about this, but most serious was the fact, reported by Angel Fojo,[47] that wage rates were substantially lower in Toluca. Fojo asserts that the wage rates in 1970 were as shown in table 4.2.[48] This meant that some workers who were moved from the Mexico City plant to Toluca experienced a wage cut.

On 3 November 1969, a Monday, when the workers arrived at the gates of the factory in Toluca they decided not to report to work. November 2nd had been an official holiday, and they wanted a day off in lieu (or compensation), as was standard practice at the Mexico City plant. There were scuffles as some workers tried to enter, and were prevented from so doing by others. The police fired warning shots in the air, and were then met with some rock-throwing by some of the workers. In the confusion, a worker was shot and wounded, producing a protest march through the streets of Toluca. A commission of workers met with the Governor of the State of México, Hank González, who arranged a conciliatory meeting among the workers' representatives, the union and the company. The workers presented a list of eight demands:
(1) a reduction in the hours of work from 9.5 to 9;
(2) a more efficient medical service;
(3) financial aid for travel between Mexico City and Toluca;
(4) a wage increase;
(5) the award of *planta* status to the workers from the Mexico City factory after they had worked in Toluca for three months;
(6) the award of *planta* status to the other workers after they had worked three three-month contracts as *eventuales*;
(7) the establishment of a savings scheme;
(8) payment for November 3.

The company agreed to pay salaries for 3 November, and began discussions on the other demands. The leaders of the protest were fired. Hostility to the union leadership was now widespread, and was increased when the union leadership refused to argue for the reinstallation of the leaders of the walkout. In January 1970 there were substantial layoffs at the Toluca plant. The response was a strike, beginning on 22 January.

Table 4.2. *Hourly wage rates in*
Chrysler (pesos)

Category	Mexico City	Toluca
Cleaners	58	28.5
4	78	47
3	93	58
2	103	68
1	117	76

Source: Fojo, 'Estudio de un conflicto industrial'.

The workers held a meeting and voted the General Secretary out of office. They then sent a commission to Mexico City to request the intervention of the Junta de Conciliación y Arbitraje.

The incumbent General Secretary counterattacked, accusing the insurgents of Communism: 'For some months a work of aggression has been carried on against our union, by professional Communist agitators and by some internal elements . . . provoking a strike in Toluca.'[49]

By now it was obvious to the company that the union was incapable of controlling its membership. Worse, the conflict over union leadership had led to a serious strike. Its response was to persuade the incumbent General Secretary to step down. At the initiative of the company, a meeting was held in Mexico City to elect a new union leadership. The striking workers held their own meeting in Toluca. Two Executive Committees were elected, one in Mexico City, one in Toluca, each claiming to be the legitimate leadership of the Chrysler union. Both meetings appear to have been well attended.[50]

The interesting thing is the nature of the persons elected in both meetings. The Toluca meeting elected the rising strong-man or *cacique*, who had, at any rate, been a likely challenger to the incumbent leadership in the forthcoming elections. The person elected by the Mexico City meeting was the previous production manager in the Mexico City plant. (It is not uncommon to hear cases of workers who have moved from union office to lower management; but the reverse career path must surely be quite unusual.)[51]

In part, the division in the workforce, which was reflected in the two Executive Committees, seems to have been a division between the established Mexico City workers and the more recently recruited Toluca workers, though the evidence for this is, naturally, impressionistic.

At any rate, the Junta Federal de Conciliación y Arbitraje saw fit to recognize the committee elected in the Mexico City meeting as the legitimate leadership of the union.

The new leadership now faced a number of problems. It was naturally anxious to solve the strike and get the men back to work. It had also to assert its authority over the supporters of the rival leadership, who were, it must be remembered, the ones still on strike in Toluca. Fidel Velázquez' assistance was solicited, a meeting was held with the strikers in Toluca, and there was an agreement to return to work on 5 February. The outcome was a clear defeat for the Toluca workers, and in the months following the return to work there were a substantial number of dismissals.[52]

Shortly after the conflict in the Toluca plant came to an end, it appeared as if some workers in the Mexico City plant were considering militant action. This movement was nipped in the bud, and a number of dismissal notices were issued there in February.

The union leadership which came to power in 1970 was to dominate the union for the next decade. No organized challenge to the monopoly of power by the General Secretary was mounted, though there were dissident movements, and he was re-elected without opposition in 1976. The PRI later recognized his valuable services in securing industrial tranquillity with a seat in the Chamber of Deputies.

The union leadership ruled in an apparently autocratic manner. Union meetings were now a thing of the past. An insurgent movement which dared challenge the leadership claimed, in April 1972, that 'In the more than two years for which the Executive Committee has been at the helm of our union, it has never called a meeting, which constitutes a violation of the statutes.'[53]

These workers sought support from their fellow unionists in other car factories. They addressed a meeting of the workers in GM's Mexico City plant, asserting that the General Secretary,

on taking control of the union, formed a non-uniformed security group, a true white guard dedicated to the imposition of terrorism and the subjection of those workers who showed their dislike; we would also like to note that in the two years of functioning of the present leadership body, there has been no rendering of union accounts, nor has a general union meeting been called; that a specific sum of money has been charged those brothers seeking work for each contract, as well as for those brothers who obtain promotion or receive *planta* status.[54]

Later, the insurgents took their case to the Ministry of Labour, arguing that 'by virtue of the fact that the Executive Committee has roundly refused to call a meeting . . . we find ourselves required to call it ourselves'.[55] This movement of protest also sank almost without a trace. Then, in the following year, trouble was caused by the workers hired by Chrysler to drive the finished vehicles to the distributors. These workers were not part of the Chrysler union, and were organized by the Frente Sindical Independiente. The company wrote to the Junta de Conciliación, asking that the strike be declared illegal.[56] Despite the fact that these events did not directly involve the Chrysler workers, they undoubtedly continued to contribute to the unrest in the company.

This unrest came to the surface once again in 1975, when the *eventuales* mounted a protest. They demanded the dismissal of the General Secretary and accused him of selling *planta* contracts. Work was interrupted for two days on this occasion. Again, the sequel to these acts of defiance was a wave of dismissals.[57]

Some notion of the nature of the subsequent purge may be gleaned from the archives of the Junta Federal de Conciliación y Arbitraje.[58] In the months following this conflict, twenty-one workers brought claims for unjust dismissal against Chrysler.[59] In initiating their actions, these workers regularly stated that they had been dismissed on the express orders of the General Secretary of the union.[60] The great majority of these workers had *planta* status and had worked for Chrysler for some years. (It is relatively simple to get rid of *eventuales;* it is only necessary to wait until the contract expires. Workers with *planta* status are more costly to lay off.)

Four workers claimed that letters of resignation produced by Chrysler as evidence had been forged. The labour court did not accept the claims that these were forgeries,[61] and ruled in favour of the company.[62] That these workers were fired for union militancy will be apparent from the following extracts from three cases.

Case 1: extract from letter sent by the lawyer for Chrysler to the Junta:

more or less at the beginning of this year, the plaintiff began to hold small meetings inside the plant which he organized among the other workers, distributing union-type propaganda and asking the workers to stop carrying out their tasks in order to listen to him. In March he was told personally and in the presence of some officers of the union that if he continued with this attitude the company would find itself obliged to take more drastic measures. On 19 March he was found distributing union propaganda and holding a meeting with 25 workers.

Case 2: extract from letter of the griever to the Junta:

[in the course of work] I was attacked by Messrs W, X and Y, who attempted to take my newspaper away from me because Mr E [General Secretary of the union] had given them instructions to take away newspapers from the workers.

The worker went to complain to the union. The next day he was fired. The union claimed that the griever 'attacked Mr W, saying that the opinion of a son of a bitch didn't matter to him'. The worker was apparently reading aloud from an open letter to *El Heraldo* of 31 May 1975 which accused the General Secretary of a series of irregularities in the conduct of the Chrysler union. This same letter figures in the third case.

Case 3: extract from letter of the griever to the Junta:

[The griever begins his letter by noting that he had read the open letter to *El Heraldo* and goes on:] On discovering such matters we, the workers, organized a delegation charged with going to talk to the union. Then we were sent to the Personnel Department and told that we were suspended indefinitely for leaving our work stations. The next day [3 June], we were not allowed to enter, some 800 workers being in this condition for the space of a fortnight, at the end of which some were readmitted, and with respect to myself it was 17 June when I was allowed to enter the union offices. The General Secretary notified me that the company no longer required my services and that I was fired.

None of these three grievers were reinstated.[63] Two accepted out-of-court settlements with Chrysler whereby they obtained financial compensation,[64] and the other lost his case.

Thus, like Ford and GM, Chrysler also experienced union insurgency in the 1970s. In part this was due to the expansion of the industry and the setting up of new plants. Two features, however, distinguished Chrysler's experience from that of Ford and GM. First, by moving more workers from Mexico City to Toluca than GM, Chrysler seemingly created greater discontent in its workforce. (Nevertheless, as the 1980 GM strike indicates, the Toluca–Mexico City tensions are still very much alive there. In Ford, the avoidance of long-distance bussing by establishing the new factories in Mexico City's industrial suburb also failed to avoid conflict completely.) Secondly, and more important, unlike GM and Ford, Chrysler opted for control by a strong and authoritarian pro-company union, rather than for compromise and negotiation. If the simple stereotype of *charrismo* as corrupt and authoritarian union leaderships, divorced from the rank and file and in league with management, has any relevance in the Mexican automobile industry, it is in Chrysler. However, this style of union leadership is different from that exercised by the kinship network of the Toluca CTM (in the case of GM's Toluca union), and different yet again from the bureaucratic control structures of the CTM unions in Ford prior to the 1977 reorganization. As the following pages attempt to demonstrate, the nature of union government in VAM is different from all of these cases.

VAM

Very little can, or need, be said about VAM. Not a great deal has happened there since the company began production in 1953. It was initially known as Willy's Jeeps and, after the integration decree, changes its name (in 1964) to VAM. Forty per cent of the equity was held by American Motors and 60 per cent by the state-owned finance company SOMEX.

The union was formed in 1952, the Sindicato de Trabajadores de la Empresa Automovilística Willys Mexicana, and affiliated with the CTM. The union leadership was changed in 1958 and again in 1959, when the person who was to be General Secretary for the next twenty years was elected. There are no indications of any internal opposition until 1962, when the union elections were seriously contested. However, on this occasion, the incumbent slate won by an overwhelming majority (532 to 28).

When the Confederación Obrera Revolucionaria split off from the CTM in 1975, the VAM union followed. Apparently the leader of Section 9 of the Federación de Trabajadores del DF (CTM), which included the VAM union, was one of the dissidents, and took the section with him into the COR. He died in the late seventies, and, the tie of personal loyalty between him and the General Secretary of the VAM union now no longer existing, the VAM union returned to the CTM in 1979.[65]

The Toluca plant, which like many others had been started after the integration decree, was unionized as a section of the existing union, and the existing Executive Committee now took both sections under its wing, though contracts for the two plants were negotiated separately.

Perhaps the most telling fact about the VAM union is that there had not been a single strike in twenty-five years. The General Secretary was routinely re-elected, worked on the shop floor, and appeared to genuinely represent the workforce. Internal union life, on the other hand, hardly existed at the time fieldwork was carried out. As the

General Secretary said, 'There ought to be meetings every two months. We don't have them; there's no need.'[66] And the *delegados departmentales* were in his words a 'formalism'; all significant problems were dealt with by the General Secretary himself.

It is not clear why VAM should have such an unusual record of trouble-free industrial relations. In part it may be due to the fact that the plant is relatively small, and was not substantially affected by the expansion of the industry in the sixties and seventies. There appear to have been no dramatic changes of personnel in VAM, such as there were in the new plants elsewhere. At the same time, there does not appear to have been any particular cause for the VAM workers to complain of a distant and unresponsive union bureaucracy. Though the present General Secretary described the early years of the union as a 'paper union', and although there appears to be little internal union democracy in VAM, there is no evidence of any worker dissatisfaction with the union as there is elsewhere in the industry.

One commentator, at least, has described the system of labour relations in VAM as 'paternalism'.[67] Despite management claims to the contrary, it cannot be denied that this is a plausible contribution to the explanation of VAM's trouble-free industrial relations.

DINA

We now move on to a discussion of the three automobile companies whose unions broke away from the CTM to form independent unions, affiliated with the UOI. The first to do so was the union at the state-owned Diesel Nacional (DINA) plant.

After several years of discussions, but apparently without any serious planning,[68] the Mexican government decided to establish a complex of metal-using factories under state control in the agricultural state of Hidalgo. In part the aim of the project was to provide employment for an acutely depressed agricultural region. The site chosen was within reasonable range, however, of the Mexico City market.

Three principal enterprises were set up in the Sahagún industrial complex: a state-owned steel plant, SIDENA; a plant producing railway rolling stock (Constructor Nacional de Carros Ferrocarril); and an auto plant, Diesel Nacional. The DINA plant began production in 1954, producing first Fiat and then Renault cars under licence, with full state ownership.

The DINA plant was unionized by the CTM, and the other plants were unionized by the Mining and Metalworkers' Union.[69] Trouble arose in the DINA union less than a year after its formation.

In September 1955 several workers from DINA wrote to the Secretaría del Trabajo requesting the cancellation of the union's registration on the grounds that the five persons who were ostensibly the members of the Executive Committee were not, and never had been, workers in DINA. They formed 'part of an Executive Committee of an organization which has never existed'. This claim was supported by the administration of DINA.[70]

When a union registers with the Secretaría del Trabajo a complete listing of the workers employed must be produced. A check of the list showed the names of the executive members included. Whatever the facts may have been, a new committee was elected in April 1955 and continued to function.

The next incident happened in 1961 when the union attempted to break away from the CTM. The actual process was quite complicated. The incumbent CTM leadership was aware of the threat to disaffiliate and sought to prevent it by organizing the re-election of the Executive Committee. According to a letter of protest sent to the Secretaría del Trabajo by a group of workers,[71] the incumbent General Secretary had allowed the *eventuales*, numbering some 225, and the catering staff, to vote. According to the union constitution, only workers with *planta* status, numbering 526, had voting rights. With the incumbent re-elected with 228 votes to the 224 of his nearest contender, the inclusion of the *eventuales* could well have tipped the balance.

But this was not all. A group of workers called for a union meeting, arguing:

As is known by everybody, in June of this year an electoral meeting should have been called and elections to select a new Executive Committee held. In violation of our [union] statutes, the committee headed by Mr X has not called elections and these have not taken place.

And if this were not much, we have discovered that X and a half-dozen of his followers have invented a supposed electoral meeting and taken the Junta Federal de Conciliación y Arbitraje by surprise, claiming to the authorities and to the company that they are the 'representatives' of the workers for another two years.[72]

The meeting was held and a new committee elected, most of whose members had been expelled from the union by the previous General Secretary. The new committee apparently made a number of overtures towards joining the CROC at this stage.[73]

Meanwhile, the incumbent group counterattacked by writing to the Secretaría del Trabajo describing the insurgents as 'a clearly defined minority group which was defeated in the electoral process, containing elements completely foreign to the members of the union which is my responsibility', and accusing them of having 'simulated the occurrence of a meeting and the election of another executive committee'.[74]

The Secretaría del Trabajo refused to recognize the insurgent group, but did call the rival groups together for discussions, together with Fidel Velázquez and other leaders of the CTM. A compromise agreement was reached. The insurgents agreed not to continue to seek affiliation with the CROC, and an Executive Committee formed from members of both groups was agreed upon. It was agreed not to use the *cláusula de exclusión* for six months.

The compromise was short-lived. In mid-December of that year both groups held separate meetings and each reconstituted the Executive Committee according to its preference. Once more there were two Executive Committees, and accusations began to fly back and forth. The pro-CTM group, for example, stated:

A future meeting will deal with the act of treason which has just been committed by three Secretaries of this union, by betraying our confederation the CTM, making overtures to a different confederation or group, which has been characterized in the struggle of the workers as Communists, saboteurs of the rhythm of work and production which reigns in Mexico, playing into the hands of capitalist interests.[75]

And it had been accused of 'subversive manoeuvres to sow discord and mistrust'.[76]

The Secretaría del Trabajo, with Solomonic wisdom, refused to accept the results of either of these two meetings, arguing that neither followed the union's own constitutional procedure.

By this time, at least three alternatives to the CTM had been mooted: the CROC; affiliation with the Mining and Metalworkers' Union (which controlled the other plants in Ciudad Sahagún);[77] and the formation of an independent union.

Seemingly, in January 1962, the insurgent group favouring independence organized a meeting that met the requirements set out in the union's statutes, once again voted out the members of the pro-CTM group from the Executive Committee, replaced them with their own members, and organized a unanimous vote for disaffiliation from the CTM.

In February, the new leadership decided to try its muscle and called a strike. The company was bitterly hostile to the new leadership, and in particular to the legal adviser, Juan Ortega Arenas.

Ortega Arenas was accused by the company of being a Communist and unpatriotic agitator.[78] It was backed up by the Centro Patronal del DF, which demanded firm government intervention ('demanded energetic measures on the part of the government in the solution of the strike, considering that it was of Communist origin').[79] In the negotiations which finally put an end to the strike, the company demanded (successfully) that Juan Ortega Arenas not be present during the discussions. The flavour of the hostility shown toward Ortega Arenas is conveyed in the following newspaper report and in the quotation from a paid advertisement immediately following.

A decisive factor in the breakdown of the conciliation talks was the union representative, Juan Ortega Arenas, whom the representatives of the company have characterized as anti-patriotic, who, carrying out a real work of agitation damaging to national interests, demanded an exorbitant 100%.[80]

Juan Ortega Arenas managed to infiltrate Dina by means of an inter-union conflict which occurred some months ago in the union, when the undeniable majority of the workers repudiated the then Executive Committee.[81]

The strike was declared non-existent by the Junta Federal de Conciliación y Arbitraje and the workers were given twenty-four hours to return to work. The Junta argued that the signatories of the strike demand were not the same as those officially registered with the Ministry as the Executive Committee. This was clearly a pretext on the part of the government to break the strike. The new Executive Committee mentioned in this dispute had been elected in a union meeting on 18 January 1962, at which the majority of workers were present. The Ministry had been duly notified. The Ministry was apparently not satisfied with this and sent a Labour Inspector out to conduct new elections on 20 February, after the strike had been called off. The same Executive Committee was again elected. But this time the legal adviser of the union was Luís Gómez, leader of the railway workers' union, and a man with the reputation for *charrismo* of the first order after his actions in the 1958–9 railway workers' strike.[82]

Despite this setback, Ortega Arenas' influence in the union continued, and he shortly thereafter resumed his function as legal adviser. His reign did not, however, go unchallenged. As late as 1967 there was an attempt by the incumbent union leadership to dispense with his services. The union published a paid advertisement in *Universal* saying:

In a general meeting on February 2, the decision was taken to revoke the agreement which designated Juan Ortega Arenas as legal adviser. This decision . . . had its origin in the confirmation of the fact that Juan Ortega Arenas, abusing his post as legal adviser, succeeded in inducing our union organization to join the so-called independent workers' movement, which he claims to direct, with political aims totally foreign to our interests.[83]

There were union elections in June of that year. The incumbents were voted out of office, and Ortega Arenas was once again back in as legal adviser.

With the exception of this incident, for ten years peace reigned. Then in May 1972 the union was once again racked by internal dissent. DINA may have had an independent union, but the incumbent Secretary General seemed to be behaving very much in the traditional manner. One of the sharp practices he was accused of was, in collusion with junior executives, to pressure *eventuales* to sign resignations and then make a show of getting them reinstated – for a certain financial consideration.[84]

An insurgent group took over the union hall by force, held a meeting, voted the Executive Committee out of office, and elected a new committee. The incumbents called a meeting, which had to be abandoned shortly after it started in order to prevent a clash between partisans of the two groups. The Secretaría del Trabajo ordered a recount, which gave the insurgents a slight majority (1040 to 935). This was followed by elections in July, which confirmed the insurgent group in office (912 to 617).[85] Their tenure of office was, however, brief. In 1973 they were ousted by an even more militant group. These were the workers in assembly, who tended to live in the same towns: Pachuca, Apán and Sahagún.[86]

In 1974, what was to be the first lengthy strike by DINA workers was called. The demands centred on the need to control the rhythms of work and to increase fringe benefits. The strike was a success for the union.

Despite the strength of the DINA union, it was unable to prevent substantial layoffs during the sharp recession of 1976–7. Something like 1400 workers, out of a total blue collar workforce of some 6000, were laid off. About half of the workers who were laid off had *planta* status. Nevertheless, the union still retained its powerful shop-floor organization based on *delegados departmentales* and twenty-four sectional committees, and continued to fight with considerable success for control over working conditions and immediate supervision.[87]

Nissan

Nissan first began operations in Mexico in 1966, in the wake of the 1962 integration decree. It chose to establish its plant in the new industrial park in Cuernavaca, Morelos. Morelos is a small state, close to Mexico City, with a predominantly agricultural economy. The establishment of the Nissan factory and several others in the new industrial park was, therefore, a significant change in the state's economy.

Initially, the contract was given to the CTM. Within a few years the CTM had lost control of the union to the UOI, and both the Nissan union and Cuernavaca had acquired a reputation for troubled industrial relations. This story, and the rise and fall of the leader of the union insurgents, Raimundo Jaimes, will be traced below.

The low level of industrial development in Morelos was one of the factors which had meant that the CTM bureaucracy in that state was relatively weak and inexperienced. The Nissan workers were organized in a plant union, the Sindicato General de Trabajadores de Nissan Mexicana del Estado de Morelos, affiliated with the CTM of that state. The fact that the archbishopric of Cuernavaca was held by a radical, Mendez Arceo, who was willing to speak out publicly in support of workers' movements, was undoubtedly another factor which explains the success of the independence movement.

The insurgent movement in Nissan developed quickly, and the first struggles within the union took place early in 1969. In the union elections of February of that year, the incumbent CTM leadership tried to manipulate the result in a vain attempt to stay in power. They used the *cláusula de exclusión* against twenty members of the union, three of whom headed the opposition slate. When these workers defied this expulsion order, the incumbent leadership wrote to the Junta Local de Conciliación y Arbitraje, requesting that the election be declared null and void.[88] The issue was resolved in favour of the challengers, but they in turn were subject to criticisms from the rank and file. At a meeting in April 1970, 474 workers, out of a total of around 570, voted them out of office. A new committee was elected. Nearly all the personnel were changed, with the exception of a worker by the name of Raimundo Jaimes, and one other. Jaimes moved from the post of Treasurer to that of Secretary for Organization. In the elections of 1971, James moved up to General Secretary. Nearly all the other members of the committee were changed. (Another worker who was to have an important union career had his first experience of office at this time: Quirino Delgado, acting as deputy for the Secretary of Political Affairs.) The union was still formally affiliated with the CTM, though real control had moved substantially away from the state-level bureaucracy and into the hands of union leaders elected by the workers themselves.

The real struggle for independence took place in 1972, achieving final success in the following year. The state-level union bureaucracy decided to levy a day's pay on the membership in order to finance the construction of a sports complex. The Nissan workers objected and, together with other factories, held a demonstration of protest. This was rapidly followed by a second protest, this time complaining about the attempts by the company to undermine the authority of the Executive Committee. The company responded by refusing to allow the members of the Executive Committee to return to work. The conflict was rapidly generalized, the Junta Local de Conciliación y Arbitraje was accused of partiality, and both FAT and the UOI established contacts with the Nissan workers.[89] Finally the union became independent in 1973, with Jaimes and most of the previous Executive Committee newly elected to office again.

By now the lines of differentiation within union politics had crystallized. Both the FAT and the UOI counted on sizeable bases of support, and the more conservative, pro-CTM workers were a minority. These divisions structured the presentation of slates in union elections in subsequent years, but few of the leaders were willing to identify absolutely with either the FAT or the UOI. Jaimes tended to incline more toward the FAT, without breaking with the UOI.

In December 1973, the leadership of the union changed hands, from Jaimes to Quirino Delgado, and then, two years later, the leadership returned to Jaimes. In the meanwhile, the Nissan workers had held their first strike, in April 1974. This strike was solved only with the intervention of the Minister of Labour three weeks later.

But before Jaimes and his group regained control of the union leadership, there were a series of manoeuvres and conflicts between the two leadership groups, with management intervening to tip the balance away from Jaimes and toward its preferred candidate, Delgado.[90] In February 1975, Jaimes and three of his associates were fired, accused of engaging in union agitation during working hours, fomenting go-slows, etc. And then in September of the same year, Jaimes was accused of fraud and misuse of union funds. He was briefly jailed, and released after the workers demonstrated on his behalf. At a union meeting called to expel Jaimes from the union as a result of the charges of fraud, a nearly unanimous vote against expulsion heralded the imminent demise of the Delgado faction. Although the Delgado group had been re-elected in September 1975, another election was held in November, and the Jaimes group was returned to power (Jaimes 798; Delgado 676; pro-CTM group 96).[91]

In April 1976, the Nissan workers went on strike for the second time, this time for seven weeks. It was a long and bitter strike, and there was some feeling among the workers that it had been badly handled. In June, the Nissan workers recalled the Executive Committee, amid accusations of misuse of union funds and inept handling of the strike, and elected a new committee. This time, Delgado held the lowly post of Secretary of Social Security. The widely held notion that the strike had been a failure marked the beginning of the end of Jaimes' leadership in the union and, with it, the implantation of firm UOI control within the union leadership.[92] After yet another election in November 1977, when the union leadership was altered, Quirino Delgado returned as General Secretary (Delgado 728; FAT group 572; CTM group 145).

Finally, in the same month, Jaimes was fired for the second time, together with four *delegados departmentales*. Once again the charges were fomenting go-slows, interference with the rhythm of work, agitation, etc. This time he was not reinstated. Seemingly, the event which precipitated the final demise of Raimundo Jaimes was an attempt at a go-slow movement which began in the factory in August 1977. Although this movement had the support of the union leadership, it failed to spread beyond three departments. With less than half of the plant involved, and with the workforce already divided in terms of union politics, there was clearly a coincidence of interest in getting rid of Jaimes between management and the UOI faction led by Quirino Delgado.[93]

The years 1977 and 1978 were each marked by brief strikes, and the new leadership under Delgado seemed for the moment to be firmly in control. But although Jaimes may have been removed from the scene, a substantial body of militants remained to challenge any incumbent leadership which might fail to deliver the goods.

In 1977, Nissan decided to establish a second factory in Mexico, producing engine blocks. In the light of the difficulties experienced in Cuernavaca, it was decided to establish the new plant in Toluca. The CTM was given the contract. (The Nissan workers in Cuernavaca seem to have been taken by surprise by this move on the part of the company. In any case, they seem not to have been particularly concerned.) In the words of a junior executive of Nissan, the new plant was to be a model enterprise with 'almost military discipline' and careful selection of the workers.[94] The contract signed by the CTM for the new plant is, indeed, a meagre affair, and gave the company complete control over the work process.

However, despite Nissan's precautions, the Toluca plant also experienced an insurgent movement which demanded disaffiliation from the CTM and led a brief wildcat strike. The company response was to fire the entire workforce of 180, close the plant for six months and start again. Their assessment of the situation was that they had made the mistake of hiring workers from the DINA plant and that these workers had provided the leadership for the insurgent movement.[95]

Interestingly, the Nissan union in Toluca has as its General Secretary not one of the four brothers who control the CTM in that city but the brother of Fidel Velázquez. This is probably another indication of the strength of the CTM apparatus in Toluca and the willingness of the CTM to fight to retain its control over the rapidly developing industrial sector in the State of México. As the histories of Chrysler and Nissan indicate, it has been successful to date.

Volkswagen

Like Nissan, VW began operations in 1966, and the plant was organized by the CTM. VW established a plant large in Mexican terms, with numbers ranging up to ten thousand workers. The plant was set up in Puebla, where, for historical reasons, the CTM was relatively weak. Puebla had been one of the centres of the textile industry, and had been organized in the early days of the Mexican revolution by the CROM and the CGT. Later, the CROC had established a sizeable base in the state. The CTM had never been able thoroughly to displace these unions.

After several years under CTM control, a well-planned mass meeting of the VW workers in April 1972 voted to recall the incumbent Executive Committee, elect a new one and join the UOI. Representatives from a wide variety of independent unions were present at this meeting. The outgoing leadership was accused of misuse of union funds, and the leader of the Puebla CTM, Blas Chumacero, was accused of menacing various members of the new union leadership with physical violence.

The meeting appears to have been a miscalculation on the part of the

CTM leadership, and the strength of the insurgent group seems to have caught them off guard. They reacted strongly. Blas Chumacero was quoted as saying, 'It doesn't matter how much money must be spent, but we will not permit the Volkswagen union to leave the Federación de Trabajadores de Puebla. We will bring them to heel.'[96]

The first strike at VW occurred in 1974, lasting a week.[97] The Minister of Labour was brought in to settle the strike.

Then, in 1975, there appear to have been a variety of attacks on the incumbent leadership, who had been in office without serious challenge since 1972. The incumbent leadership blamed the CTM for attempting to stir up trouble, and for interfering in union elections. A quite different account emerged from the opposition group themselves. Seven distinct oppositional slates were presented in the 1975 elections, and these eventually formed a coalition against the incumbent leadership. According to the challengers, the *cláusula de exclusión* was used against them and their supporters, and the election results were falsified. It is clear that an entire opposition slate was deprived of their union rights for 'lack of respect for union representatives and making baseless accusations'.[98]

Another group of oppositionists wrote to the President of the republic, claiming that there had been:

union reprisals, culminating in the application of the *cláusula de exclusión*, ordering the company to fire workers who had protested and demanded their rights. But the union, notwithstanding that it itself applies the union sanction of loss of job, requires, through the use of threats, that the workers sign a letter to the company in which they 'voluntarily' resign without receiving remuneration or compensation in return . . .
Since the present executive committee took office, approximately 400 workers have been laid off.[99]

In what appears to have been something of a putsch, the union leadership was displaced and a new leadership elected in elections whose results were fiercely challenged.

In January 1976, discontent among the VW workers brought them out in a public meeting to protest against the new union leadership and the wave of redundancies. At a second protest meeting, held in a sports stadium, there was an attempt by a group of men to disrupt the meeting. Shots were fired, some workers were injured, and the newcomers attempted to get the workers to leave and go to another meeting elsewhere. Workers claimed that the aggressors were led by the previous Secretary General, who had been deposed in the 1975 putsch.[100]

There was also an attempt by the slate which had not been allowed to run to unseat the group which had come to office in 1975, and the insurgents elected their own Executive Committee. The incumbents counterattacked, and accused the insurgents of a variety of anti-union practices.

Since last November, with the participation and leadership of labour relations officers of the company, union representation has been practically ignored and a series of acts of divisionism, interference and dissolution of our organization have been carried out, violating the contract and signed agreements . . . a systematic campaign of slanders, injuries, kidnapping of transportation vehicles, falsification of signatures and pressures . . . in order to simulate a fake meeting with simulated documentation, trying to ignore the Executive Committee constituted by ourselves and trying to fool the Secretaría del Trabajo into recognizing the group of provocateurs as the Executive Committee.[101]

The Secretaría de Trabajo intervened at this point, ruling against the insurgents and in favour of the leadership group which had come to power in 1975.

There was a brief strike in 1976. And in 1977, the company apparently threatened to close down production unless the union accepted massive redundancies.[102] The recession in the auto industry notwithstanding, there was another brief strike in July 1977, and the union leadership appeared to have, for the moment at least, consolidated their position. In July 1978 the VW union called a strike for a wage increase and increased employment.[103] The strike lasted two weeks, and the union broke the government's wage policy with a 16 per cent increase.[104] After the return to work, VW fired twelve of the strike leaders.[105]

The independents

It is perhaps interesting to compare Nissan and VW, since both factories were set up at the same time, and were organized by the CTM in states where the CTM apparatus was relatively weak. In both cases there were successful insurgent movements in 1972, and both unions joined the UOI. In the years after 1972 both unions appear to have been the scene of confused and drawn-out struggles between the more radical elements and the moderates, with the companies and the CTM doing their best to intervene in the disputes. In both cases the radicals were defeated, and some of the more irregular union practices, such as the widespread use of the *cláusula de exclusión*, became common events.

It might appear that this signals the triumph of Michels' iron law of oligarchy. But reality is rather more complicated than that. In the first place, the 'moderate' leaderships of Nissan and VW are, in Mexican terms, quite militant on the industrial front. It should be remembered that the 'militancy' of the radical, Jaimes, in Nissan brought about a disastrous strike and his subsequent removal from union leadership. 'Moderate' leaderships may perhaps prove more effective bargainers in certain circumstances.

In the second place, there is considerable rank-and-file pressure on the leaderships of both unions. There is, however, an important difference in this respect between Nissan and VW. Whereas the opposition in Nissan is institutionalized around support for the more radical policies of the FAT (and to some extent around the myth of Raimundo Jaimes), the radicals in VW are more fragmented and dispersed. This is possibly a result of the ease with which the UOI gained control of the VW union, whilst it had to contend with the FAT in Nissan.

Moreover, discontent with the policies of the UOI, and in particular with its leader, Juan Ortega Arenas, continued to provide material for intra-union conflicts. In July 1980, a mass meeting of the Nissan workers voted to dispense with Ortega Arenas' services as union adviser. This gave rise to a particularly factious election for the union leadership in January 1981. Opponents of Ortega Arenas claimed that he forced his way into a union meeting with a group of armed men, and subsequently obtained recognition of the Secretaría del Trabajo for the new union committee. This occurred in the context of contract negotiations, a speed-up of the assembly line, and the dismissal of some 200 workers.[106] For the time being, at least, the UOI had thwarted yet another challenge to its control.

A similar movement in Puebla had more success. As we have seen, the VW union has had a turbulent history, with the lines of division among the various factions being less clearly defined than in the case of Nissan. Given this history, an accusation by Ortega Arenas in May 1981 that a recently deposed (October 1980) General Secretary of the VW union had been guilty of financial irregularities may have appeared as just another skirmish. In fact, it led to a sequence of events which ended with the VW union leaving the UOI. In October, during a union meeting, a substantial minority of workers demanded the ouster of Ortega Arenas, and the union committee subsequently decided to dismiss him as union adviser. On the twenty-second of that month, a group of some four hundred men entered the plant and demanded a meeting to elect a new committee. According to the incumbent General Secretary, these men were not VW workers and 'were headed by a group of traitors to the union who had democratically been excluded from work by legal expulsion from the union organization'.[107] Apparently, this manoeuvre backfired and the mass of workers backed the incumbent committee. Four days later, the union disaffiliated from the UOI and became a totally 'independent' union.

Although the 1970s saw the rise of independent unions affiliated with the UOI, the 1980s may well see a different pattern. Although the UOI unions did introduce a measure of union democracy and were quite militant, they were clearly also failing to satisfy the expectations of large sections of the rank and file. Movements to disaffiliate from the UOI have occurred in Nissan and VW, and also in unions in other industries.[108] Why this should be, and the likely outcome of this new phase of conflict, must remain, for some while, a matter of conjecture.

It does seem plausible, however, to argue that in a rather difficult economic situation, the institutionalization of shop-floor democracy in these unions severely constrains the ability of 'accommodationist' leaders to act in a 'moderate' and 'responsible' manner. Short of massive repression of the rank and file it is highly likely that the future history of these unions will continue to be turbulent and conflict-ridden.

Discussion

This chapter has discussed the individual history of each of the nine unions in some detail. At the risk of not seeing the wood for the trees, the aim has been twofold: to establish that factory-level conflicts are an important factor in union behaviour; and to examine, in a preliminary manner, the factors involved in union militancy. To show that union politics are, at least in part, determined by shop-floor issues and struggles is important as a corrective to those analyses of union behaviour in Latin America which focus on political bargaining at the national level as the central issue.[109] Of course, the point here is not that national political bargaining and state intervention are unimportant. Indeed, this issue is discussed extensively in chapter 10. Rather, the aim is simply to establish that an accurate account of working class struggles cannot ignore the day-to-day skirmishing on the shop floor and in union meetings.

As the materials presented in this chapter indicate, these conflicts revolve around wages, the successful conduct of strikes, hiring and firing, and, not least, demands for union democracy. The issue of union democracy has produced insurgent movements in Ford, Chrysler, DINA, Nissan and VW. It has produced protracted internal conflicts in one of the GM unions (Mexico City), in Ford and in the three independent unions in DINA, VW and Nissan.

Sometimes insurgent movements have been successful. Elsewhere (in Chrysler and the Nissan Toluca plant) they have been firmly and successfully resisted. It is possible that the success or failure of insurgent movements depended, to some extent, on the strength of the regional CTM bureaucracy. In all three cases where unions left the CTM and joined the UOI the state-level CTM apparatus was relatively weak. Conversely, insurgent movements have failed in Toluca, where the CTM appears to be quite strong. Clearly, the considerable regional variations in the organization of official unionism need to be taken into account in any analysis of the Mexican labour movement. The ability to resist attempts to form breakaway independent unions seems to be a function of the organizational strength and coherence of the CTM bureaucracy at the state level. In many of the regions with limited industrialization, such as Ciudad Sahagún and Cuernavaca, the official union structure is weak and unable to resist such attempts. Similarly, the continuing strength of the CROM in Puebla has somewhat weakened the CTM apparatus in that state, as has the factionalism within the CTM in the Federal District. By way of contrast, the coherence of the CTM apparatus in Toluca has meant that this city has successfully resisted a series of challenges to the official unions.

All nine unions (with the possible exception of VAM) have had their share of internal conflict. Nowhere in the Mexican automobile industry is there a 100 per cent pure revolutionary union. But only day-dreamers would expect such a thing. What does exist, however, is a relatively clear division into militant and democratic unions on the one hand and conservative and oligarchic unions on the other. In this context, for a union to be independent of the CTM amounts to an increase in its autonomy to bargain freely with the employer. In the auto industry, where unions are organized by plant or by company, autonomy tends to be translated into a concern with the day-to-day shop-floor conflicts with management. As will be shown in subsequent chapters, this increased concern with shop-floor issues is bound up with an increase in the importance of shop-floor union representatives, the *delegados departmentales*, and with a greater measure of democracy in union government. What is crucial in all this is not the formal affiliation of a union to one or other of the official confederations versus a formal affiliation to the UOI; rather, what matters is the degree of real autonomy from the official union structure enjoyed by the union local. As a result, the unions in Ford and in GM's Mexico City plant, both of which belong to official confederations but which are allowed substantial autonomy in contract bargaining, resemble the three UOI unions more than they do the remaining official unions.

Some accounts of struggles in Mexican unions have portrayed these largely in terms of an opposition between a conservative union bureaucracy and a militant, democratic rank and file.[110] There is a substantial measure of truth in such a picture. It is, however, only part of the dynamic. In the auto industry, as elsewhere in Mexico, conflict also occurs between rival groups of leaders, and this interacts with conflicts between the rank and file and the leadership. The most obvious way that this happens is when there are institutionalized factions within unions. But even in the absence of clear-cut factions, it would be foolish to treat the workforce as a homogeneous group. The widespread image of a union bureaucracy dominating an amorphous rank and file is, as this chapter has attempted to show, implausible. There are indeed cases where a union bureaucracy has imposed itself through violence or through an organizational monopoly. In other cases a union leadership has continued unchallenged because it has secured a measure of acceptance by its membership. Finally, there are unions where institutions and traditions mean that the rank and file exert pressure on the leadership. The following chapters take up these differences and explore them systematically.

The evidence presented in this chapter has been of a largely 'qualitative' nature. Interviews, periodicals and a variety of documentary sources have been drawn on to build up a picture of unions in the automobile industry. In chapters 5 through 8, a more systematic attempt at analysis is made using, wherever possible, data that are susceptible to quantification. Neither approach is intrinsically superior to the other. They are, rather, intended to be complementary.

5

The unions: power and organization

The aspect of union power which is considered in this chapter is primarily organizational. It concerns the ability of the union to function effectively as an organization at the plant and company levels, dealing with a range of industrial conflicts. In addition to the yearly or biennial negotiations over wages and contract revisions,[1] trade unions are involved in a complex web of daily negotiations and conflicts with management. For the union to operate effectively in this sphere, a certain minimum level of institutionalization is required. This implies some degree of acceptance by management, some level of support and legitimacy from the workforce, and some measure of organizational resources for the union apparatus.

The autonomy and effectiveness of the union in the workplace can vary enormously, from situations where the workplace union is a mere cipher and real power rests with the union federation or with a political party, to situations where the workplace union is wholly autonomous and operates effectively entirely on the basis of its own resources. The unions in the Mexican automobile industry vary considerably along this continuum, as will be illustrated below.

The importance of this organizational power of unions is twofold. In the first place it affects the locus of economic bargaining. Only unions with a certain measure of organizational autonomy and power will be able to bargain independently of the support of national union federations. One reason for the importance of national union federations in Mexico is the weakness of the constituent locals. This is particularly the case with the CTM.[2] Changes in the locus of economic bargaining could well have important repercussions for the strength of national union confederations. This matter will be taken up again later.

In the second place, organizational power means that control over the union local is highly meaningful for the workforce. There is an immediate and direct connection between control over the union and the existential reality of the workers. For this reason, union democracy becomes a potentially meaningful issue.

In general, unions in the Mexican automobile industry are capable of bargaining directly with transnational companies and have secured important gains. They are by no means dependent on state intervention for success in contract negotiations, as certain analyses would suggest.[3] However, empirical measurement of unions' specifically economic power is a complex and difficult matter, requiring good data. Since the aims of the research project had more to do with politics than economics, a discussion of economic power has been omitted on the grounds that any serious attempt to address such questions is beyond the scope of this work and deserves a fuller, and separate, treatment.[4]

Nor, on the other hand, is this chapter primarily concerned with political power in a direct and narrow sense. Chapter 10 discusses the possible impact which changing styles of unionism in the Mexican automobile industry might have on national politics. This is, indeed, one of the central preoccupations of the research. However, the political impact of auto unionism is not a direct one. A rather long and complex causal chain is involved, and this chapter will be concerned mainly with some of the first steps in that causal chain.

Mexican labour law

In Mexico, industrial relations take place in the context of a corporatist labour law. First promulgated as a law with national scope in 1931,[5] the Federal Labour Law closely regulates many aspects of Mexican industrial relations. Several aspects of this complex law provide unions with rights which can be used to enhance their power. Those aspects which are relevant for the automobile industry include hiring and firing provisions, the system of labour courts and the closed-shop provision (*cláusula de exclusión*).

Perhaps the key feature of industrial relations in the Mexican automobile industry is the formalization of the system in the biennial contract negotiations. There is a tendency for custom and practice to become codified and, hence, subject to the jurisdiction of the labour courts.[6] The labour courts in Mexico are bifurcated into those with local jurisdiction and those with federal jurisdiction. This is not a two-tier system; rather, industries of national importance are subject to the federal labour courts and the remainder fall under the jurisdiction of the local labour courts, which are constituted at the state level. In 1975, the automobile industry passed from local to federal jurisdiction.⁷ The structure and functioning of the federal labour court is discussed in chapter 8.

One interesting feature of Mexican labour relations is that the union, which has exclusive jurisdiction, has the right to propose candidates for vacancies in the firm where a contract has been signed. This right is qualified, and usually amounts to the following: if a company has a vacancy, it must notify the union. The union then has a brief period (usually forty-eight or seventy-two hours) to propose a candidate for the job. (Sometimes the contract stipulates that the union provide two candidates for each vacancy.) The company is obliged to hire this person if he/she meets the requirements for the job (including aptitude and appropriate references). If the union fails to provide suitable candidates in the time allowed, the company may then hire freely.

The effect of this is to create a permanent pool of potential applicants which is administered by the union. The result is to strengthen particularistic ties among workers, since applicants who are friends or relatives are given preference in hiring. (In some unions, such as DINA, there are clauses in the contract stating that relatives be given preference. Many companies, such as Ford, also clearly prefer such a system.) In administering this system, union leaderships tend to acquire a certain amount of power.

Another major source of power for the union leadership is the closed-shop provision, the *cláusula de exclusión*. This can be used to expel a worker from the union, whereupon the company is obliged to fire him/her, since only union members may be hired.

However, workers have clearly defined rights to compensation for layoffs or dismissals, and may have the right to be rehired in cases of wrongful dismissal. Such rights vary according to whether the worker has *planta* or *eventual* status. As explained previously, *eventuales* are hired for a specified time or task and have few rights in their jobs, whereas *planta* workers are hired indefinitely and have seniority-related rights to compensation for loss of job. The result is that there is a cost to companies of reducing their workforces.

In this situation, companies have two options: they may seek to keep a large number of *eventuales*, since the cost of laying off these workers is not too high. Or they may decide to operate with a stable labour force. While this has several advantages for the company, it also is a potential source of union power. Particularly when most workers have *planta* status, widespread dismissals as a way of disciplining the labour force tend to be prohibitively costly.[8]

These provisions of the Labour Law, in a country of considerable unemployment and underemployment, provide a social base for the power of union leaderships in the automobile industry. This has consequences for the size of the union apparatus, as well as for its manner of functioning.

The union apparatus

If the union is organized as a section of a larger industrial union, then it is often the case that the General Secretary will be a full-time CTM union official, with his office in a CTM headquarters. This was the case in Ford prior to 1977. In this kind of structure, provision may also be made for the section leader and/or *delegados departmentales* to have time off with pay to attend to union duties. While the section leader may spend all or most of his time engaged in union duties, the *delegados departmentales* will generally be required to work in the plant, and will be released from work only in order to deal with immediate grievances.

In this industrial union structure, the union leadership is basically located outside the factory, and is recruited from the official union apparatus. By and large, it appears that the *delegados* tend to have reduced powers, though in some factories they might well come to exert considerable influence.

In some cases, the union was organized at plant level rather than as a section of a larger industrial union, and the General Secretary was a full-time union official drawn from the CTM's professional leadership. There appear to be no substantial differences between this case and the preceding. What is important is not the formal structure of the union *per se*, but whether the leadership is drawn from the professional cadres of the official union movement, or from the workers themselves. Clearly, in certain circumstances an industrial union structure can act as a serious obstacle to recruitment of leaders from the rank and file. This is particularly the case where union meetings are not held at the workplace. Unless there are organized factions which command widespread support among the rank and file, the structural conditions for effective democracy will be absent. In this situation, the CTM hierarchy can effectively impose a candidate who may have little or no real connection with the workforce and its problems.

In those unions where the leadership of the union is drawn from the factory workers themselves, these leaderships are institutionalized to varying degrees. In some cases (VAM), union officials are allowed to attend to union business only on a part-time basis. No union officer is completely exempted from working in the factory. In other instances, as many as eighteen union officers (the whole of the Executive Committee or the most important members) are full-time officials, with no obligation to work in the plant. There may in addition be a number of *delegados* with rights of part-time activity, and the contract revision negotiating committee may also be given time off with pay for a certain period. All these costs are borne by the company. In one instance (Nissan), the company also agreed to supplement the monthly wages of the two top union officials by a fixed amount.

By 1976–8, most unions had established a full-time bureaucracy. Notable exceptions were VAM,[9] the Nissan plant in Toluca and the Chrysler union. (Chrysler's 1977 contracts contain no information on this matter, though it is known that only the General Secretary has a full-time post. Whether his salary is paid by the company or by the CTM is not known.) The existence of a number of union officials who are able to devote their full working week to union business clearly strengthens the union *vis-à-vis* management. There is, naturally, the possibility that the full-time union officials may come to adopt a posture which is conciliatory toward management, and that they may become estranged from their base. However, although the data are susceptible to this sort of interpretation, it should be borne in mind that the unions in the Mexican auto industry are quite small, and cover at most a few plants in the same company. The likelihood of a union bureaucracy becoming alienated from an active membership is low, and the size of the union apparatus seems to reflect union militancy rather than conservatism. As can be seen from table 5.1, there is a clear association between militancy and the number of full-time union officers on company payrolls. A more interesting question concerns trends over time. According to the hypotheses, the more militant unions ought to increase the number of full-time union officials at a faster rate than is the case in the conservative unions, and this also appears to be borne out by the data in table 5.1.

Unions in the Mexican automobile industry have been successful in increasingly strengthening their position over time, in the sense of maintaining a plant-level union apparatus. The overall trend, quite clearly, has been a steady increase in the number of union officers whose salaries are paid for by the company, and who are not required to work in the factory. By the end of the 1960s only DINA and the GM union in

Table 5.1. *Number of full-time union officers on company payrolls*

Company	Year														
	1966	1967	1968	1969	1970	1971	1972	1973	1974	1975	1976	1977	1978	1979	1980
Ford	—	—	—	0	—	0	—	0	—	3	—	4	—	15	*
GM–DF	—	—	—	—	—	8	—	*	—	8	—	9	—	—	9
GM–Toluca	—	—	—	—	—	—	—	—	—	—	3	—	5	—	5
VAM–DF	—	—	0	—	0	—	0	—	0	—	0	—	*	—	0
VAM–Toluca	—	—	—	—	—	—	*	—	*	—	*	—	*	—	*
VW	—	—	—	—	—	—	7	—	9	—	*	—	9	—	10
DINA	—	—	3	—	4	—	5	—	6	—	6	—	8	—	18
Nissan–Cuernavaca	0	—	0	—	0	—	2	—	3	—	4	—	5	—	5
Nissan–Toluca	—	—	—	—	—	—	—	—	—	—	—	—	0	0	*

Note: The table presents data from the first year for which data were available for each company. Subsequent missing data are indicated by *.

Mexico City had any full-time union officers. VW and Nissan–Cuernavaca soon joined them, and were followed later by Ford and the other GM union. While the general trend appears to be one of steady growth, both DINA and Ford had dramatic increases (from 8 to 18 and from 4 to 15 respectively) in the number of full-time union officers in the late seventies.

With the possible exception of the Toluca GM union, the data presented in table 5.1 are clearly compatible with the hypothesis that militancy and the increase in the number of full-time union officials are correlated.

The number of full-time union officers on the company's payroll is, of course, only one aspect of the institutionalization of the union apparatus. As indicated above, there is also a closely associated trend toward increasing the status and power of *delegados departmentales*, and toward increasing the size of the contract negotiating team.

The increase in the number of persons on the contract renegotiation committee (and the increase in the duration of their paid appointment to the committee) is another particularly interesting aspect of the increase in union power. To some extent, an increase in the size of the negotiating committee must increase its effectiveness in bargaining (but only up to a point) and its legitimacy in the eyes of the union membership. At the same time, for many of the members of the committee, this must signify a welcome break from work on the shop floor, and will often be viewed as a perk. In so far as this is the case, then, offers of membership of the negotiating committee become instruments of patronage for the union's Executive Committee. What evidence there is suggests that the negotiating committees are composed of the Executive Committee plus the *delegados departmentales*.[10]

By its very nature, evidence on the role of the *delegados departmentales* is hard to come by. Nevertheless, the trends observed in this chapter appear to hold here. The rights and duties, as well as the number, of *delegados* tend to increase in those unions which are more militant. One interesting index of the role of *delegados* is whether they are specifically mentioned in union contracts. While this is by no means an infallible indicator, it may well be significant that it was only toward the end of the decade of the seventies that references began to be made to *delegados* in contracts, and that it was in the VW, Nissan–Cuernavaca, Ford, and GM–DF unions where such mention was made. Although *delegados* existed in these and other unions well before 1978 (which is the first time, apparently, that the rights and duties of *delegados* were specified in a contract), the inclusion of specific clauses detailing their number and function surely indicates, on the one hand, an institution-alization of their role and, on the other hand, conflict over their power.

There is also a recent push by some unions to (a) link increases in the number of full-time officers to increases in the workforce, and (b) ensure that, for every x workers present in a given workplace at a given time, one full-time union official is also present. Some unions have also obtained cars (often several) from the company in order to carry out union business more effectively.

Finally, the Nissan–Cuernavaca union contract has a clause specify-ing (a) top union officers will be paid a substantial additional monthly stipend by the company, in addition to their regular pay, and (b) will, on cessation of office, return to a job category one place higher than when they entered office. It is only too likely, as Michels argued, that increasing the monetary rewards for union office will decrease turnover, as office-holders acquire a venal interest in prolonging their tenure.

Nevertheless, with this one exception, it seems reasonable to argue that these increases in the size of the union apparatus are union gains at management expense. Of course the expense in money terms (a handful of non-productive workers added to the payroll) is not high. And the increased institutionalization of the union will in the long run tend to produce more stable industrial relations. But it also has the result of increasing the effectiveness of the union. With a stronger union apparatus, the union is in a better position to investigate grievances and mobilize shop-floor support. Whether the stronger union apparatus is used to represent and mobilize shop-floor grievances will depend largely on the existence or otherwise of internal union democracy. This is considered in detail in chapter 7.

Union finances

In addition to automatic check-off of union dues, some unions have also negotiated the regular payment of monthly subsidies by the company to the union. Some have also negotiated a lump-sum payment by the company which is intended to cover the 'costs of the contract revision'; this is apparently a substantial fee which goes to the legal adviser and to the confederation with which the union is affiliated.[11] Reliable data on union finances were not collected and it is therefore not possible to estimate accurately the amounts involved in these payments by companies to unions, the purposes to which this money is put, nor even its importance *vis-à-vis* union dues as a source of income.

However, an illustration of what may be achieved by the more militant unions is provided by table 5.2, which shows payments by the company to the union in Nissan–Cuernavaca. It is evident that the sums involved are not insignificant.

This table must be interpreted with care. It summarizes data obtained from the collective contracts of the union. It does not, therefore, cover any payments which may have been made informally or by separate agreements. This is important, since many commentators assert that backhanders and bribes of various kinds are common in relations between unions and management in Mexico. In the research carried out by the auto industry, no evidence of such behaviour was uncovered, and it is not possible to say with any certainty whether or not such payments are common in that industry.

The table also only covers payments made direct to the union. It does not cover fringe benefits which are paid direct to the workers, such as transport subsidies. Some items are earmarked for specific purposes, such as the construction of a union hall, or sporting activities; others are provided to the union to spend at its discretion. The table contains a row indicating the subtotal of payments which are not specifically earmarked (i.e. discretionary expenditure). It is likely that this is an underestimate of the real discretionary power of the union, since it is possible that some part of the sums allocated for specific expenditure might be used for other purposes.

In examining these payments, one obvious question arises: what is the role of these payments in the union's overall finances? It is difficult to answer this question directly.[12] We can, however, make a reasonable estimate of the magnitude of direct company payments in total union finances. The other principal source of funds is the compulsory deduction of union dues from the payroll. Some data are available on this.

In Nissan, union dues were 1 per cent of gross weekly wages of union members. For 1974, Nissan's total payroll amounted to 81,848,859 pesos for a total of 2452 employees. Of these 2452 employees, 1590 were *obreros* and therefore union members. As a rough estimate, we may calculate that the total payroll to union members in 1974 was of the order of 53,074,912 pesos. (This is probably an overestimate.) At a rate of 1 per cent, union dues for the year would amount to something on the order of 530,749 pesos. In that year, total union income resulting from direct payments by the company came to 272,520 pesos, an increment of

Table 5.2. Company payments to the union: Nissan–Cuernavaca, 1966–80

	1966	1968	1970	1972	1974	1976	1978	1980
No. full-time officials	—	—	1	2	3	4	5	5
No. part-time officials[a]	—	—	9	13	15	14	13	13
Negotiating committee: membership	—	—	—	20	24	27	30	30
Negotiating committee: duration (days)	—	—	—	60	60	60	60	60
Monthly payment to union (pesos)	—	—	—	4,000	5,000	6,000	10,000	15,000
Contract revision fee (pesos)	—	—	—	—	—	150,000	200,000	—
Other, unspecified payments (pesos)[b]	—	—	—	—	—	—	—	—
Construction of union building (pesos)[c]	—	—	—	—	—	1,000,000	—	—
Social and cultural activities (monthly) (pesos)[d]	800	1,600	2,000	—	—	—	—	—
Sport (pesos per worker per month)[d]	—	3	4	5	5	7	7	10
Attendance at union events (annually) (pesos)	—	—	—	3,000	3,000	4,000	4,000	6,000
Salary increment for union officials (monthly) (pesos)	—	—	—	—	2,700	3,300	3,300	8,000
Consumer co-operative (pesos)	—	—	—	—	30,000	—	—	—
Total yearly union income from all of above	9,600	55,200	77,424	158,940	272,520	298,792	264,866	312,380
Total yearly discretionary union income from above[e]	9,600	19,200	24,000	51,000	95,400	115,600	239,600	276,000

[a] The number of officials with paid periods of leave is specified as (1) from 1970, the Executive Committee (ten members, from which the full-time officials must be discounted), (2) from 1972, the members of the hygiene and security committee, numbering five union members, (3) from 1974, the committee on seniority, numbering three union members. In 1974, the times permitted to the part-time union officials were as follows: Treasurer and Organizational Secretary: two days per week each; hygiene committee: a minimum of five hours per week per member; seniority committee: six hours per week; the other members of the Executive Committee: two hours per week each.

[b] This sum was not included in the total union income for 1976 as it was not clear that the money had actually been paid over to the union. It was in the form of an intent to do so.

[c] This seems to have been a direct subsidy to the union to be used for discretionary purposes.

[d] Sizeable sums are involved here. I have used the following figures as estimates of the number of workers: 1968 – 1000; 1970 – 1113; 1972 – 1799; 1974 – 2452; 1976 – 3038; 1980 – 3038.

[e] This includes monthly payments to the union, contract revision fees, social and cultural activities, and the salary increment for the union

51.35 per cent on union dues. Discretionary payments were 95,400, amounting to 17.97 per cent over union dues. It will readily be seen that the payments agreed to in the contract almost certainly represent a substantial addition to union finances.

These conclusions, tentative though they may be, directly contradict a more widely held belief that 'despite their political and economic strength, Mexican labour unions tend to be weak financially'.[13] It is this financial weakness which forces unions, according to Schlagheck, to seek additional financial support from employers. He mentions the 1974 VW contract to illustrate his case, and goes on to claim that 'even these kinds of employer outlays do not significantly complement union incomes. Some sources, therefore, have suggested that extensive government support and donations by religious groups have been necessary to sustain Mexico's many labour groups. It is not known to what extent such contributions actually do take place.'[14]

Two brief comments appear to be in order here. In the first place, the need for some substantial research on Mexican union finances is obvious. In the second place, it is important not to generalize too rapidly from a limited number of cases. Union finances will vary in a number of important ways. The incidence of financial malpractice and corruption by union leaders in Mexico probably varies considerably. The widespread belief that all Mexican unions are thoroughly corrupt is almost certainly an exaggeration. There are, doubtless, many instances of financial malpractice by union officials for personal gain, but this is not a universal phenomenon. It would certainly be difficult to substantiate such a claim for the Mexican automobile unions.

Perhaps more important than personal enrichment are financial flows between union locals and the federations and confederations with which they are affiliated. Here we are in uncharted terrain and there is a strong temptation to abandon further speculation as fruitless. However, despite all these caveats, it does seem to be the case that the militant unions in the Mexican automobile industry have managed to establish, and extend, a substantial base of real power *vis-à-vis* management.

6

Control over work processes

Control over work processes

In day-to-day industrial relations in Western Europe and the United States, a host of formal and informal agreements about work loads and speeds have developed. This has created a complex of 'custom and practice', which is often at the heart of industrial conflict. Custom and practice are the result of the struggle of several generations of trade unionists to bargain, at the plant level, over effort. There have, of course, been managerial counter-offensives, and the outcome of this unceasing struggle has not always been to labour's advantage.[1]

The fact that custom and practice are embedded in the concrete work situation makes investigation and measurement difficult. It indicates that a study of formal agreements such as collective contracts may seriously misrepresent the situation, by underestimating the importance of unwritten, but real, custom and practice.

Because the research in Mexico did not have the resources to investigate the reality of day-to-day industrial relations on the shop floor, the results reported below must necessarily be treated with a certain degree of caution. Nevertheless, as was argued in the preceding chapter, the highly formal and legalistic features of Mexican industrial relations mean that important gains by unions and management tend to be explicitly acknowledged in collective contracts. This may be in the nature of a *post factum* assertion about previous practice, designed to prevent gains achieved in daily negotiations from subsequently being eroded on the shop floor, or these issues may be raised and fought for primarily around the negotiating table. Whatever the situation is, an analysis of clauses in union contracts pertaining to working practices, supplemented of course by interviews, is surely indicative of trends in the industry. The assumption is that the collective contract forms a framework around which conflict is organized. Both parties seek to interpret, selectively implement or evade clauses in the contract in so far as they believe this will be to their advantage. When there are rules they will be bent, broken and ignored. But to say this is not to suggest that the rules themselves are irrelevant. On the contrary, they both channel and express real conflicts and grievances. As a result, alterations in the clauses of the collective contract are a good indicator of trends in workplace conflict. As an illustration of the utility of this approach, we will consider the Nissan contracts.

Nissan

In 1966, the Nissan contract mentioned work processes in a single, brief clause:

The workers are obliged to fulfil normally the quantity and quality of work assigned them, which they will execute with absolute honour and care.

This clause was retained in subsequent contracts. In 1972, for the first time, the following clause appeared:

Union and company agree that the plant should operate at a normal rhythm. In the case of lost time, the company will not use the workers affected in other posts; said workers will have no obligation to make up lost time.

This was amplified in the next contract (1974). It was now explicitly stated that

In the case of lost time imputable to the company, the company will recognize that time as part of the normal working day, retaining a normal rhythm during the rest of the same.

It seems reasonable to infer that the union had, over the years (and particularly since leaving the CTM in 1972), gained from the company the explicit acknowledgement that workers would not be required to produce extra effort in order to make up for work lost, and that there would be no attempt to reallocate the workers who were immediately affected by stoppages. The 1974 contract also stipulated that

The company will train four members of the union in time-and-motion study.

The union was clearly preparing to engage in a prolonged struggle over work measurement and, obviously, its efforts to date had been hampered by lack of confidence in disputing the results of time-and-motion studies.

But while the union was proving more troublesome than the company wished, Nissan management had won an important position in its new plant in Toluca. As explained in chapter 4, Nissan management were determined that the Toluca plant should be run with quasi-military discipline. A contract was signed in 1978 with the CTM covering the new plant which gave the company a completely free hand in terms of work practices:

The intensity of work executed by the workers will be that determined by the requirements of production. The company will issue all technical and administrative dispositions considered appropriate.

The company may entrust its workers with any task other than the one they normally carry out, without prejudice to their category and salary.

The company may change machines and equipment, introduce new ones or eliminate old ones, as well as alter its present procedures, methods of work and schedules.

As if this were insufficient, the 1979 contract added for good measure:

both parts [to this contract] recognize that Nissan is an industry with special characteristics . . . consider necessary and indispensable that its personnel be trained and under a scrupulous system of control and supervision, so that work is executed according to the strictest norms of work, cleanliness, quality control and security.

Thus, at a distance and interpreted with due caution, the shop-floor struggle for control over work processes becomes accessible through the study of these documents. We will now attempt to investigate trends over time, and examine the differences between unions and companies in terms of work practices.

Work processes

By the 1970s, a number of union contracts included clauses suggesting some form of union influence on work practices. This achievement was not general throughout the industry and in some contracts there is no indication of any union control over work processes, or there are simply references to the employees' obligations to work hard. In addition to the Nissan–Toluca contract mentioned above, this is also true of Chrysler, GM–Toluca and VW. That this should be the case in VW contradicts our general hypothesis, and is somewhat surprising. The VW management do seem to have won a concession from the union in this respect. In the 1978 contract we find a clause expressly stating that

The intensity and quality of work will be that which produces efficiency in production, the workers strictly following the norms of quality and efficiency set by the company, the company empowered to change its workers temporarily, in terms of shift or activity.

Quite possibly, the somewhat chaotic situation in the VW union at this time (see chapter 4) enabled management to tighten its control over work practices.

From the point of view of the general hypotheses, perhaps even more surprising are the explicit statements in the VAM contracts that

The intensity and quality of work will be the usual.

This appears in the 1968 Toluca and 1970 Mexico City contracts, and is repeated with each new contract. From the point of view of the hypotheses set out in chapter 2, the VAM union, which is both official and conservative, would be expected to have little control over work processes. In fact, the reverse appears to be the case. It is, perhaps, yet another indicator of the general stability of industrial relations in VAM, as contrasted with the dramatic changes elsewhere in the industry. These changes are evident in Nissan–Cuernavaca, Ford and GM-Mexico City.

Whereas the DINA union (like the VAM union) had already won an agreement on 'customary' work loads by 1968, statements of this nature appear in the contracts of Nissan, Ford and GM only in the 1970s. We have already examined the case of Nissan. In Ford, the first mention of work processes appears in 1977 with the statement that

The company recognizes the right of the workers to develop their work in a balanced form during the workday, at a normal rhythm of work, which is understood to be that of an average worker. Company and union agree that excessive workloads will not be created by alterations in the speed of the line, pulling or pushing units or any other abnormal situation not the responsibility of the worker.

And in GM–Mexico City in 1977, for the first time, we find:

The company will maintain a distance on the assembly lines approximately one metre between units, to protect the security of the worker.

By 1981 the union had won the right to be notified in writing by management of any intended change in line speed, together with a written explanation of the reasons for the change.

Indeed, in VAM the union won the right, in 1976, with respect to any introduction of new methods, to retain existing custom and practice:

The incentives most favourable to the workers will be retained as a right . . . The union may request a revision of operating times as well as the line speed . . . The union may request the checking of the application of time-and-motion studies.

Summarizing these results, we find a very uneven and differentiated situation in the Mexican automobile industry. A concern with work loads, and with custom and practice more generally, seems to be widespread in the industry. There are, however, marked disparities in the extent to which unions and management have formalized these matters in negotiated contracts. Generally the differences are much as would be expected, with the important exceptions of VAM and VW, which clearly run counter to our expectations. These two cases apart, the general trend is for the more militant unions also to initiate relatively successful attempts to control workloads on the shop floor. In the cases of Ford and Nissan this was clearly linked with the move away from direct control by the CTM.

Moreover, it seems reasonable to infer from this evidence that conflicts over working practices are becoming an increasingly salient aspect of union–management negotiations and may be expected to increase in the near future. The possible implications of this apparent trend are discussed in chapter 9.

Supervisors

One other issue which is relevant to control over work processes concerns supervisors and white collar *empleados de confianza*. It is quite common to find clauses in collective contracts forbidding supervisors to work on the machines. It is also quite common to find clauses such as the following, dealing directly with the relationship of authority:

Workers and *empleados de confianza* are obliged to treat each other with the required consideration and respect, abstaining from verbal or physical ill-treatment. (VAM, 1972)

There is no smoke without fire, and the appearance of these admonitions to treat subordinates with due respect suggests a certain degree of dissatisfaction with previous treatment. One might speculate as to the origins of this situation, invoking cultural and/or pre-industrial notions of dignity and status. Alternatively, demands for more respectful treatment by supervisors may be a direct function of the growth of shop-floor and union power. When interviewed, managers frequently expressed concern about the quality of shop-floor supervision and saw the workers' notions of their personal dignity as a sensitive issue. Whatever construction is put on it, it is clear that authority relations in the Mexican automobile industry are subject to considerable contention.

Movement of labour

The clauses about normal working arrangements are only one of several ways in which unions in the Mexican automobile industry have sought to challenge 'managerial prerogatives'. Another, related, issue concerns movements of workers from one job to another. It is clearly in management's interest to have clauses such as the following (taken from the 1972 GM–Toluca contract):

When in the judgement of the company the necessities of production so require, it may move workers from one department to another or from one category to another, without prejudice to the workers' salary.

Although no union has been able to prevent any horizontal movement within the plant, some have been able to put restrictions on management's right to move labour freely and without consultation with the union. (Wages are not at issue. It is accepted that workers who are moved to a new job will not suffer a loss in pay, and will be paid the rate for the new job if this is higher than their previous salary.)

In general, gains have been limited to an agreement to consult or inform the union prior to such movements. In DINA there is clear evidence of a growth of union control in this respect. The 1968 DINA contract states:

The company may effect movements of personnel in its sections and departments . . . When dealing with permanent changes, the seniority scale will be used.

In the next contract (1970) this is altered to:

The enterprise may not effect movements of workers in its workshops and departments, except when there is good reason.

More important than horizontal movements, from the union point of view, are temporary and permanent promotions from one category to another. It is at this point that job control issues merge with the question of the internal labour market, and it is perhaps simpler and clearer to deal with vertical movements as part of a wider discussion of internal markets.

Internal labour markets

All the Mexican auto companies operate with a clearly defined, hierarchical scale of job categories. Each job is classified as falling into one of these categories, and each worker is assigned to a particular category. Any change from one job to another, therefore, raises the possibility of a promotion or demotion in category and, hence, salary. In so far as purely temporary movements are concerned, the universal practice in the industry is to continue to pay the worker at the old rate if the alteration would result in a drop in pay, and to pay him at the new rate if the change involves an increase in pay.

The question of permanent movements (almost always promotions) is, however, a matter of dispute in the Mexican auto industry. It is clearly in management's interest to exercise discretion in promotions. The unions, on the other hand, have tended to push for automatic upgrading by seniority. A clear illustration of this is the change in the Ford contract between 1975 and 1977. The earlier version states:

In the case of temporary or permanent promotions the company, the union representatives or the relevant *delegado departmental* will jointly agree such cases, the selected worker being required to collect the maximum of requisites listed below: that he is competent, efficient, has a sense of responsibility and a good work record, and in the event of equality of circumstances the company will choose the worker with greater seniority.

This was revised in 1977 to a simple statement about seniority:

The worker will be selected according to the pre-established order of seniority.

An automatic seniority-determined promotion clause had already been formally agreed in 1968 by DINA and VAM. However, in all these cases, too literal an interpretation would be unwise. Interviews suggest that the automatic seniority agreed to was more real in DINA than in VAM or Ford. The caution that the data presented indicate trends, rather than precise point estimates, should perhaps be repeated.

In some companies, promotion from one category to another depended solely on length of service. In VAM this was the case after 1972 for one of the lower categories. In GM–Mexico City, the two highest positions open to manual workers were subject to a length-of-service restriction and, in addition, there was an agreed-upon quota of these positions. According to the 1971 contract, there were sixty positions corresponding to the first category and ninety corresponding to the second category. To be eligible for promotion to the first category, fourteen years of service were a prerequisite; and for the second category, nine years of service.

In Nissan we find, in 1974, an attempt to remove an obvious promotion bottleneck in a particular department, together with (for the first time) a statement about how recruitment policy and promotions might be connected:

The company will give the workers in the paintshop the opportunity to be promoted to other departments with higher job category levels when vacancies occur. The company accepts that all new personnel, with the exception of skilled workers, shall go to the departments with low job category levels.

In other companies, there is little indication of successful union struggles over this issue.

From a long-term perspective, one of the factors which directly affect promotion prospects is the relative balance of *eventuales* and workers with *planta* status. The unions are clearly interested in increasing the job security of their members, and this is most easily done by increasing the percentage of workers on *planta* contracts.[2] This is clearly not in the short-term interests of employers. The following statements of the rationale for hiring *eventuales* indicate why:

Each year, due to model changes, the company needs to intensify production during part of the year, for which it has the right to hire temporary workers. (Ford, 1969)

Taking into account the nature of the business, which has large changes in the volume of work, which in turn requires a frequent increase or decrease in the number of workers, both parties to the contract agree that, excepting the *planta* personnel, the remaining operatives will be *eventuales*, hired for a specific time or task. (DINA, 1968)

In both cases, it was also specified that *eventuales* would have first claim on any new vacancy in the *planta* category.

It is interesting to trace the increasing percentage of *planta* jobs in the industry. Some firms make no mention of this in the collective contracts (Chrysler, VW, Nissan–Toluca and Ford fall into this category), though this does not necessarily indicate that it is not the subject of informal bargaining.

In the Mexico City GM plant, the 1975 contract specifies that all workers with five years' experience would automatically receive *planta* status. By 1981 this had been reduced to eighteen months. The Toluca plant contract had a similar provision in 1976. By 1978 the time required for *planta* status had been lowered to three years and by 1980 to two years. More usual are agreements about the absolute number or the percentage of *planta* places. In Nissan the 1974 contract limited the number of *eventuales* to 15 per cent of the total workforce. In 1976 this was altered to 10 per cent and by 1978 all *eventuales* had been given

Table 6.1. Eventuales *as percentage of all
workers*

	DINA	VAM–DF	Nissan–Cuernavaca
1970	55	54	15[a]
1972	35	52	—
1974	25	49	15
1976	14	39	10
1978	14	—	0
1980	14[b]	31	5[c]

[a] Nissan contracts prior to 1974 do not specify any fixed ratio of
planta : *eventuales*. The figure for 1970 refers to the actual percentage of *eventuales* working at that time.
[b] The DINA figures represent the number of *eventuales* the
company may hire. In 1980 all *eventuales* were given *planta*
status.
[c] The 1980 Nissan contract once again makes reference to *eventuales*, and there is no mention of any limit to the number of
eventuales the company hire. The figure of 5% refers to the actual
number of *eventuales* working at that time.
Note: The VAM figures refer to the actual numbers of *eventuales*
working in any given year.

planta status. In DINA, the number of *eventuales* (expressed as a
percentage of the total unionized workforce) agreed upon in collective
bargaining was as shown in table 6.1.

The evidence presented here and in chapter 3 strongly suggests that
there is a correlation between union militancy and the percentage of the
workforce who have the job security of *planta* status. Particularly
interesting is the comparison of DINA and VAM in the decade of the
1970s. Both began the decade with 55 and 54 per cent of their respective
workforces in *planta* categories. By the end of the decade, both unions
had achieved significant gains in increasing job security for their
constituents. However, the DINA union both took the lead and
achieved greater success.

On the other hand, although the Nissan union was able to codify
agreement to its initially high level of *planta* positions, and was
subsequently (like DINA) able to achieve *planta* status for all its
constituents, there appears to have been some backsliding in the 1980
contract.

However, the cautionary note of chapter 3 must be repeated. As the data for Ford show, the ratio of *eventuales* to *planta* workers may vary dramatically in a very brief period (fig. 1), and the data presented here should be taken as indicative of trends in the industry.

External labour markets

Since hiring is carried out through the agency of the union, there is, at first sight, little necessity for controls over recruitment to be written into the contract. Nevertheless, recruitment is not entirely under union control, and management does have a substantial, though variable, influence. The company usually requires that the union present more than one candidate for each post. Candidates must also meet educational and health requirements, pass a technical aptitude test, and present certificates of good conduct from the police.[3]

Hence, sometimes the union has inserted a clause in the contract specifying some aspects of the recruitment process in more detail. (In most cases this is an unwritten, rather than a formal convention.) The classic statement of this concern over recruitment comes from the DINA contracts:

Sons or family members of *planta* workers have priority in filling vacancies.

In DINA, this was a long-established clause. In Nissan, it appears for the first time in 1972. (Again, the connection with the union's departure from the CTM should be noted.) Preference in hiring to sons and relatives must reduce the scope for patronage on the part of union officialdom. From the point of view of the permanent workforce, these preferential hiring clauses are more universalistic than leaving the selection of candidates to the union leadership. Although there is no direct evidence that it occurs widely in the automobile industry, some Mexican union leaders sell jobs to workers. It is widely believed, for example, that employment in the petroleum industry necessitates prior payment of a bribe to union leaders. In this way, control over the selection of job applications can be transformed into a source of income and patronage for union leaders. In the auto industry a number of allegations have been made that the General Secretary of the Chrysler union sold jobs in this way. Hence, the stipulation that sons of workers be given preference is by no means so particularistic as it may at first appear.

The situation described above may usefully be compared with that in Ford, where there was a much more ambiguous statement in the 1977 contract (for the first time), though company policy was to favour relatives of the workers:

Job application forms will be given to all applicants recommended by anyone in the company.

As suggested in chapter 3, with the partial exception of a few firms like Chrysler which have higher than average turnover rates for the industry, there is a widespread tendency toward the creation of stable labour forces which are increasingly linked together by ties of kinship and residence.[4] Although this tendency is most fully developed in the DINA plant, it is by no means negligible elsewhere. The possible implications of this trend are discussed in chapter 9.

Before leaving the subject of labour markets, a few brief remarks about layoff policy and alterations in company operations are in order.

Company expansion and contraction

The long-term prospect for the Mexican automobile industry – and for most, if not all, of the firms in it – appears to be one of growth. Several companies have plans for the construction of new plants in the immediate future or for expansion of existing plants. The likely impact of these expansion plans is discussed in chapter 9, particularly with regard to union jurisdiction. In this chapter, however, mention must be made of the fact that, within this long-term panorama, there may be cyclical contractions in the industry and, quite apart from this, companies may wish to reduce or shut down operations at some specific plant.[5] The following paragraphs discuss union responses to threats of layoffs.

After a period of sustained growth from the mid-sixties, the Mexican auto industry experienced a sharp recession in 1975–7. The economy as a whole experienced a series of substantial difficulties from 1973 onwards.[6] This recession did not hit all the auto companies equally. Its effects depended on a variety of factors and had to be placed within the global perspectives of the various firms. Nevertheless, the severity of the recession may be judged from the rumours current in 1976 that VW was considering pulling out of the Mexican market.[7]

Strangely enough, in some companies a foretaste of the recession had happened with the initial expansion in the mid-sixties. Those companies with established operations in Mexico City which intended to develop new plants elsewhere (i.e. in Toluca) had to persuade the existing workforce that they would not suffer. Hence we find in the GM contract for the Mexico City plant the following clause:

The company agrees that, for the duration of the present contract, it will not move any of its installations in the assembly plant out of Mexico City, and if it removes any other of its installations, this will be done without prejudice to unionized personnel.

The problem of companies shifting operations may be a double one for the unions concerned. In the first place, they are concerned to minimize the impact of possible redundancies. Secondly, where – as in Nissan and GM – there is more than one union in the company, movements of personnel may directly threaten one of these unions. Significantly, both of these militant unions have attempted – unsuccessfully – to win bargaining rights for new plants.

In general, the recession caused severe problems for the industry and a worsening of industrial relations. In some companies workers with *planta* status were paid off, and in DINA there were bitter conflicts over layoffs. In 1976 in GM, VAM and DINA there appear, for the first time, clauses pertaining to layoffs, stipulating that there will be consultation with the union and that seniority will be used as the principal criterion in deciding which workers will be laid off. The Ford union included a similar clause in its 1977 contract; Nissan–Cuernavaca did the same in 1978. By the end of the 1970s, such clauses had not appeared in contracts signed by the VW and Chrysler unions, nor by Nissan's Toluca union.[8] Once again (with the exceptions of VW, VAM and GM's Toluca union) the results are those predicted by the general hypotheses.

Health and safety

Mexican labour law is quite favourable to the workforce in terms of health and safety provisions, though whether or not these are implemented depends to a considerable extent, of course, on actual industrial relations practice.[9] All unions have some sort of health and safety committee, though these appear to have the greatest facilities in Nissan–Cuernavaca, DINA and Ford. By the end of the seventies, annual contract negotiations for these unions included clauses detailing alterations in work systems and plant layout to minimize health hazards.

7

Union government

As indicated in chapter 1, the prevailing notion concerning union government in Mexico is expressed in the concept of *charrismo*. This has come to be used as a catch-all epithet to describe a variety of union practices. The term is largely devoid of analytic utility, as may be seen from the following representative statement:

Charrismo is a particular form of trade union control which is characterized by: (a) the use of the repressive forces of the state to support a trade union leadership; (b) the systematic use of violence; (c) the permanent violation of workers' union rights; (d) misuse and theft of trade union funds; (e) dishonest dealing with the workers' interests; (f) connivance between union leaders and the government and capitalists; (g) corruption in all its forms.[1]

In this usage, *charrismo* simply indicates that the author or speaker disapproves of the union leadership in some way. Furthermore, there is a generalized belief that Mexican unions typically are *charro* unions. Yet there appear to be very few serious studies of internal union government in Mexican unions. This belief is a generalization from a number of specific cases, such as the 1958–9 railway strike.

Two questions immediately spring to mind: (a) to what extent is this picture of *charrismo* an accurate description of Mexican unionism? (b) If non-*charro* unions exist, are they more likely to be found among the 'independent' unions, or are these also breeding grounds for *charrismo*? In this section we will look at one key aspect of the concept of *charrismo*, namely, the existence or otherwise of democracy in unions.

The presence of internal democracy in trade unions has long been a subject of political concern and scholarly investigation. Perhaps the most influential study has been the 1915 polemic by Roberto Michels, *Political Parties*.[2] Michels argued that all organizations tended to be dominated by a leadership oligarchy as a result of the indispensability of the leaders (itself a result of specialization and division of labour) and the incompetence of the rank and file. This became a generally accepted

132

theme within social science and it has generally been held that unions are, by and large, characterized by oligarchic internal government.

The classic 1956 study by Lipset, Trow and Coleman, *Union Democracy*, takes this supposed general absence of union democracy as the starting point, and proceeds to ask why it should be the case that the International Typographical Union had been able to maintain a functioning and viable two-party democracy. The answer provided by the authors, rather than disproving the Michels thesis, gives it additional empirical support.[3] In brief, the study by Lipset *et al.* concludes that the organization of work in the printing industry is atypical of that in the rest of industry. The unique features of printing are highly conducive to the existence of a viable two-party democracy in the printing union. Precisely because there are unique circumstances in this case, Michels' general rule about union oligarchies continues to hold.

More recent studies, however, indicate that the prevailing supposition that trade unions are generally oligarchic in nature may well be an inaccurate description of reality. A recent survey by Edelstein and Warner suggests that there exists a wide range of forms of union government in Great Britain and the United States.[4] In addition, some published work on union government in Mexico clearly demonstrates that some unions in that country can legitimately be described as democratic.[5] It seems, therefore, quite reasonable to ask to what extent union democracy exists in the Mexican automobile industry.

In the analysis below, no precise and formal definition of democracy has been attempted. Instead, four indicators have been singled out. They are as follows:

(1) The existence of *contested elections*. Where elections are not held, or are not contested, the leadership may be popular and representative of the membership, but such a system would not usually be termed democratic. Long periods of unchallenged leadership almost certainly point to an oligarchy. In the Mexican context, contested elections where the majority faction invariably wins, as occur in national politics, would also indicate the presence of an oligarchy.

(2) The *turnover of leaders*. Although one leader might be sufficiently popular to assure continual re-election, this situation should be relatively rare, and low turnover may imply the absence of democracy. In union terms, the defeat of incumbents (or their unwilling retirement from office) would indicate more democracy, although the regular rotation of officers might indicate a dominant oligarchy using union office to enrich itself.

(3) The *closeness of elections* provides evidence of the strength of opposition, including its ability to influence union policy or defeat incumbent leaders.

(4) A factor linked to elections is the existence of *permanent and organized opposition*. The greater the degree of organization and the more permanent the opposition, the greater the probability that the opposition will be able to influence the leadership.

None of these indicators is infallible by itself, and all are open to criticism. Although no single variable is an acceptable indicator of democracy, taken together they constitute a reasonable approximation to formal democracy.

By confining the analysis to elections for the post of General Secretary, we are introducing an element of distortion in the analysis. Very often, there may be intense competition for other union posts while the position of General Secretary may be uncontested or unchanged. In this way, our analysis may understate the degree of democracy in the unions studied here. On the other hand, there are good reasons for concentrating on the post of General Secretary. This is the most important post, and if this post does not change hands, it is unlikely that other changes in the composition of the Executive Committee will be of great relevance. This is particularly so in a system, such as the Mexican, which is prone to clientelistic behaviour. Summary data on union elections are presented in table 7.1. The Nissan union in Toluca had not begun to operate when the data were gathered and was excluded from the analysis. In addition, owing to the recent changes in the Ford union, the complexities of which are indicated in chapter 4, this has been omitted from the analysis below. It was only in 1976 that any meaningful internal democracy emerged in that union. As the historical description of the Ford union in chapter 4 indicates, the early years were turbulent ones, with rival leadership groups struggling for control over the union and with the Ford union moving between the CROM, the CSUM and the CGT. During these struggles in the 1936–7 period, rival leadership groups would hold separate meetings, and each group would attempt to persuade the labour courts to rule in its favour. These struggles probably had little impact on the rank-and-file Ford workers, and in any case in the 1970s only the oldest Ford workers would have had any experience and recollection of those struggles.

Apart from a brief challenge in 1941, Vicente Rendón controlled the Ford union from 1939 to 1948, when he was succeeded by his second-in-command (the Secretary of the Interior). The new leader died two years

Table 7.1. *Elections for General Secretaries of Mexican auto unions*

Union	Period covered	No. of elections	No. of contested elections	Contested elections/ 10 years	Ratio of contested/ non-contested elections	No. of office-holders	Average length of office (years)	Incumbent stands & is defeated (frequency)	Incumbent re-elected (frequency)	Re-election as ratio of all elections	Accusations of electoral fraud (frequency)
Nissan	1966–77	9	6	5.0	0.67	7	1.71	2	0	0	1
DINA	1954–77	18	15	3.7	0.83	16	1.50	3	3	0.17	4
VW	1972–8	2	2	2.9	1.0	2	3.50	1	0	0	1
Ford	—	—	—	—	—	—	—	—	—	—	—
GM–DF	1937–77	28	22	7.9	0.78	21	1.95	8	7	0.25	3
GM–Toluca	1966–78	5	0	0	0	1	13.0	0	4	0.80	0
Chrysler	1964–76	5	1	0.8	0.20	5	3.85	0	1	0.20	2
VAM	1952–74	10	2	0.9	0.20	3	7.67	0	7	0.70	0
Nissan–Toluca	—	—	—	—	—	—	—	—	—	—	—

later, to be succeeded by *his* second-in-command, who ruled until 1953, when he also died. The transfer of power in all these elections was a unanimous and uncontested vote for the incumbent General Secretary or his heir-designate. In 1953, a man who had never previously held office took over the top post in an uncontested election, being re-elected in 1959 and again in 1965.

None of these three elections for the post of General Secretary was contested, though there appear to have been genuine contests for some of the other union positions (such as the Secretary of Conflict, with voting between two candidates in 1953 of 628 and 187 votes, and in 1959 637 versus 203 votes). Basically, throughout the post-war period the Ford union was under bureaucratic control, with elections gradually becoming less frequent (every two years up to 1950; every three years up to 1953; and every six years thereafter).

This situation continued up to the revolt of 1976–7. Ford had expanded its operations in the late sixties and set up two new plants (Cuautitlán and Tlalnepantla) in the northern industrial suburbs of Mexico City. As these plants were located in the State of México, they were organized by the CTM in that state. The organizational structure of the union was essentially the same as in the La Villa plant in the Federal District. As was noted in chapter 4, the threat of a rank-and-file movement in 1976–7 to take the Ford unions out of the CTM brought about a compromise reorganization. All three plants were now organized into a single national union, affiliated to the CTM. However, the two-tier structure, and the multi-enterprise base of the previous Ford unions disappeared. This meant that the new leadership had to be more responsive to rank-and-file pressures. At the same time, the national leadership of the CTM were willing to allow the new Ford union a greater degree of autonomy to pursue its own goals. Because of this complex situation, and because the electoral information on the older Ford unions refers to other workers in addition to those in Ford, it was decided to omit Ford from the quantitative analysis.

The data in table 7.1 indicate a wide range of electoral practices in the Mexican auto industry. Nissan, DINA and GM (Mexico City union) have all had frequent contested elections for the top post of General Secretary. On the other hand, VAM, Chrysler and GM (Toluca union) have had few contested elections for General Secretary. The VW union is an intermediate case (column 5). If, however, a different measure is used (ratio of contested to uncontested elections), the distortions due to the short time over which some unions were observed are eliminated and VW moves up into the frequent contest category (column 6).

There is also a wide range when it comes to turnover of union office. GM–DF, DINA and Nissan have all had a number of General Secretaries and the average length of tenure of office has been under two years. VAM and GM–Toluca, at the other extreme, have had stable leaderships. VW and Chrysler represent intermediate cases, though there are reasons to believe that the special circumstances of the 1970 Chrysler conflict overstate the turnover of leadership in that union.

There is considerable coincidence between these two sets of rankings (frequency of contested elections and rotation of leadership) and on this basis the unions might be lined up as indicated in table 7.2. Given the fairly limited information about VW and its intermediate position on these two criteria, it is difficult to assign it unambiguously to either the 'democratic' or the 'oligarchic' camp. In table 7.2 it has been put in the 'democratic' column, though with considerable reservation. On the basis of a qualitative analysis of the Ford union, it would be reasonable to argue that it was predominantly oligarchical up to the 1977 reorganization, and has since become 'democratic'. However, as I will argue below, this simple dichotomy between democratic and oligarchic union governments may not be entirely adequate for our purposes.

The data discussed so far indicate whether or not stable oligarchical leaderships retain power. They have little to say about the nature of the opposition to union leaderships and whether opposition groups can defeat or influence incumbent leaderships. This aspect of union government – the effectiveness of opposition – is tapped by the third and fourth indicators, closeness of elections and permanent and organized opposition.

Here, one of the key questions is whether or not incumbents can be voted out of office. Column 9 of table 7.1 provides data on the number of times incumbents have been out-voted by challengers. This has never been the case in Chrysler, VAM or GM–Toluca. These data confirm the previous analyses of turnover and frequency of contested elections. Indeed, in 80 per cent of the elections in GM–Toluca and 70 per cent of the VAM elections, the incumbent was re-elected. This contrasts with Nissan and VW, where incumbents have never been re-elected, and GM-DF and DINA, where incumbents have been re-elected in 25 and 17 per cent respectively of all elections. (The figure for Chrysler is unreliable owing to the peculiarities of that case.)

One index of the authenticity of contested elections for General Secretaries is the percentage of the vote going to the winner. Even if

Table 7.2. *Union government in Mexican auto unions*

Democratic	Oligarchic
GM–DF	GM–Toluca
DINA	Chrysler
Nissan–Cuernavaca	VAM
VW (?)	Ford (before 1976)
Ford (after 1976)	Nissan–Toluca (?)

there are opposition candidates, if an incumbent is persistently re-elected with very substantial majorities, it would be reasonable to describe the opposition as weak and ineffectual. This might happen as a result of electoral fraud; because the incumbent is, in fact, a genuine popular choice of the workers; or because the opposition, for one reason or another, was unable to present an effective challenge. It is of some interest, therefore, to look at voting behaviour in union elections.

Voting figures were not always available from the records of the Secretaría de Trabajo, and in some cases (Chrysler, GM–Toluca, VAM) most elections for the General Secretary were uncontested. In other cases, the election was decided by acclamation rather than by a vote of some kind. Such practices do not really indicate the existence of institutionalized democracy.[6] The fact that voting data are not available for Chrysler and GM–Toluca is hardly surprising in the light of the foregoing analysis. In only two of the ten elections in VAM were voting figures available, since only two elections were ever contested. In both cases incumbents were re-elected with sizeable majorities (79 and 89 per cent of the total vote). These majorities are high enough to suggest that the opposition to the incumbents was extremely weak. In the elections for VW, Nissan, DINA and GM–DF for which data are available, elections are won more narrowly. The average vote obtained by the winner in elections in these unions was as shown in table 7.3.

Only in DINA and GM–DF do we have enough cases to analyse the data further. For our purposes, there are three kinds of election: (a) the incumbent is re-elected, (b) the incumbent is defeated, (c) the incumbent does not stand for re-election. Tables 7.4 and 7.5 present the number of elections falling into each of these three categories for the two unions. The data are broken down by a dichotomous variable, high versus low vote.[7] It will be seen from the tables that there is a tendency for incumbents, when they are re-elected, to capture a high percentage

Table 7.3. *Average vote cast for winner in union elections*

Union	Average winning vote	No. of elections considered
GM–DF	62.5	14
DINA	51.2	12
Nissan	68.0	5
VAM	84.0	2
VW	58.8	1

Table 7.4. *GM–DF: contested union elections for General Secretary*

	Won by incumbent	Incumbent defeated	Incumbent didn't stand	All elections
Above-average winning vote	3	2	1	6
Below-average winning vote	0	6	2	8
Total	3	8	3	14

Table 7.5. *DINA: contested union elections for General Secretary*

	Won by incumbent	Incumbent defeated	Incumbent didn't stand	All elections
Above-average winning vote	2	1	5	8
Below-average winning vote	1	2	1	4
Total	3	3	6	12

of the total votes, and for successful challengers to scrape into office with a lower percentage of the total vote. The differences between the types of election are summarized in table 7.6.

These data are consistent with our analysis of both DINA and GM having a substantial degree of internal union democracy. In the case of the GM union, additional data on turnout at twelve of these elections were available. The turnout at the three elections where incumbents

Table 7.6. *Average winning vote in union elections*

	Won by incumbent	Incumbent defeated	Incumbent didn't stand	All elections
DINA	54.1	41.2	54.7	51.2
GM	79.9	56.4	61.5	62.5

were re-elected averaged 73.3 per cent, while at the six elections (where data were available) where incumbents were defeated turnout averaged 69.1 per cent. This does not appear to be a significant difference.

On the whole, turnout at union meetings and elections appears to be high in those unions which are democratic. Union meetings tend to be held about once a month and are attended by something like 80 per cent of the membership. In part, this is owing to the fact that, according to union constitutions, attendance at meetings is compulsory and non-attendance may be sanctioned with loss of a day's pay.[8]

The final indicator of union democracy is the existence of permanent and organized opposition. In some ways this is the most important factor in the long run, as both Lipset *et al.* and Edelstein and Warner have suggested. (At this point, the reader may wish occasionally to refer back to chapter 4, where the histories of the various unions are chronicled.) The evidence in the cases of Ford (after 1976), Nissan, GM–DF and VW indicates fairly unambiguously the continued existence of electoral slates representing more or less defined tendencies. In Nissan there is a clear three-way split among factions which are oriented to the larger world of union politics, and which derive their identity from their association with pro-UOI, pro-FAT or pro-CTM positions. In VW and Ford the tendencies are much less clear, and the factions which exist in DINA appear to reflect the politics of kinship and residence networks rather than more 'universalistic' orientations.

The factions which exist in GM–DF seem to have a more complicated basis, and to a considerable degree are organized around particular sections and departments. No evidence for organized factions could be found in the cases of Chrysler, GM–Toluca or VAM. Once again, we have the same dichotomous line-up as before.

The GM case, however, suggests that it is important to move away from a simple notion of 'democracy' towards a more complex typology. GM's history contains periods when a formal two/three party contest was the norm, with regular transfers of power between the rival forces.

It also has periods of highly personalistic and anarchic democracy in which organized competition between factions based on some principled position gives place to a scramble by individuals for office. And GM also has periods when an autocratic leadership maintains itself in office until overthrown by a rank-and-file revolt in a form of 'caesarist democracy'.

My purpose here is not to elaborate such a typology. Rather, it is the more modest one of suggesting that the substantive content of union democracy can vary widely. A similar comment is called for when talking about oligarchy. As the cases discussed below suggest, there can be great variations in the form and substance of union oligarchy. Let us take first the case of Chrysler, in some ways the union which comes closest to the commonly accepted notion of *charrismo*.

Essentially, the Chrysler union has always been controlled by a single professional leader who is re-elected unopposed at six-yearly intervals. As explained in chapter 4, a rank-and-file revolt deposed the incumbent leadership in 1970 but the new men were defeated in the course of a confused and drawn-out strike. The company and the new union leadership then oversaw a massive purge of the 'troublemakers'. Since then, potential oppositions have been threatened with physical violence and/or fired from the company after the application of the *cláusula de exclusión*. The present leader is a Federal Deputy. Chrysler seems to be a classic case of rule by a union boss in a quite direct way.

In contrast, although the GM union in Toluca is every bit as undemocratic, the union appears to control the rank and file in a more bureaucratic and impersonal manner. The key to this particular mechanism of control resides in the very considerable power of the CTM in Toluca and the domination of the CTM apparatus in Toluca by a small group of leaders, knit together by family ties.

In Mexico City (despite the fact that it is one of the CTM's strongholds), it is not so easy for the CTM to control the situation. Here, in the Ford plants, the CTM controlled the union through a two-tier structure. Prior to its 1977 reorganization, the Ford union was a branch of a metallurgical union. The General Secretary of this metallurgical union was a PRI Senator. He was always elected unopposed at meetings of the delegates from the various branches. In turn, the delegate in Ford acted as a liaison between the General Secretary and management. The General Secretary never set foot in the plant, and the delegate handled all the day-to-day problems directly with management. But when it came to negotiation of the collective contract, this was carried out by the General Secretary. This meant that management, delegate and General Secretary were able each to deny responsibility and diffuse any incipient worker protest. Both the situation in Ford and that in GM–Toluca seem to be typical of CTM control mechanisms. They both rely heavily on organizational structure (a two-tiered, multi-factory union) to diffuse potential rank-and-file opposition to self-perpetuating leaderships. Elections are uncontested and by acclamation of picked delegates. Certainly, the leadership in both cases were drawn from the professional cadres of the CTM. The leader of the Chrysler union did not start out in this way (he was, as noted above, from middle management), and came into the CTM from outside. He also was elected in the middle of a crisis. These factors seem to account for the higher levels of overt repression in Chrysler, which seems to be atypical of the CTM as a whole.

Finally, the case of VAM illustrates yet another form of oligarchic control. From the formation of the union in 1952 until the present, the only office with any power has been that of the General Secretary. There have been contests for the other offices in the union, and a considerable degree of turnover of personnel among them. However, the position of the General Secretary has basically been unchallenged, and there is no evidence of any organized alignments in internal union politics. The only disturbance came with a rather ineffectual challenge to the incumbent in 1958, which failed. However, the incumbent General Secretary and two other members of the Executive Committee left the firm the following year, and the opposition leadership was elected to office. Since then, there has been a steady move to unanimous re-election of the incumbents by acclamation. At the same time, the length of tenure of office has been increased from two to four years (in 1962) and to six years (in 1974).

Although this may appear similar to the other oligarchic cases, there is a crucial difference. The union General Secretary in VAM works on the shop floor. In no way is he a full-time, professional union leader. Moreover, VAM is a small company with a stable workforce with high average seniority. (This is more true of the Mexico City plant than of the more recently established Toluca factory.) In the case of VAM, there is very little reason to suppose that there is any widespread rank-and-file discontent with the union leadership. (In contrast, the evidence for rank-and-file discontent in Ford before 1977 and in Chrysler is obvious and abundant.) Moreover, unlike the GM union in Toluca, the VAM union (although it has always belonged to an 'official' confederation) appears to have a considerable degree of autonomy from the national confederation when it comes to plant-level bargaining. On the other hand, both the VAM and the GM–Toluca unions appear to be heavily dependent on the legal departments of their respective federations during contract negotiations.

It seems, then, that the oligarchic unions are controlled in a variety of ways; in an authoritarian–repressive manner in Chrysler; in a two-tiered bureaucratic way in Ford (before 1977) and GM–Toluca; and in a personalistic–clientelistic way in VAM. Once again, the aim here is less the formal elaboration of a typology than to indicate the range of variation in union government.

One final point about the data needs to be made. In a number of instances there were accusations of irregularity in elections. These occurred with more frequency in the unions which I have described as democratic. The analysis of the GM–DF case has perhaps given some indication of the events which give rise to such accusations (other instances are to be found in chapter 4). Apart from the obvious fact that union democracy does not necessarily mean that contenders always behave like perfect gentlemen, these accusations of irregularities, and the appeals to the Secretaría del Trabajo to intervene, indicate three things. In the first place, in these unions, elections are seen as meaningful and legitimate forms of access to power. Secondly, control over union government is seen as a meaningful thing, not only by small groups seeking a source of personal power and patronage, but also by the majority of the workers who want to influence union behaviour. Thirdly, the fact that insurgents appeal to the Secretaría del Trabajo in itself suggests that they do not see it as absolutely committed to the defence of *charro* union leadership. And, as a reading of the archives of the Secretaría del Trabajo suggests, the insurgents were right to appeal, since the Secretaría del Trabajo frequently intervened on their behalf. This is in complete contrast with the rather mechanical assumption made by some commentators that the state will always intervene to support the *charros*.

The panorama, then, is a rich and varied one. Unions which resemble the picture of *charrismo* clearly do exist. But, at least in the automobile industry, this is by no means the entire picture. There is clear and unambiguous evidence that several unions in the Mexican auto industry are characterized by lively and meaningful internal democracy. They include the 'independent' unions and also the other two militant unions (GM–DF, and Ford after 1977). It is difficult to infer anything about trends from the data, but there are no obvious reasons to assume that union democracy will be on the wane in the next few years in Mexico.

Given the variety and complexity of union government in the Mexican auto industry, and the existence of union democracy, it may well be time for a reassessment of union government in Mexican industry as a whole. This issue is taken up again in chapter 10.

8

The labour courts

The labour courts

According to the Mexican labour law, workers in specified industries fall under the jurisdiction either of the Juntas Locales de Conciliación y Arbitraje or of the Junta Federal de Conciliación y Arbitraje. This is not a two-tiered system; there are two separate labour court systems, the local and the federal. There are a number of differences in the operation of the two systems, of which the principal is that the local Juntas appear to be much more open to political pressure from the state Governors and local political forces.[1]

Generally speaking, the industries which are of national importance, such as railways, steel, textiles, etc. fall under federal jurisdiction. In 1975 the automobile assembly industry was transferred from local to federal jurisdiction. Since federal records are centralized in Mexico City whereas local records are not, this makes data collection considerably easier and the federal records only were consulted. This meant that the universe of cases was considerably reduced, and clearly any thorough study would have to utilize the records of the local Juntas as well.

The labour courts have three judges. These judges are supposed to represent the interests of capital, of labour and of the government. The representatives of labour and of capital are designated by trade unions and employers' associations, and the representative of government is, of course, a functionary of the Ministry of Labour. As can be seen, the labour courts reproduce the corporatist tripartite formula.

One of the more important functions of these labour courts is to rule whether a strike is to be considered legal or not. According to the Constitution and the Labour Law, workers have the right to strike in order to equilibrate the factors of production. If the court rules that the strike does not fulfil this requirement, it can declare the strike non-existent. If certain legal requirements are not met, the courts may declare

145

the strike illegal, rather than non-existent. In either case, this clearly puts the strikers at a disadvantage in terms of bargaining power. In addition the courts are empowered to rule on a wide range of industrial conflicts, including individual grievances brought by workers against the company and/or the trade union. The Juntas act as a control mechanism over industrial conflict, channelling it in certain directions and predisposing certain kinds of outcomes.

One of the functions of the Mexican labour courts is to consider cases where there is a claim that the contractual obligations between employer and employee have not been fulfilled. A great number of such disputes about individual work contracts arise from cases where unjust dismissal is alleged. In the automobile industry, as in most industries, workers are either temporary (*eventual*) or permanent (*planta*). The legal rights and job security of these two sections of the labour force are different. The permanent workers enjoy a considerable degree of security and may only be dismissed for certain causes. If a labour court rules that the worker has been unjustly dismissed, he or she may legally be reinstated in the previous position. Although temporary workers are also covered by a law on unjust dismissal, their security of tenure within the firm (together with the wages and fringe benefits which they enjoy) is less. These individual contract disputes, however, often turn out to be a three-way contest, involving the union as well as the employer and employee. That this should be so arises from two causes: in the first place, it is sometimes the case that unions offer legal assistance to their members and help them in the defence of their cases in the labour courts. However, it is also often the case that the principal dispute is between the griever and the union itself. This conflict between the individual worker and the union usually stems from the application of the *cláusula de exclusión*.

According to the general hypotheses advanced in this book, the more militant unions in the auto industry should be more likely to act as representatives of their members, defending them in the labour courts against the employers. The more conservative unions, on the other hand, are more likely to be involved in conflicts with their own members. The dismissed workers are likely to be viewed by the leadership of the conservative unions as troublemakers, and if they have not been dismissed directly by the company, they may well have had the *cláusula de exclusión* applied to them.

The data

The automobile industry came under federal jurisdiction in April 1975. By 21 April 1978, 216 individual grievances had been started. Of these, 196 had terminated by that date. A sample of 100 of these cases was analysed.

The sample of cases terminated is not entirely representative of the universe of cases initiated by April 1978. Biases in the sample were unavoidable, owing to the short period during which the automobile industry had been under federal jurisdiction. It would be interesting to draw a more representative sample at some future date and compare the results.

Causes of conflict

One question that must be answered is: what kind of conflict comes to the labour courts, and what kind of conflict is settled with the plant? Ninety-nine cases were initiated by workers and one was initiated by a company. The majority of the grievances taken to the labour courts resulted from claims of unjust dismissal.[2] Of the 89 cases alleging unjust dismissal, 61 demanded reinstatement and 28 demanded constitutional compensation. Two more cases were indirectly related to dismissal issues, since the workers were claiming that they were owed money from the union mutual aid funds. Another 8 cases dealt with the question of who should be the beneficiary of deceased workers.

The outcomes

Of the 89 cases, only 2 resulted in the reinstatement of the worker. If this is taken as the criterion against which the operation of the labour courts is to be measured then one of two conclusions must be drawn: either the vast majority of individual grievances are groundless, or the courts display a marked anti-worker bias. However, such a simple interpretation is probably not warranted.

In 60 cases an out-of-court settlement was reached in which the worker dropped his action in return for compensation. In another 10 cases the worker dropped the action without obtaining compensation. In the remaining cases dealing with unjust dismissal a court settlement was obtained. There were 15 decisions expressly against workers. If we add to these 15 cases the 10 in which the workers dropped their action at some point, we have a total of 25 cases with outcomes clearly unfavourable to the workers.

Nevertheless, this does not mean that the court ruled against the firm. There was only one case of the court ordering reinstatement plus compensation and there were only two other cases in which the court ordered the firm to pay compensation. As mentioned above, the vast majority of cases (60) concluded with an out-of-court settlement. In one of these cases the worker was rehired; in the other cases the workers were not rehired but were given compensation. In fact, irrespective of whether the worker demanded reinstatement or simply compensation it appears that he could only reasonably hope for compensation.

Given the importance of out-of-court settlements, it is of some interest to look at the size of such settlements. Mexican labour law provides that when a worker has been unjustly dismissed he or she is entitled to financial compensation. In the case of workers with *planta* contracts, the worker is entitled to ninety days' pay, plus twenty days' pay for each year of service. *Eventuales* are entitled to half the length of time served (i.e. up to five and a half months' pay). In both cases, the court may also order the payment of wages for the period between the initiation and the termination of the court case.[3]

It is therefore relatively straightforward to calculate the minimum amount to which a griever would be entitled, if the court were to rule in his favour. There were 57 cases of out-of-court settlements in unjust dismissal cases with sufficient information to permit an analysis of the settlements. The procedure was as follows. In the case of *planta* workers, the daily wage was multiplied by a factor of 90 plus 20 for each year of service, as stipulated by the law. Years of service were rounded down, in order to produce a minimum estimate. In the case of *eventuales* the legal formula was applied exactly.

In many cases, the worker would also be entitled to certain other compensations – vacations owed, punctuality payments, overtime, etc. Thus, it should be clear that the calculations of what the worker could expect if the court ruled in his favour are absolute minima. In many cases, the worker might well expect substantially more than the calculations made here.

The formula of 90 plus 20 days per year was checked by examining the only instance in the sample where the court records indicated that they had followed this procedure. (This was a case involving twenty VW workers fired during the conflicts in December 1975 at that plant.) The formula worked exactly, and there is every reason to believe that the computations made here accord with the procedure outlined in the Mexican labour law.

Our interest lies in part in the percentage of out-of-court settlements which are substantially less than the minimum calculated as the workers' legitimate compensation if the court had ruled in his favour.[4]

Twenty-six of the 57 cases involved full payment of the worker's claims. In the other 31 cases, the out-of-court settlement involved a substantial reduction of the griever's minimum claim. The range was quite large, with an average settlement being some 54 per cent of the minimum claim. It should be stressed that these figures probably seriously underestimate the extent to which workers agree to reductions in their claims in out-of-court settlements, both in terms of frequency and in terms of money forgone.

Given how little is known about the actual operation of Mexican labour courts, it is risky to speculate about these out-of-court settlements. It may perhaps be the case that these grievers had weak cases and were happy to accept an out-of-court settlement. On the other hand, it is entirely possible that many of these grievers were in the right and settled as a result of financial, and other, pressures. Whether any of this was due to unscrupulous lawyers putting pressure on their clients for a speedy, but certain, settlement is, of course, impossible to say.

The fact that most of the grievances examined concern claims of unjust dismissal raises a number of questions. In the first place, the total number of dismissals is, of course, considerably greater than the number of cases which appear in the labour courts. What is it that differentiates the grievers from the rest of the individual dismissals, and from the labour force in general?

One speculation, and one that fits in well with the evidence presented here about the generally unsympathetic role played by the union, is that the grievers are workers who, for one reason or another, have not maintained good relations with the union. It might be the case, for example, that the union helps the bulk of laid-off workers to get appropriate compensation but fails to do so in those cases where there has been some antagonism between the worker and the union. This is, it must be repeated, only a surmise, and needs to be investigated in more detail.

Following this line of thought, one might also ask whether or not the layoffs were deliberately engineered by the union to disembarrass itself of these troublesome workers. This is perhaps not as far-fetched as it sounds. The very real power which the Mexican unions have in the structure of control (unlike the situation in Brazil) will generate pressures towards the development of clientele systems. One consequence of the operation of patron–client systems is the personal victimization of actors who fail to display appropriate client behaviour.

The union

Of the sample of 100 cases, 40 involved the union, either as co-defendant with the company or in its capacity as defender of the worker's rights. Of these 40 cases, no fewer than 29 involved the union as co-defendant. In only 11 cases was there clear evidence of union support for the worker.

The breakdown of cases by company (given in table 8.1) is interesting. Of the 29 cases in which the union was cited as co-defendant, 25 occurred in Chrysler, 1 in Volkswagen, 2 in Ford and 1 in GM–DF. Of the cases in which the union actively supported the worker, 1 occurred in GM-DF and 10 in Nissan–Cuernavaca. These cases concerned union activists who had been fired for union-related activities.[5]

In the complaints of the Chrysler workers, after the statement that the worker had been fired, the following phrase occurred with monotonous regularity: 'these were also the orders of Mr X, General Secretary of the union'. And in every case where the union was accused, its officers replied by denying any such intervention. According to the testimony of the union all the firings were exclusively a company affair. And in no case did the Junta rule against the union.

Other cases involved workers who had been fired for distributing leaflets criticizing the incumbent union leadership, both in Chrysler and in GM. Moreover, this figure of 29 cases of union–worker conflict is probably an underestimate. The transcripts and documentation in many cases are so sparse as to preclude any informed judgement about the causes of the conflict.

It is likely that in some cases the involvement of the union is not immediately apparent from the court proceedings. The following extract from a letter written by the lawyer of Volkswagen to the Junta certainly indicates this: 'the plaintiff told my client that, as a result of the problems which he had been having with the Executive Committee of the union he wished to terminate his work contract'. (In his evidence, the worker claimed that he had been fired and that he had never had any difficulties with the Executive Committee of the union.)

Several cases did not involve the union directly. For example, in eight cases workers were accused of stealing auto parts or tools, or of

Table 8.1. *Cases involving the union, by company*

	VW	Chrysler	GM	Ford	VAM	Nissan	DINA	Total
Union cited as defendant[a]	1	25	1	2	—	—	—	29
Union support for griever	—	—	1	—	—	10	—	11
Others	26	6	6	13	3	5	1	60
Total	27	31	8	15	3	15	1	100

[a] Or there is clear evidence of union complicity in the firing.

systematically fiddling overtime records. Another two cases documented acts of gross misdemeanour. While in most of these cases the evidence was such that it would have been difficult for the union to attempt to defend the workers involved, the mere fact that the workers went to court indicates that the cases were not entirely open and shut. Even though the union could not condone such action, it could be argued that one of its functions is to defend its members where possible. Minor theft and fiddling the books are, after all, a frequent, if somewhat individualistic, expression of class conflict and worker dissatisfaction, and the fact that the unions played no part in these disputes is surely some indication of the extent to which unions are part of an institutional system of control over the labour force.

In presenting the results of the analysis of the sample of 100 labour court cases, the figures have not been deflated by the size of the workforce in each company. This information is provided in chapter 2 and the reader may perform his or her own calculations if desired. It was felt that both the total number of grievances filed and the size of the sample were so low that great restraint needed to be exercised in interpreting the data. More substantially, it was felt that the absolute number of individual grievances (rather than that number divided by the size of the workforce) was a good indicator of worker–union relations. Essentially, it appears that individual grievances are likely to be filed in two situations: (a) when a union leadership is attempting to purge dissidents, as appears to have been the case in Chrysler and (more problematically) in VW, and (b) when the company is using devious means to rid itself of 'undesirable' elements, and the union is willing to contest this (as in Nissan).

Support for this interpretation comes from the numerous cases in which there is a claim by the worker that he was fired for opposition to the incumbent union leadership. Instances of this have already been noted, particularly in the case of Chrysler. In addition, it should be noted that the sample contains several cases involving actual or deposed union leaders. In Nissan, one of the members of the union's Executive Committee was fired in 1975 for organizing a work stoppage: 'inciting groups of workers to engage in a slow-down and work as slowly as possible and indicating to them that they should have a stoppage'.[6] Another six Nissan workers were also fired for involvement in the work stoppage. These two court cases were defended by the union lawyer. Two years later another member of the Nissan union's Executive Committee was fired for 'causing material damage to 26 units by allowing units to pass without putting water in the part'.[7]

Another case in the sample also had to do with a Nissan worker accused of slowing down production, and there were two cases of workers fired for 'being responsible for affecting discipline in the canteen, material damages and disobedience'.[8]

In all these cases, the union defended the workers involved, as they had clearly been fired for being union 'troublemakers'.

Equally common, and probably more typical of the industry as a whole, were conflicts between the incumbent union administration and rank-and-file militants or ex-leaders. The conflicts in VW in 1975 had their echoes in the federal labour court. The ousted General Secretary was fired by the company and took his case to court. He accepted a generous out-of-court settlement. And the group which had been barred from presenting its slate in the elections of 1975 also had reason to complain. The leader of the faction and twenty-one of his fellow workers were fired by VW in December 1975. They also accepted an out-of-court settlement (of three months' pay and twenty days for each year of service).

The dismissals in Chrysler have been extensively commented on elsewhere. There was a similar case in GM. In GM, a man who had been the Secretary of Labour during 1967–8 as part of the Coalición faction was fired in June 1975 for distributing leaflets criticizing the incumbent General Secretary. This must be put in the context of the twenty-two-day strike of March 1975 in which the General Secretary had been accused of 'selling' the contract and after which there had been an abortive move to suspend his union rights.[9] (In the elections of September of that year, a new leadership was voted into office by 926 votes to the 617 votes for the previous General Secretary.)

Dirty tricks?

One of the more interesting phenomena was the accusation by workers that either (a) they had been forced to sign letters of resignation or (b) these letters of resignation were forgeries. I quote below some statements made by workers to this effect:

I was pressured emotionally and physically to make me sign a document which purports to be a voluntary resignation. (Ford)

They offered me a cheque for $8,920, suggesting that I sign some papers, that in the event of not doing so I would not be given a single cent . . . I felt obliged to accept that amount, [and when] I asked for a copy of the documentation and of my contract, I was laughed at, being told that the policy of the enterprise was not give out any documents. (Ford)

[I demand] that whatever document which claims to be a resignation from my work be declared null and void . . . as I have never signed such or any similar document. (Chrysler)

In 7 cases (all Chrysler) the workers involved claimed that they had been fired, yet the company produced signed letters of resignation. In another similar case (VW) the worker claimed that he was made to sign a blank sheet of paper and was threatened with jail if he refused. A worker in Ford claimed that he was similarly threatened with jail if he didn't sign a resignation. All told, there were 12 cases in which some doubt was cast by the worker on the authenticity of letters of resignation.

It is difficult to know what to make of these cases. In every case the Junta accepted as genuine the letters of resignation and, as it is a law court, it might be assumed *a priori* that their findings are to be accepted. On the other hand, it is equally unlikely, *a priori*, that workers who have written letters of resignation would bring a case of unjust dismissal against their former employers. If this line of reasoning is followed, the possibility that the resignations were either coerced or forged cannot be discounted.[10]

The workers

The fact that the grievances were concerned with dismissals may have been a result of the unusual contraction in the automobile industry in 1975. However, whether or not this is the case does not affect the general findings of this chapter to any significant extent.

The dismissals which caused the grievances did not simply involve recently hired workers. Indeed, the average length of time worked in the firm by the workers in the sample was seven and a half years. Since most of the workers had long periods of service, most already had been upgraded to permanent status and this was not therefore a major issue. It was not always possible to infer from the records whether workers were permanent or temporary. In 30 cases there was information on this; of these 30, 21 were permanent and 9 were temporary. Of the remaining cases, there is no reason to assume anything about whether the workers were permanent or temporary. There was only one case in which an *eventual* (successfully) demanded upgrading to permanent status.

Conclusion

The most interesting statistic is that in only 11 per cent of the cases was there clear evidence of union support for the worker's grievance, whereas in 29 per cent of the cases the union was cited as co-defendant. Unions everywhere play a dual role, as defenders of their members and as supporters of a specific institutional order which maintains industrial discipline in capitalist enterprises. However, these figures suggest that the balancing of the two roles by unions in the Mexican automobile industry is somewhat lopsided.

On the basis of data available, it is not possible to make definitive statements about whether the labour courts function equitably. However, it should be noted that in only one case was a worker reinstated. Most grievances were, in fact, settled out of court. The implications of this fact are not entirely clear. On the whole, though, it cannot be said with any degree of conviction that the labour courts function with any great efficiency to defend the rights of individual workers.

One result of the investigation has been to lend circumstantial support to the hypothesis that a significant proportion of the cases that come to the labour courts are actually cases in which a union bureaucracy has dealt with a recalcitrant or dissident worker by using the closed-shop provisions of the Labour Law to get the worker fired. It should be noted, however, that nearly all the cases examined which fell into this category occurred in one company (Chrysler). Although the distribution of cases among companies is highly skewed, the evidence reviewed in this chapter is highly compatible with the general pattern of correlation established throughout this book.

9

The empirical findings and the dynamics of industrial militancy

Chapter 2 presented a number of hypotheses about unions in the Mexican automobile industry. The point of departure was an interest in the question of whether there were systematic differences in union behaviour between the new 'independent' unions and the old-style 'official' unions. A number of different dimensions of union behaviour – militancy, control over work processes, internal democracy, representation of workers in the labour courts, etc. – were examined in subsequent chapters. The present chapter will tie together the results of previous chapters in order to clear the way for a discussion (in chapter 10) of the implications of the findings of this research for political processes in Mexico.

The first dimension of union behaviour which was examined was union militancy, defined here as strike-proneness. The hypothesis that the three independent unions would be more strike-prone than the six official unions received only qualified support. The three independent unions (Nissan–Cuernavaca, VW and DINA) were, indeed, among the most strike-prone in the industry. However, two of the official unions (GM–DF and Ford) were also strike-prone. It was therefore decided to amend the original hypotheses, and see whether the dichotomy militant–conservative was a better predictor of union behaviour than the dichotomy independent–official.

As the available evidence on the various dimensions of union behaviour was reviewed in chapters 4 to 8, a strikingly consistent pattern of intercorrelations emerged. On all the dimensions surveyed, the behaviour of the five militant unions was consistently different from that of the four conservative unions. There were, of course, some minor exceptions, and these are discussed in detail below. Nevertheless, the overall pattern shown in table 9.1 is clear: those unions which have a high strike frequency are also characterized by the presence of internal union democracy, by a larger number of full-time union officers paid for

Table 9.1. *Summary*

Union	Location	Affiliation	No. of strikes 1970–80	Democratic	No. of union officials	Court case[a]	Control over work processes	Wage increase 1975–80[b]
Nissan	Cuernavaca	UOI	6	Yes	4	10+	Yes	274
DINA	Cuidad Sahagún	UOI	5	Yes	8	0	Yes	ND
VW	Puebla	UOI	4	?	9	−1	No	281
Ford	Mexico City	CTM	3	Yes	4	−2	Yes	293
GM	Mexico City	CROC	6	Yes	9	−1/1+	Yes.	251
GM	Toluca	CTM	0	No	5	0	No	255
Chrysler	Toluca & Mexico City	CTM	0	No	0	−25	No	253
VAM	Toluca & Mexico City	COR	0	No	0	0	Yes	248
Nissan	Toluca	CTM	0	No	0	0	No	ND

Data are for 1978 unless otherwise indicated.

[a] A plus sign indicates union support for the griever; a minus sign indicates that the union was cited as co-defendant.

[b] 1975 = 100; ND = no data; source, Ford Motor Company, *Proyección*, No. 14 (1981).

by the company, by a greater degree of control over work loads and line speeds, by a more supportive attitude to their constituents in the labour courts, and by somewhat faster rates of wage growth. The converse is generally true for the conservative unions.

Table 9.1 does not include information on the bargaining role of *delegados departmentales* or on the percentage of the workforce on permanent *planta* contracts. This is owing to problems of securing reliable comparative data. These two issues, are, however, discussed in preceding chapters and there is every indication that the same pattern of correlation also holds for these two dimensions.

It is also clear from table 9.1 that, while it seems correct to say that the independent unions are quite different in behaviour from the majority of official unions, some official unions behave in ways that are not dissimilar to the pattern displayed by the independent unions. Clearly, union affiliation alone is an inadequate predictor of behaviour in the Mexican automobile industry.

Nor are the characteristics of the enterprise (its nationality or bargaining style, for example) likely to explain much of the variance in union behaviour in this case. Both General Motors and Nissan have two unions. In each case, one union is militant and the other is conservative. Of course, there is no suggestion here that management or enterprise characteristics are irrelevant or uninteresting, but for the hypotheses considered in this study these do not seem to be the most salient explanatory variables.

The exceptions

Very few correlations in social science are perfect; considerable suspicion would be aroused if such were the case in this study. In fact, there are a number of interesting exceptions to the pattern of correlations which characterizes the industry as a whole. Some are merely artifacts of particular measures. For example, in the Ford union, the column referring to the number of court cases shows that there were two cases in which the union was cited as a defendant. This is contrary to our theoretical expectations. However, both cases were initiated prior to the reorganization of the union in 1977 and refer to the *ancien régime* in Ford, whereas the interest for this study lies with the Ford union after its 1977 reorganization. Owing to the fact that this particular union underwent a radical change during the period covered by this study, this particular measure (and only this one) fails to reflect the true state of affairs.

In the case of the GM union in Mexico City, the statistics on union involvement in court cases are also contrary to expectation, and here the problem is slightly different. In this case, it is a matter of the interpretation to be placed on the quantitative data. Here, the bald statistics need to be supplemented with more qualitative data. The case in which the union was cited as defendant arose out of an internal struggle for control of the union. It does, indeed, indicate the presence of dubious union practices, such as the use of the *cláusula de exclusión*, which characterize the more oligarchic unions. Nevertheless, this should be placed in the context of a lively and permanent rank-and-file opposition to union oligarchs.

A more serious deviation from our expectations in this area involves the case against the VW union. This cannot be qualified in the same way as has just been done for the GM union, and must remain an exception to the overall pattern. We shall return to this case shortly.

There are three other exceptions which need explicit comment: the GM union in Toluca is deviant in that it has a sizeable number of union representatives; the other GM union is deviant in not achieving wage increases as large as the other militant unions; and VAM is deviant in that this conservative union appears to exercise a strong measure of control over the work process.

None of these deviations are easily explained away. Perhaps the easiest to explain is the poor wage performance in GM's Mexico City union. A combination of a highly militant union, management plans to expand operations elsewhere in Mexico (to the possible detriment of employment in the Mexico City plant), and inept handling of some lengthy strikes may go some way to account for this.

In the absence of reliable data about the role and bargaining power of shop-floor union representatives, there is no easy way to account for the presence of a union officialdom in GM's Toluca union, given its otherwise totally conservative nature. Interviews with management and union officers in this case do tend to suggest, however, that this expansion of the union apparatus is a form of bureaucratic clientelism.

The control over line speeds in VAM is particularly interesting, since the union apparatus in this firm is exiguous, to say the least. It is possible that the small size of the company, together with the fact that there is a sizeable element of state ownership, may partially explain this exception to our expectations. If this is so, then one might be inclined to conclude that VAM's relatively trouble-free industrial relations record and the apparent absence of widespread rank-and-file discontent with union leadership may be the result of a generalized satisfaction on the part of the workforce. On the other hand, this general absence of discontent needs itself to be explained, and it is possible that the industrial relations philosophy of the management, described by one analyst as 'paternalism', may be a major factor in producing this outcome.[1]

Before leaving this section, we must return briefly to the union in VW. As noted above, this union was deviant from expectations in terms of behaviour in the labour courts. It is also deviant in that, as of 1980, the union had not achieved any control over work processes. Moreover, we saw in chapter 7 that it was difficult unambiguously to characterize the internal government of the VW union as 'democratic'. For this reason, a question mark has been placed in the appropriate column of table 9.1. Such a collection of deviant results requires a major reappraisal. All the other cases of deviant results are relatively minor and do not materially alter the overall findings. The VW case is, however, more consistently at odds with expectations derived from the fact that it is a strike-prone independent union.

It may well be that the most appropriate conclusion would be to described the VW case as an intermediate one.[2] It is the one case which does not fit either the militant or the conservative pattern. There is, however, a way in which even the VW case can be reconciled with the general interpretative scheme advanced in this book. Up to now, the discussion has been couched entirely in terms of correlations among the various dimensions of union behaviour. The time has come to move on to a discussion of the causal processes underlying this pattern of correlations.

The chains of causality

As the data on the various aspects of union behaviour have been gradually introduced throughout this book, they have been discussed in terms of the patterns of correlations which appeared to emerge. In the original hypotheses there lurked an implicit theory of causality: namely that union affiliation (independent or official) was the factor which determined union militancy, and that this, in turn, brought about higher wages, more control over work processes, etc.

Since it was immediately obvious that union affiliation was not directly related to militancy, the first step of this implicit causal chain (union affiliation determined militancy) was quietly dropped, and a new implicit theory of causality adopted: union militancy determines wage increases, control over work processes, etc. Taking strike frequency as the measure of union militancy, this causal theory is compatible with the available data, with the major exception of the VW union.

There is, however, at least one other causal theory which is both compatible with the data and which can incorporate the VW case without resort to *ad hoc* explanations. It is illustrated in figure 2.

The theory presented here gives considerable weight to the type of union government as a determinant of other types of union behaviour. It is assumed that when a union is directly responsible to its rank and file (and it must be borne in mind that we are dealing with very small unions which are often restricted to a single plant) the leadership will be under pressure to 'deliver the goods' to its membership. In democratically run unions, leaderships which consistently fail to deliver the goods will be voted out of office. (It will be remembered that the measures of union democracy used in chapter 7 stressed the importance of rank-and-file constraints on leadership.)

Therefore, in those unions which are democratic, and given the appropriate economic situation, one should find high levels of strikes, rapid increases in wages, a high percentage of workers on *planta* contracts and control over work processes. To attempt to represent the workers more effectively, the number of full-time union officers paid for by the company will increase, as will the size of the contract revision committee, and the *delegados departmentales* will play an important role. One possible company response to increased militancy on the part of the union may be to dismiss what it sees as 'troublemakers'. As a result, the more militant unions will be drawn into the labour court system as defenders of their constituents.

In those unions which have oligarchic leaderships, there will be little or no membership pressure to go on strike; hence, wage rates will rise more slowly, and the union will exert less control over line speeds and there will be a smaller percentage of workers on *planta* contracts. Since union office in these unions is largely viewed as a source of power and income, the number of full-time officers paid for by the company will be small. If there is an increase in the number of union officers paid for by the company this will be used to extend clientelistic networks. *Delegados* will be unimportant, and contracts will be negotiated without active membership involvement. Opposition to leadership policies by the rank and file will be dealt with by applying the *cláusula de exclusión*,

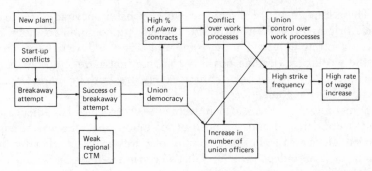

Fig. 2. Militancy in the Mexican automobile industry

and there will therefore be a tendency for these unions to be cited as defendants in grievances brought before the labour courts.

In addition to these differences among unions, some factors in the industry will be common to all types of union. Thus, although one would expect the percentage of workers on *planta* contracts to be higher in the democratic unions, the general tendency in the industry as a whole is probably for the number of *planta* workers to increase over time, and, as with wages, the important differences between unions may well be in terms of rates of change, rather than absolute levels.

Some of the changes outlined above will also interact with each other. For example, as the percentage of workers on *planta* contracts increases, it is likely that there will be greater pressure by management to utilize this labour force more efficiently to respond to fluctuations in output, rather than rely on the hiring and firing of *eventuales*. This, in turn, is likely to lead to increased conflict over labour processes, and to enhance the need for a large and active shop-floor union representation.

Thus, differences in types of union government, it is hypothesized, may have these sorts of implication for union militancy. But why are some unions democratic and others oligarchic?

Origins of union democracy

Almost without exception, when the new automobile plants were started in the post-war period, there were major crises in industrial relations within a few years. Since all these plants were organized by official unions (usually affiliated with the CTM), some of this discontent took the form of movements to break away from the CTM and form independent unions.

These movements of discontent were probably inevitable, and had their origins in start-up difficulties which are common to much of manufacturing industry, in the youth and lack of industrial experience of the workforce (leading possibly to somewhat anomic outbursts of discontent), and in the lack of union experience, both by union leaders and by the workforce.[3]

Sometimes these breakaway movements succeeded and in other cases they were defeated and the position of union oligarchs was strengthened. In one case (Ford), a compromise was achieved whereby the union became independent in substance while remaining within the CTM. Where breakaway movements were successful, the experiences and divisions resulting from those movements provided the basis for meaningful union democracy. Once institutionalized, such democratic practices tended to be relatively stable.

The one exception to this pattern is the GM union in Mexico City. This union had been established during the pro-labour regime of President Lázaro Cárdenas (1934–40). This was a time of political effervescence in which left-wing currents were particularly influential in the union sector. The origins of democracy in the GM union can clearly be traced to this period, and the fact that the union was affiliated with a relatively weak (and marginally more progressive than the CTM) official confederation (the CROC) may have enabled it to retain its independence of action throughout the post-war period.[4]

Returning to the sixties and seventies, it is reasonable to enquire as to why some breakaway movements succeeded while others failed. A possible answer to this may be sought in the regions in which the plants were located.

Many of the new plants were set up in a concentric ring around Mexico City, partly as a result of government support for industrial decentralization. In three of these locations, the regional apparatus of the CTM was relatively weak. The DINA and Nissan plants were both located in states with very little industry (Hidalgo and Morelos). Here the CTM was weak because the industrial underdevelopment of these states had precluded the formation of a cohesive and experienced CTM bureaucracy. Interestingly, both Ciudad Sahagún and the industrial park in Cuernavaca became sites of union militancy; the results were by no means confined to the automobile industry.

The VW plant was set up in Puebla. Although this was an industrial city, the area was predominantly a textile centre, and this industry had originally been organized by the CROM and CGT. Even in the 1970s both of these confederations retained enough power in the region to prevent the development of a really strong state-owned CTM bureaucracy. Conversely, the industrial city of Toluca, in the State of Mexico, was a CTM stronghold. All attempts at breakaway movements to date in this city have been effectively quashed.

The control of the CTM in Mexico City and its immediate environs is difficult to assess. Although the CTM controls many unions in this region, its capacity to resist oppositional movements is unclear. In part this is due to the fact that the CTM in Mexico City is heavily factionalized, as is indicated by the breakaway of the COR. At the same time, the fact that there are fissures within the CTM bureaucracy is, in a paradoxical way, a hindrance to the emergence of independent unions in the city, since there is a tendency for oppositional movements to become co-opted by bureaucratic cliques within the CTM.

Although much of the analysis presented above on the antecedents of union democracy and its possible consequences for union militancy must necessarily remain somewhat speculative, it does appear to offer some interesting insights into the effects of industrialization in Mexico on the development of the labour movement.

If it is indeed the case that the combination of the establishment of a new plant and its location in a region of the country with a weak CTM tends to set in train a series of processes leading to greater industrial conflict, then this is something to be borne in mind when considering plans for industrial decentralization. It should be possible to explore this question in the next few years. Several automobile manufacturers have announced plans for, or have already begun to build, new plants in the northern regions of Mexico. In all of these cases, union jurisdiction has gone to the CTM. These new plants are, however, being established in regions where the CTM is quite weak. If the analysis presented in this book is valid, then the 1980s may well see a number of serious industrial conflicts in these new plants.

10

Unions and political stability in Mexico

Mexico's authoritarian political system

Many recent analyses of Mexican politics stress the authoritarian features of the political system and the way in which the stability of the regime rests, at least in part, on the control and co-optation of organized labour.[1] According to Lawrence Whitehead,

what one might almost call the establishment view of Mexican and foreign social scientists is that twentieth-century Mexico underwent a bourgeois revolution, clearing the way for a strong state to emerge, one that would be firmly committed to the process of capitalist industrialization. In pursuit of this aim, semi-corporatist forms of political control have been elaborated, peasant, working class and intellectual resistance have been curbed or co-opted, and a powerful process for the redistribution of resources toward the rich (often allied with foreign corporations) have been set in motion.[2]

This orthodox vision of the Mexican polity clearly implies that insurgent movements within the ranks of organized labour are likely to be ephemeral or irrelevant. If they pose any threat to the *status quo* such movements will be either repressed or brought into the official system of control.[3] As was noted in chapter 1, such arguments are frequently made for other Latin American countries as well.

The argument, elaborated by Guillermo O'Donnell and others, may be summarized briefly as follows: the exigencies of capital accumulation in certain types of peripheral regimes require a strong and autonomous state which will, *inter alia*, exert control over unions in order to prevent wages from rising too fast (i.e. to the detriment of capital accumulation) and will keep strike activity to a low and manageable level so as not to scare off potential investors.[4] Industrial growth in such countries is based on the rapid expansion of the consumer durables sector rather than on the more 'traditional' final goods industries such as textiles. Since only the higher income groups are able to purchase consumer durables such as automobiles, TVs, washing machines, etc., industrial growth will be accompanied by an increasingly unequal distribution of income. Since workers, according to this theory, will not be consuming these products,[5] raising wages will not stimulate demand and therefore Keynesian arguments for increased wages are inapplicable. With this pattern of growth and capital accumulation the state will have little legitimacy and will, therefore, tend to be increasingly authoritarian. At the same time, its technical intervention in the economy will increase; hence the label 'bureaucratic authoritarianism' for this sort of regime. It has been argued that the theory is applicable to Mexico,[6] and this implies that, so long as the PRI is successful in maintaining a commitment to rapid accumulation of capital, there will be no liberalization of the control structures of Mexican unionism. This theory has been criticized on a number of grounds,[7] including its empirical validity.

In any event, the theory merely asserts (in its non-teleological versions, at least) that if capital accumulation is to proceed apace, then there must be effective control over union militancy. But Mexico's rulers – however much they may desire to achieve high growth rates – may not be able to control union militancy in the ways that the theory of bureaucratic authoritarianism suggests is necessary.

For one thing, the PRI has other imperatives, such as maintaining its legitimacy and controlling the level of political opposition, and these may militate against rapid capital accumulation. Nor, despite the impressive skill of the Mexican political elite, is the political process entirely subject to their control. One area where political control is not total is precisely in what is regarded as the principal pillar of the regime, organized labour.

The possible ways in which political control over organized labour is subject to strain are discussed below. Before proceeding with the main line of argument, however, it is necessary to discuss a variant of these theories of authoritarianism, one that stresses the 'populist' basis of the Mexican state.

Populism and inclusionary corporatism

A number of analysts have pointed to a major difference between the Mexican political system and authoritarian systems in other Latin American countries such as Brazil and Argentina. Within the framework of theories of corporatism, Mexico is usually seen as a case of *inclusionary* corporatism, and contrasted with the *exclusionary* corporatism of, say, Brazil.[8] The key difference here seems to be that organized labour is controlled by bringing it into the state apparatus, and giving union leaders real political power (which they use to support the system) rather than restricting the power of the unions and actively preventing them from acting in anti-system ways.

The reason for this difference has been suggested by Robert Kaufman. He argues that, at the time when the exigencies of capital accumulation required effective state control, the prior incorporation of labour into the political system under Cárdenas meant that existing institutional structures could be utilized to control labour. He argues that 'populism . . . died a premature death in Mexico' and therefore 'The only imperative with respect to import-substitution politics was that the workers be "kept in line" – a task that could be relatively easily accomplished by drawing on the political capital built up by earlier reforms, by occasional new concessions, and by the substantial threat of coercion.'[9]

Thus, the heritage of populism in Mexico was a set of stable institutions which could be utilized to restrain labour militancy. Other analysts have suggested, however, that the Mexican political system is marked by continuing populist features. Indeed, one author has described the Mexican political system as one of 'structural populism'.[10] Presumably, the intention is to stress the extent to which the PRI rules through consensus, with a high degree of legitimacy, and the extent to which subordinate classes are organized and mobilized by the state.

There is an important element of truth in this perspective. All stable political systems need some degree of legitimacy, and one which does not rely on direct military force must clearly seek a fair measure of popular acceptance. But whether such a system should be described as 'populist' is, however, a matter for dispute.

The term 'populism' has been so widely used that one might despair of finding agreement on its empirical referent. Without going into the details of a necessarily complex discussion about the term, it seems reasonable to note that the salient aspect for the purposes of this book concerns the degree to which governments are under some sort of pressure to take popular concerns into consideration. That the Mexican government does not behave toward organized labour in a thoroughly authoritarian manner has been a central argument of this book. Analyses of the 'populist' basis of Mexican politics, misleading though they may be in some respects, do at least emphasize the importance of legitimacy. Contrary to the thrust of most analyses of the authoritarian nature of Mexican politics, the state does not have a free hand in its dealings with labour. Despite its very considerable power, the Mexican state faces a complex and problematic task in its efforts to subordinate labour to the tasks of capital accumulation.

Labour insurgency

At first sight, the results of the empirical research on the automobile industry presented in this book are difficult to reconcile with the 'establishment' view of Mexican politics. Insurgent movements were successful in the face of opposition from the CTM, and the institutional structures which predispose unions toward militancy appear to be reasonably firmly grounded in half of the unions studied. Nor is there much evidence that either the leaderships or the rank and file in these militant unions have been co-opted in any meaningful sense.[11] Leaders are under more or less constant pressure from their members to 'deliver the goods' and this puts constraints on their ability to negotiate the sorts of compromise with management which might be regarded as instances of co-optation.

The rank and file, on the other hand, are not easily described, for the reasons suggested in chapter 3, as a labour aristocracy. It is certainly true that, in terms of job tenure and wages, the workers in the Mexican automobile industry are privileged compared to many other workers. It is also true that the workers in each factory appear increasingly to form a coherent quasi-class. Nevertheless, and this is central to any meaningful definition of a labour aristocracy, there is very little evidence of any widespread conservative support for the *status quo* among automobile workers.[12]

Naturally, whether workers are judged to be conservative or not depends to some extent on prior theoretical expectations about the political responses 'appropriate' to such workers. If an analyst believes that Mexican auto workers ought, in some sense, to be imbued with a revolutionary class consciousness, and ought to use their unions as instruments of struggle against the capitalist state, then these workers – like most workers in Mexico – must be regarded as being profoundly conservative.[13]

Mexican automobile workers engage in predominantly 'economistic' struggles. They do not agitate for specifically political demands. Their concerns are with wages, working conditions, control over labour processes, hiring and firing, etc. They resemble the 'instrumentalist' workers of the Luton car factory studied by Goldthorpe and his associates more than a politically conscious Leninist vanguard.[14]

This is hardly surprising. Trade unions are institutions which function within a capitalist economy and, by regulating and institutionalizing labour conflicts, tend to contribute to the maintenance of that system.

But the 'Leninist' expectation is surely an unreasonable one in any case. As Lenin himself was at pains to point out, most workers in capitalist societies tend to have a trade union consciousness most of the time, and the actions of their unions reflect this.[15] It is only in exceptional circumstances that the social scientist might expect anything different. To be useful in the analysis of social reality, terms like 'conservative' and 'militant' must be defined in terms of the context in which action occurs.

Further, such contextual analysis must explore the effects which union actions have on the political system as a whole. While the conscious intentions of actors are not unimportant, for certain questions it is the 'objective' outcomes rather than the 'subjective' meanings which are of interest to the social scientist. It will be argued below that the kind of union militancy described in this book may well have important and far-reaching implications for the functioning of the Mexican political system.

Before proceeding, however, we must consider one other argument about whether the evidence presented in this book is incompatible with the 'establishment' view of the Mexican political system.

One of the most impressive features of the Mexican political system is its flexibility.[16] The system is complex and all-inclusive. There are few areas of life that are not brought into the political system. A myriad of local-level organizations and special interest groups are aggregated into a sprawling state apparatus. In this way, the Mexican polity is riddled with clientelistic networks and widespread corruption.[17] These phenomena have two interesting effects: on the one hand, they serve as mechanisms of integration of a variety of particularistic interests into the system; on the other hand, they inhibit the capacity of the central parts of the state apparatus to implement coherent policies effectively. This, together with the operation of a number of important checks and balances in the system,[18] markedly reduces some of the authoritarian features of Mexican politics.

The control mechanisms of the Mexican polity are not confined to repression or co-optation by the central state apparatus. Rather, in addition to the actions of the central state apparatus, there also exist a host of mechanisms of control and co-optation in a wide variety of institutional spheres which serve to prevent conflict getting out of hand. Only when these mechanisms fail to operate effectively need the central state apparatus intervene.

According to this interpretation of the Mexican political system, the complexity and flexibility of the system are such that isolated instances of union insurgency can be allowed to exist without posing a real threat to the system as a whole. Such an interpretation would reconcile the data presented in this book with the establishment view of the Mexican political system by arguing that the cases of union militancy identified here are isolated and relatively minor cases which leave the overall panorama unaltered.

It would require a much larger research project to answer this question satisfactorily. Nevertheless, some comments are in order. First, the automobile industry may be relatively small in terms of total employment, but it is both strategically placed within the economy and highly visible. The effects of union militancy in the automobile industry are likely to have considerable ramifications elsewhere. Secondly, the automobile industry is a modern industry and, therefore, somewhat representative of the kinds of industrial establishment which may be set up in the next decade or so in Mexico. More and more Mexican workers will be employed in enterprises similar to the ones studied here. A certain degree of generalization of the results of this study seems legitimate.

In the third place, a desultory survey of union insurgency in Mexico suggests that the automobile industry is by no means an isolated example. Chapter 1 provided a historical review of the development of Mexican unionism, and drew attention to the widespread occurrence of insurgent movements. Such movements continue in contemporary Mexico. Important oppositional movements exist in the mining and metalworking union, in electricity generation and supply, in the teachers' union and elsewhere. Of course, not all these movements have prospered. On the other hand, neither have they been totally and permanently defeated. Union militancy and rank-and-file insurgency are not isolated and peripheral features of Mexican unionism; they are an integral part of the dynamic of the industrial system, and one which continually poses difficulties for the stability of Mexican politics.[19]

Up to the present, however, the continued insurgency of sections of the Mexican working class has rarely been able seriously to challenge the dominance of the official union apparatus. Nonetheless, there are some possible indications that the situation may be changing.

Recent developments

A major impetus to the development of union militancy, particularly in the form of independent unionism, was given during the term of office of President Echeverría (1970–6). The way in which President Echeverría distanced himself from the CTM and created a climate propitious for the development of independent unions has been described in chapter 1. This sort of political permissiveness goes some considerable way toward explaining why the insurgent movements of the 1970s were successful, though it is only part of the explanation. Such presidential support was not forthcoming under President López Portillo (1976–82), and there is little reason to suppose that this will change under the regime of President Miguel de la Madrid, since he is generally regarded as having technocratic and pro-business orientations.

On the other hand, there is little sign of a general crackdown on union militancy, and insurgent movements, both within national industrial unions and in the form of the independent union confederation (UOI), appear to be here to stay. It is possible, indeed likely, that the UOI will enter the pro-government umbrella organization, the Labour Congress (Congreso del Trabajo). Such a move would undoubtedly be seen by much of the Mexican left as the final proof, if any were needed, that the process of 'neo-charrification' of the independent unions was proceeding apace. It is also possible that a substantial number of unions will break away from the UOI, in a manner similar to the VW union, and create a nucleus of 'independent' unions. Such a development could easily be construed as further evidence of the bureaucratization and 'charrification' of the UOI. There are grounds, however, for a rather different interpretation of the existing tendencies in contemporary Mexican unionism.

There can be little doubt that the leaders of organized labour in Mexico wish to preserve political stability and that they favour a considerable amount of private investment. But, at the same time, the leaders of the official labour movement must respond to the challenge posed by insurgents, either within their own unions or in the form of breakaway independent unions. In recent years, this response has taken two forms: an increased militancy in the public pronouncements of the CTM, and increasing organization rivalry among the various official union confederations.

While the increased militancy of the CTM is a direct response to the challenge posed by union insurgency, the in-fighting within the ranks of official labour has its immediate origins in an incipient leadership conflict. Throughout the post-war period, the CTM has been led by one man, Fidel Velázquez, with no serious rivals for the post of General Secretary. Born in 1901, he is now quite old and his retirement from active work in the labour movement is not unlikely. This raises the spectre of a struggle for leadership of the CTM by the handful of top leaders. Given the widespread clientelism and bureaucratic factionalism which characterize the CTM (and many other Mexican political organizations), such a conflict may well prove to be energy-consuming. The other official union confederations and the large national industrial unions outside the CTM could take advantage of a momentary weakness of the CTM to increase their own political standing *vis-à-vis* that organization.

If these conjectures turn out to be correct, the next few years may see an intensification of internal conflict within the ranks of official labour, which will create a series of opportunities for insurgent movements to make gains. Nevertheless, this potential leadership struggle is a minor element in the industrial relations panorama in Mexico. Of more importance are structural shifts in the economy.

Workplace conflict

Despite the severity of the recession induced by the 1982 foreign debt crisis and the extremely gloomy short-term prospects for the Mexican economy, it is not unreasonable to suppose that industrial growth will resume, though possibly under rather different circumstances. The very process of industrial growth itself is likely to increase the level of union militancy in a number of ways. It is not very likely that industrial growth will increase union militancy by way of increased employment and a general tightening of the labour market. Although some evidence indicates that industrial growth is contributing in the long run to the process of job creation,[20] there is such a huge pool of unemployed and underemployed, and population growth rates are so high, that no major changes are foreseeable in the immediate future. In any case, labour markets in Mexico are often quite tight for individual firms, owing to the operation of *planta* clauses in employment contracts.

It is, however, highly likely that a number of modern industries will be the site of conflicts over working conditions in a manner not dissimilar to the automobile industry. If such conflicts develop, then it would not be unreasonable to expect an increase in the importance of shop-floor union representation. This development, if the theory advanced in chapter 9 of this book has any validity, will be a powerful force in the institutionalization of union militancy.

Policies of industrial decentralization may also, as indicated in the previous chapter, prove to be major stimuli for industrial militancy. For a variety of reasons, it may well be the case that the level of industrial conflict in the newer industrial zones outside Mexico City will tend to rise in the near future. However, the likelihood that such conflicts will coalesce into an organized national movement is low. Both regional dispersion and occupational fragmentation will probably continue to characterize the Mexican working class.

In this sense, the Mexican working class has been composed of a number of heterogeneous segments: railwaymen, industrial workers, miners, etc., with a considerable degree of homogeneity and structuration within industries but very little across industries. This book has suggested that similar trends may be developing in the automobile industry, as fathers exert pressure to hire sons, and all workers exert pressure to make employment a life-long commitment. This may be contrasted with recent experiences in Brazil and Argentina where, apparently, high rates of labour turnover[21] are tending to produce a more homogeneous working class, one whose experiences and life chances are similar for all members.

While class-wide political action is possible in countries where the working class has a relatively high degree of homogeneity, collective action in countries like Mexico is more likely to take the form of a series of sectional conflicts. Industrial conflicts are likely to be both economistic and uncoordinated. As a result, the successful formation of a political party of labour in Mexico is improbable and nationally coordinated general strikes will probably be a rare occurrence. Industrial militancy will probably remain confined to a series of discrete and isolated conflicts. The likelihood that a unified labour movement will pose a direct challenge to political stability seems remote.

This does not mean, however, that future developments in Mexican labour will not be destabilizing for the regime. The volume of industrial conflict may be expected to rise, and the institutional structures of the labour movement will probably undergo changes leading to greater shop-floor power. Moreover, while the trend will be toward a fragmentation of industrial conflict, the pursuit of growth and balance of payments equilibrium in an inflationary context means that the Mexican government will seek to implement some form of incomes policy.

Inflation and incomes policy

Recourse to the use of incomes policy as a way of controlling wage drift began in the second half of the seventies. The government relied on the agreement of the CTM and other official union confederations to establish a ceiling above which wage settlements would be discouraged. While the success of incomes policies (both in Mexico and elsewhere) will continue to be a matter of considerable debate, they do seem to have one clear effect. Those workers who are able to win wage increases above the norm will disregard the incomes policy wherever possible, and this will generate considerable discontent elsewhere in the ranks of organized labour. The successful implementation of incomes policy requires a unified and disciplined labour movement. However, the argument presented in this chapter is that the probable future prospect for the Mexican labour movement is one in which centripetal forces will be strong, and the conditions for a successful incomes policy will therefore be continually eroded.

This inability to control the rate of growth of wages, particularly in the modern industrial sector, may perhaps be an important destabilizing force in the Mexican political system.[22] The reality of a severe recession, with its attendant layoffs and unemployment, will of course do much to moderate wage growth. However, the segmentation of the labour market, and the relative security of workers with *planta* contracts, will mean that, in an inflationary situation, different sections of the work-force will be able to defend their real incomes with differing degrees of success. The strength of unionism in the modern industrial sector may mean that wages continue to be high, threatening both the government's anti-inflationary policies and its efforts to attract foreign capital.

A possible response to this threat might be an attempt to shore up, or modify, the authoritarian features of official labour organizations in order to re-establish the dominance of the *charro* leaderships or, alternatively, to replace the old system of labour control with a newer and more authoritarian one. According to José Luís Reyna, 'Mexico is on her way to a more authoritarian, corporatist political regime. Social exclusion and high social costs are inevitable within an economic model like the Mexican one . . . Repression will be more intense because it is becoming more difficult to meet popular demands'.[23] Such repressive responses, while well within the bounds of possibility, nevertheless run up against an important constraint.

In the 1970s the Mexican state embarked on a long-term programme of political reform. Although many critics of the regime contend that the political reform is merely a form of window-dressing and point out, quite rightly, that its aim is to conserve the PRI in political power, it cannot be dismissed too lightly. The stated aims of the reform are to move gradually away from a political system where the PRI always 'won' 90 per cent of the vote and totally dominated the legislature to a slightly more pluralistic system. The aim is not to create a viable multi-party democracy, but rather to give legitimacy to a broad range of oppositional political tendencies. This means legalizing a number of opposition parties on the political left as well as on the right, and providing certain guarantees that these organizations will be able to function in a regular and effective manner. The reform also implies that oppositional groups may be represented in the legislature and that this will become a more active forum for criticism of government policy. The political reform does *not* envisage any diminution in the power of the President, and it does not contemplate a situation where the PRI would lose its hegemonic role. Clearly, the intention is to liberalize the system in order that growing dissatisfaction with the regime be incorporated into the system to some extent. The political reform is designed to move from an alienated to a 'loyal' opposition.

The basic aim, obviously, is to strengthen the dominant role of the PRI by means of a programme of concessions and 'openings'. Such a process naturally has its risks, and may prove to be the harbinger of broader and more fundamental changes.[24] But even if the reform is effective, it will produce a situation in which the suppression of union dissidence becomes more problematic. In a situation of even limited pluralism, the scope for manoeuvre of trade union militants is greatly enhanced, and the task faced by the government of ensuring compliance with its macroeconomic policies becomes much more complex. Although Mexico's vast oil reserves are a tremendous asset, there are considerable inflationary tendencies in the economy. This, in conjunction with a sizeable foreign debt and the ease with which pesos can be transferred into dollars, means that the achievement of stable economic growth in the 1980s will require sophisticated economic management. The continuing pressures on the government to deal simultaneously with problems of poverty, income distribution and unemployment will compound the difficulties faced by economic planners. In such a situation, the willingness of the labour movement to cooperate with the government's macroeconomic policy is both essential and highly problematic.

In twentieth-century Mexico the state has been a leviathan, dominating civil society and marshalling it into a ramshackle complex of corporatist and clientelistic institutions. But, according to some analysts of Mexican society, things are now changing and 'civil society' is seeking a place in the sun.[25] In this theoretical framework, the political reform may be seen as an attempt on the part of the state to accommodate to the changing situation. The final result of such an accommodation, however, must remain in doubt. Authoritarian political systems have considerable difficulties in managing political reforms. Mexico's leaders have simultaneously to fight their way out of a major economic crisis and attempt a reform from within of the political system. In their attempt to carry out both economic recovery and political reform the Mexican elite must rely heavily on the cooperation of organized labour. Yet the ability of organized labour to deliver support for the system is being steadily eroded by the factors which have given rise to the emergence of the militant unions described in this book. Although in the short run the economic crisis will undoubtedly hit hard at the independent unions, rank-and-file militancy is unlikely to disappear. In a diffuse and unorganized manner, such grass-roots insurgency will continue to weaken organized labour's ability to prop up the system. In such a situation the temptation of an authoritarian solution must be very great. There are, however, alternative courses open to the Mexican state. It remains to be seen whether the political skills of Mexico's governing elite are adequate to the task in hand.

Notes

1 Organized labour in Mexico

1 Recent overviews of the discussions are contained in B. Roberts, *Cities of Peasants* (London, Edward Arnold, 1978) and P. Lloyd, *A Third World Proletariat?* (London, Allen and Unwin, 1982).

2 L. Martins Rodrigues, *Trabalhadores, sindicatos e industrialização* (São Paulo, Brasiliense, 1974); J. Payne, *Labor and Politics in Peru* (New Haven, Yale University Press, 1965).

3 K. Mericle, 'Corporatist Control of the Working Class: Authoritarian Brazil since 1964' in J. Malloy (ed.), *Authoritarianism and Corporatism in Latin America* (Pittsburgh, University of Pittsburgh Press, 1977); P. Schmitter, *Interest Conflict and Political Change in Brazil* (Stanford, Stanford University Press, 1971); R. B. Collier and D. Collier, 'Inducements *versus* Constraints: Disaggregating Corporatism', *American Political Science Review*, vol. 73, no. 4 (Dec. 1979); H. Wiarda, 'Corporative Origins of the Iberian and Latin American Labor Relations Systems', *Studies in Comparative International Development*, vol. 13, no. 1 (Spring 1978). A somewhat different perspective, focussing on the British case, is contained in O. Newman, *The Challenge of Corporatism* (London, Macmillan, 1981).

4 Wiarda, 'Corporative Origins'.

5 G. O'Donnell, *Modernization and Bureaucratic-Authoritarianism* (Berkeley, Institute of International Studies, University of California, 1973); *id.*, 'Tensions in the Bureaucratic-Authoritarian State and the Question of Democracy' in D. Collier (ed.), *The New Authoritarianism in Latin America* (Princeton, Princeton University Press, 1979); *id.*, 'Reflections on the Pattern of Change in the Bureaucratic-Authoritarian State', *Latin American Research Review*, vol. 13, no. 1 (1978); K. L. Remmer and G. W. Merkx, 'Bureaucratic-Authoritarianism Revisited', *Latin American Research Review*, vol. 17, no. 2 (1982); G. O'Donnell, 'Reply to Remmer and Merkx', *Latin American Research Review*, vol. 17, no. 2 (1982).

6 Such accounts of the rise of populism include A. Hennessy, 'Latin America' in G. Ionescu and E. Gellner (eds.), *Populism* (London, Weidenfeld and Nicolson, 1969); T. di Tella, 'Populism and Reform in Latin America' in C. Veliz (ed.), *Obstacles to Change in Latin America* (Oxford, Oxford University Press, 1965).

7 Mericle, 'Corporatist Control'; D. Collier (ed.), *The New Authoritarianism in Latin America*; J. Malloy, 'Authoritarianism and Corporatism in Latin America: The Modal Pattern' in Malloy (ed.), *Authoritarianism and Corporatism*.

8 A. Quijano, 'The Marginal Pole of the Economy and the Marginalized Labour Force', *Economy and Society*, vol. 3, no. 4 (1974).

9 Among the voluminous literature, see R. Hyman, *Industrial Relations* (London, Macmillan, 1975); G. Hildebrand, *American Unionism* (Reading, Mass., Addison-Wesley, 1979).

10 A. Schonfield, *Modern Capitalism* (Oxford, Oxford University Press, 1965); C. Crouch, *The Politics of Industrial Relations* (London, Fontana, 1979); Newman, *Challenge of Corporatism*; N. Harris, *Competition and the Corporate Society* (London, Methuen, 1972).

11 K. P. Erickson, *The Brazilian Corporative State and Working Class Politics* (Berkeley, University of California Press, 1977) is, I think, a case in point. His aim is to demonstrate that the Brazilian labour movement was 'political', in the sense that bargaining was oriented toward the state rather than toward employers. However, by neglecting to investigate anything other than large-scale national disputes, the author hardly proves his case.

12 M. Murmis and J. C. Portantiero, *Estudios sobre los orígines del Peronismo*, vol. 1 (Buenos Aires, Siglo XXI, 1971).

13 W. Little, 'Popular Origins of Peronism', in D. Rock (ed.), *Argentina in the Twentieth Century* (London, Duckworth, 1975).

14 J. C. Torre, 'Sobre as origens do Peronismo', *Estudos CEBRAP*, no. 16 (April–June 1976).

15 T. Harding, 'The Political History of Organized Labor in Brazil', unpublished Ph.D. thesis, Stanford University, 1973.

16 T. Skidmore, 'Workers and Soldiers: Urban Labor Movements and Elite Responses in Twentieth Century Latin America' in V. Bernhard (ed.), *Elites, Masses and Modernization in Latin America 1850–1930* (Austin, University of Texas Press, 1979); J. Moises, *Greve de massa e crise política* (São, Paulo Polis, 1978).

17 J. F. Leal and J. Woldenberg, *Del estado liberal a los inicios de la dictadura porfirista*, La clase obrera en la historia de México, vol. 2 (México, Siglo XXI, 1980); C. F. S. Cardoso *et al.*, *De la dictadura porfirista a los tiempos libertarios*, La clase obrera en la historia de México, vol. 3 (México, Siglo XXI, 1980); J. Hart, *Anarchists and the Mexican Working Class 1860–1931* (Austin, University of Texas Press, 1978); J. Basurto, *El proletariado industrial en México (1850–1930)* (México, Universidad Nacional Autónoma de México, 1975).

18 R. Anderson, *Outcasts in their Own Land* (De Kalb, Northern Illinois University Press, 1976); M. González Ramírez (ed.), *La huelga de Cananea* (México, Fondo de Cultura Económica, 1956).

19 S. Hernández, 'Tiempos libertarios: el magonismo en México: Cananea, Rio Blanco y Baja California' in C. F. S. Cardoso *et al.*, *De la dictadura porfirista*.

20 R. Ruiz, *The Great Rebellion* (New York, Norton, 1980); D. Brading

(ed.), *Caudillo and Peasant in the Mexican Revolution* (Cambridge, Cambridge University Press, 1980).

21 J. Hart, 'The Urban Working Class and the Mexican Revolution: The Case of the Casa del Obrero Mundial', *Hispanic American Historical Review*, vol. 58, no. 1 (1978), P. González Casanova, *En el primer gobierno constitucional*, La clase obrera en la historia de México, vol. 6 (México, Siglo XXI, 1980); V. M. Sánchez, *El surgimiento del sindicalismo electricista* (México, Universidad Nacional Autónoma de México, 1978).

22 Hart states that they 'constituted a massive augmentation of the small Constitutionalist army' ('The Urban Working Class' p. 14). A somewhat different appreciation is J. Meyer, 'Los obreros en la revolución mexicana: los batallones rojos', *Historia Mexicana* (July–Sept. 1971).

23 J. Cockcroft, *Intellectual Precursors of the Mexican Revolution* (Austin, University of Texas Press, 1968).

24 F. Barbosa Cano, *La CROM, de Luís Morones a Antonio J. Hernández* (Puebla, Universidad Autónoma de Puebla, 1980); F. Chassen de López, *Lombardo Toledano y el movimiento obrero mexicano, 1917–1940* (México, Extemporáneos, 1977); R. Guadarrama, *Los sindicatos y la política en México: la CROM* (México, ERA, 1981); M. R. Clark, *Organized Labor in Mexico* (Durham, University of North Carolina Press, 1934); B. Carr, *El movimiento obrero y la política en México 1910–1929*, 2 vols. (México, Sepsetentas, 1976); M. Rodríguez, *Los tranviarios y el anarquismo en México* (Puebla, Universidad Autónoma de Puebla, 1980); R. Ruiz, *Labor and the Ambivalent Revolutionaries: Mexico 1911–1923* (Baltimore, Johns Hopkins University Press, 1976).

25 A. Córdova, *En una época de crisis*, La clase obrera en la historia de México, vol. 9 (México, Siglo XXI, 1980). On the CGT, see also G. Baena Paz, 'La Confederación General de Trabajadores (1921–31)', *Revista Mexicana de Ciencias Políticas y Sociales*, no. 83 (Jan.–March 1976).

26 Ruiz, *Labor and the Ambivalent Revolutionaries*; Clark, *Organized Labor in Mexico*.

27 Clark, *Organized Labor in Mexico*; E. Barrios, *El escuadrón de hierro* (México, Cultura Popular, 1978); V. Campa, *Mi testimonio* (México, Cultura Popular, 1978).

28 J. Meyer, *La Cristiada*, 3 vols. (México, Siglo XXI, 1973).

29 Rodríguez, *Los tranviarios y el anarquismo en México*.

30 Barbosa Cano, *La CROM*, p. 25.

31 R. Loyola Díaz, *La crisis Obregón–Calles y el estado mexicano* (México, Siglo XXI, 1980).

32 A. Hernández Chávez, *La mecánica cardenista*, Historia de la revolución mexicana, vol. 16 (México, El Colegio de México, 1979), p. 124.

33 G. Peláez, *Partido Comunista Mexicano: 60 años de historia* (Culiacán, Universidad Autónoma de Sinaloa, 1980); M. Márquez and O. Rodríguez, *El Partido Comunista Mexicano* (México, El Caballito, 1973); M. de Neymet, *Cronología del Partido Comunista Mexicano* (Mexico, Cultura Popular, 1981).

34 W. Cornelius, 'Nation-Building, Participation, and Distribution: The Politics of Social Reform under Cardenas', in G. Almond *et al.* (eds.),

Crisis, Choice and Change (Boston, Little Brown, 1973); S. León, 'El Comité Nacional de Defensa Proletaria', *Revista Mexicana de Sociología*, vol. 40, no. 2 (April–June 1978).

35 A. Anguiano, *El estado y la política obrera del Cardenismo* (México, ERA, 1975); A. Córdova, *La política de masas del Cardenismo* (México, ERA, 1974); J. Ashby, *Organized Labor and the Mexican Revolution under Lazaro Cardenas* (Chapel Hill, University of North Carolina Press, 1963); J. F. Leal, *México: estado, burocracia y sindicatos* (México, El Caballito, 1975); A. Shulgovski, *México en la encrucijada de su historia* (México, Cultura Popular, 1968); N. Hamilton, *The Limits of State Autonomy* (Princeton, Princeton University Press, 1982); H. F. Salamini, *Agrarian Radicalism in Veracruz, 1920–1938* (London, University of Nebraska Press, 1971).

36 Chassen de López, *Lombardo Toledano*, p. 237; Hernández Chávez, *La mecánica cardenista*.

37 H. Levenstein, 'Leninists Undone by Leninism: Communism and Unionism in the United States and Mexico 1935–1939', *Labor History*, vol. 22, no. 2 (Spring 1981).

38 Hernández Chávez, *La mecánica cardenista*; A. J. Contreras, *México 1940* (México, Siglo XXI, 1977).

39 L. Medina, *Civilismo y modernización del autoritarismo*, Historia de la revolución mexicana, vol. 20 (México, El Colegio de México, 1979); *id.*, *Del Cardenismo al Avilacamachismo*, Historia de la revolución mexicana, vol. 18 (México, El Colegio de México, 1978); A. Loyo, 'El movimiento obrero y la Segunda Guerra Mundial' in J. Woldenberg *et al.*, *Memorias del encuentro sobre historia del movimiento obrero*, vol. 2 (Puebla, Universidad Autónoma de Puebla, 1981).

40 A. Rivera Flores, 'UGOCM, 1946–52' in Woldenberg *et al.*, *Memorias del encuentro sobre historia del movimiento obrero*, vol. 2, p. 238.

41 F. Barbosa Cano, 'El charrazo contra el STPRM' in *ibid.* p. 361.

42 Medina, *Civilismo y modernización*, p. 162.

43 *Ibid.* p. 164.

44 *Ibid.* p. 166.

45 Barbosa Cano, 'El charrazo contra el STPRM'.

46 Medina, *Civilismo y modernización*, p. 132.

47 O. Pellicer de Brody and J. L. Reyna, *El afianzamiento de la estabilidad política*, Historia de la revolución mexicana, vol. 22 (México, El Colegio de México, 1978), p. 197.

48 W. van Ginneken, *Socio-Economic Groups and Income Distribution in Mexico* (London, Croom Helm, 1980).

49 M. Everett, 'La evolución de la estructura salarial en México: 1939–1963', *Revista Mexicana de Sociología*, vol. 42, no. 1, (Jan.–March 1980), p. 119.

50 J. Bortz, 'El Salario Obrero en el Distrito Federal, 1939–1975', *Investigación Económica*, no. 4 (Oct.–Dec. 1977).

51 F. Zapata, 'Afiliación y organización sindical en Mexico' in J. L. Reyna *et al.*, *Tres estudios sobre el movimiento obrero en México* (México, El Colegio de México, 1976); C. Zazueta and S. Geluda, *Población, planta industrial y sindicatos* (México, Centro Nacional de Información y Esta-

dísticas del Trabajo, 1981); C. Zazueta and R. de la Peña, *Estructura dual y piramidal del sindicalismo mexicano* (México, CENIET, 1981).

52 Zapata, 'Afiliación y organización sindical', p. 97.

53 The figures published in the ILO Yearbook sometimes correspond to the strikes under local jurisdiction only.

54 I. Bizberg and L. Barraza, 'La acción obrera en las truchas', *Revista Mexicana de Sociología*, vol. 42, no. 4 (Oct.–Dec. 1980); S. Gómez Tagle, *Insurgencia y democracia en los sindicatos electricistas* (México, El Colegio de México, 1980); A. Alonso, *El movimiento ferrocarrilero en México 1958–59* (México, ERA, 1972).

55 On the independent unions, see: E. Contreras and G. Silva, 'Los recientes movimientos mexicanos pro independencia sindical y el reformismo obrero', *Revista Mexicana de Sociología*, vol. 34, nos. 3–4 (1972); L. Alafita Méndez, 'Sindicalismo independiente en México: algunos indicadores, 1971–1976' in Miguel Angel Manzano *et al.*, *Memoria del Primer Coloquio Regional de Historia Mexicana* (México, CEHSMO, 1977); M. Galindo, 'El Movimiento obrero en el sexenio echeverrista', *Investigación Económica*, no. 4 (1977); R. Trejo and J. Woldenberg, 'Los trabajadores y la crisis' in R. Cordera (ed.), *Desarrollo y crisis de la economía mexicana* (México, Fondo de Cultura Económica, 1981); M. Camacho, *El futuro inmediato*, La clase obrera en la historia de México, vol. 15 (México, Siglo XXI, 1980); R. Trejo, 'Notas sobre la insurgencia obrera y la burocracia sindical' in J. Woldenberg *et al.*, *Memorias del encuentro sobre historia del movimiento obrero*, vol. 3 (Puebla, Universidad Autónoma de Puebla, 1980); S. G. Sánchez Díaz, 'Sobre la Unidad Obrera Independiente' in Woldenberg *et al.*, *Memorias del encuentro*, vol. 3; L. Bázan, 'El sindicato independiente de Nissan Mexicana', in Woldenberg *et al.*, *Memorias del encuentro*, vol. 3; D. Molina, 'La política laboral y el movimiento obrero, 1970–76', *Cuadernos Políticos*, no. 12 (1977); J. O. Quiroz Trejo, 'Proletariado e industria automotríz' in E. Suárez Gaona (ed.), *Memoria del Segundo Coloquio Regional de Historia Obrera*, vol. 2 (México, CEHSMO, 1979); B. Acevedo and J. M. Ramos, 'Unidad Obrera Independiente' in Suárez Gaona (ed.), *Memoria del Segundo Coloquio Regional de Historia Obrera*, vol. 2.

56 Student demonstrations at the time of the Olympic Games in 1968 led to the shooting of several hundred people by the army during a meeting in the Tlatelolco housing complex in Mexico City. See S. Zermeño, *México: una democracia utópica* (México, Siglo XXI, 1978); E. Poniatowska, *La noche de Tlatelolco* (México, ERA, 1971).

57 A typical statement is contained in G. Grayson, *The Politics of Mexican Oil* (Pittsburgh, Pittsburgh University Press, 1980), p. 100

58 K. de Schweinitz, *Industrialization and Democracy* (London, Collier-Macmillan, 1964).

59 Malloy, 'Authoritarianism and Corporatism'; D. Collier (ed.), *The New Authoritarianism*.

2 The Mexican automobile industry

1 R. Michels, *Political Parties* (New York, Collier-Macmillan, 1962; 1st edn., 1911).
2 E. Stevens, *Protest and Response in Mexico* (Cambridge, Mass., MIT Press, 1974), pp. 27–9.
3 *Ibid.*, p. 63.
4 F. J. Aguilar, 'El sindicalismo del sector automotríz', *Cuadernos Políticos*, no. 16 (April–June 1978).
5 Among such studies are Bizberg and Barraza, 'La acción obrera'; F. Zapata (ed.), *Las Truchas* (México, El Colegio de México, 1978); M. Vellinga, *Economic Development and the Dynamics of Class* (The Hague, Van Gorcum, 1979).
6 D. C. Bennett and K. E. Sharpe, 'Agenda Setting and Bargaining Power: The Mexican State *versus* Transnational Automobile Corporations', *World Politics*, vol. 32, no. 1 (Oct. 1979), p. 65.
7 R. O. Jenkins, *Dependent Industrialization in Latin America* (New York, Praeger, 1977); W. Gudger, 'The Regulation of Multinational Corporations in the Mexican Automotive Industry', unpublished Ph.D. thesis, University of Wisconsin, 1975; Bennett and Sharpe, 'Agenda Setting'.
8 H. Vázquez Trejo, *Una década de política sobre industria automotríz* (México, Tecnos, 1975), p. 11.
9 Secretaría de Programación y Presupuesto, *La industria automotríz en México* (México, Secretaría de Programación y Presupuesto, 1981), p. 10.

3 Wages and workers in the Mexican automobile industry

1 M. Everett, 'La evolución de la estructura salarial en México: 1939–63', *Revista Mexicana de Sociología*, vol. 42, no. 1 (Jan.–March 1980), p. 115.
2 These data, and the time-series comparison of GM and Chrysler, were obtained from the archives of the Secretaría del Trabajo y Previsión Social and from the Junta Local de Conciliación y Arbitraje of the Federal District.
3 O. de Oliveira, *Migración y absorción de mano de obra en la Ciudad de México, 1930–1970*, Cuadernos del CES, no. 14 (México, El Colegio de México, 1976); H. Garcia Muñoz et al., *Migración y desiqualidad social en la Ciudad de México* (México, El Colegio de México, 1977).
4 I. Bizberg, *La acción obrera* (México, El Colegio de México, 1982), pp. 146, 273.
5 G. Faba, 'Características del mercado de trabajo industrial: dos estudios realizados en México', *Revista Mexicana del Trabajo*, vol. 3, no. 1 (Jan.–March 1980), p. 70.
6 *Ibid.*
7 J. Balan et al., *Men in a Developing Society* (Austin, University of Texas Press, 1973).
8 O. de Oliveira, 'Industralization, Migration and Entry Labor Force Changes in Mexico City, 1930–1970', unpublished Ph.D. thesis, University of Texas, 1975, p. 222.

9 E. Contreras Suárez, *Estratificación y movilidad social en la Ciudad de México* (México, UNAM, 1978), p. 195; M. Vellinga, *Economic Development and the Dynamics of Class* (The Hague, Van Gorcum, 1979).

10 G. Campero *et al.*, *La incorporación obrera en un medio de industrialización reciente* (México, Instituto Nacional de Estudios del Trabajo, 1977).

11 V. Novelo and A. Urteaga, *La industria en los magueyales* (México, Nueva Imagen, 1979).

12 Professors Coleman and Zapata kindly made their data available to me.

13 P. Arias and L. Bazán, *CIVAC: un proceso de industrialización en una zona campesina* (México, La Casa Chata, 1977), p. 121.

14 Campero *et al.*, *La incorporación obrera*, p. 10.

15 Novelo and Urteaga, *La industria en los magueyales*, pp. 90–1.

16 R. U. Miller *et al.*, 'Modern Sector Internal Labor Market Structure and Urban Occupational Mobility', mimeographed, 1976.

17 S. Amin, *Accumulation on a World Scale* (New York, Monthly Review Press, 1974).

18 J. Foster, *Class Struggle and the Industrial Revolution* (London, Weidenfeld and Nicolson, 1974).

19 Some of the critiques may be found in H. F. Moorehouse, 'The Marxist Theory of the Labour Aristocracy', *Social History*, vol. 3, no. 1 (Jan. 1978); D. S. Gadian, 'Class Consciousness in Oldham and Other North-West Industrial Towns', *Historical Journal*, vol. 21, no. 1 (March 1978).

20 An interesting discussion of labour processes in the automotive industry is contained in A. L. Friedman, *Industry and Labour* (London, Macmillan, 1977).

21 R. Q. Gray, *The Labour Aristocracy in Victorian Edinburgh* (Oxford, Oxford University Press, 1976); G. Crossick, *An Artisan Elite in Victorian Society* (London, Croom Helm, 1978).

22 Cf. R. Hamilton, *Class and Politics in the United States* (New York, Wiley, 1972); *id.*, *Affluence and the French Worker in the Fourth Republic* (Princeton, Princeton University Press, 1967).

23 J. Humphrey, 'Operários da indústria automovilística no Brasil', *Estudos CEBRAP*, no. 23 (1979); *id.*, *Capitalist Control and Workers' Struggle in the Brazilian Auto Industry* (Princeton, Princeton University Press, 1982).

24 A. Reid, 'Politics and Economics in the Formation of the British Working Class', *Social History*, vol. 3, no. 3 (Oct. 1978).

4 The unions: a historical analysis

1 For attempts to establish closer ties among the Mexican auto unions, see K. Middlebrook, 'International Implications of Labor Change: The Automobile Industry', in J. Dominguez (ed.), *Mexico's Political Economy* (Beverly Hills, Sage, 1982).

2 Junta Local del Conciliación y Arbitraje, DF, archives.

3 On the slow decline of the CROM, see Arnaldo Córdova, 'El movimiento obrero mexicano en los albores de la crisis de 1929', *Estudios Políticos*, vol. 4, nos. 13–14 (Jan.–June 1978).

4 Richard U. Miller, 'The Role of Labor Organization in a Developing

Country: The Case of Mexico', unpublished Ph.D. thesis, Cornell University, 1966, p. 176.

5 Córdova, 'El movimiento obrero mexicano', p. 85.

6 Registro de Asociaciones, archives.

7 GM union minutes, 17 Feb, 1949; Miller, 'Role of Labor Organization', pp. 176–7. On the abortive breakaway attempt in June 1949, see L. Medina, *Civilismo y modernización del autoritarismo*, Historia de la revolución mexicana, vol. 20 (México, El Colegio de México, 1979), p. 173.

8 The social background of the Mexican auto workers is discussed in chapter 3.

9 F. J. Aguilar, 'El sindicalismo del sector automotríz', *Cuadernos Políticos*, no. 16 (April–June 1978), p. 49.

10 Interview, Ford industrial relations executive, 16 May 1978.

11 *Ibid.*

12 *Ibid..*; *Excelsior*, 31 Aug. 1975.

13 Interview, Ford industrial relations executive, 16 May 1978.

14 The Sindicato Nacional de Trabajadores de la Industria Automotríz, Similares y Conexos de la Republica Mexicana.

15 *Punto Crítico*, no. 50 (April 1976), p. 11.

16 *Ibid.* no. 60 (Aug. 1976), p. 15; no. 62 (Sept. 1976), p. 19.

17 Interview, Ford industrial relations executive, 16 May 1978.

18 In the struggle to break with the old leadership, the Ford insurgents were helped by the GM union, which, among other things, lent them their union hall so that they could hold elections outside the CTM headquarters (*Punto Crítico*, no. 73 (April 1977), p. 11).

19 The way in which corporatist fringe benefits are allocated to specific groups of workers is by no means clear. However, it is highly probable that CTM-affiliated workers have a disproportionate access to such benefits. With regard to subsidized housing, the General Assembly of the state-financed union housing agency, INFONAVIT, is composed as follows: CTM, 8 members; CROC, 2; CROM, 1; COR, 1; miners, 1; railways, 1; electricians, 1.

20 Interview, 25 Aug. 1978; *Uno Más Uno*, 2 Aug. 1978. The union obtained a 16 per cent increase.

21 Interview, Ford industrial relations executive, 16 May 1978.

22 *Uno Más Uno*, 11 April 1978.

23 L. Araiza, *Historia de movimiento obrero mexicano*, 2nd edn. 4 vols. (México, Ediciones Casa del Obrero Mundial, 1975), vol. 4, pp. 190–2.

24 The CUT was founded in 1947 under the leadership of Luís Gómez Z and Valentín Campa, and included the railway, mining and petroleum unions which had recently split from the CTM (J. L. Reyna *et al.*, *Tres estudios sobre el movimiento obrero en México* (México, El Colegio de México, 1976), p. 57).

25 The CROC was founded 1952. It brought together the Confederación de Obreros y Campesinos de México, the Confederación Proletaria Nacional, the Confederación Nacional de Trabajadores and the CUT (*Estatutos de la CROC* (México, Cuadernos Obreros, 1976)). The CROC was a rival to the CTM, but always remained firmly within the ambit of official PRI politics

(R. Trejo, 'The Mexican Labor Movement', *Latin American Perspectives*, vol. 3, no. 1 (1976)).

26 W. Würtele, 'International Trade Union Solidarity and the Internationalization of Capital', unpublished paper, 1977. It should be noted that the existing union contract contained a clause specifying that any movement of GM's operations would occur only if it did not adversely affect the Mexico City workers. Cf. also F. J. Aguilar, 'Historia sindical de General Motors y la huelga de 1980', *Azcapotzalco*, vol. 1, no. 1 (1980).

27 J. Schlagheck, *The Political, Economic and Labor Climate in Mexico*, Wharton School Multinational Industrial Relations Series (Philadelphia, University of Pennsylvania, 1977), p. 143 suggests the GM union received $7,000 in strike fund donations from these sources.

28 Schlagheck, *The Political, Economic and Labor Climate.*

29 Made by a FITIM official (interview 25 April 1978).

30 Industrial relations executive, interview, 26 June 1978.

31 F. Zapata, 'Afiliación y organización sindical en México' in Reyna *et al.*, *Tres estudios.*

32 Interview, 9 Aug. 1978.

33 More detailed information on union elections is presented in chapter 7 below.

34 GM union minutes makes several references to this problem.

35 Registro de Asociaciones, archives.

36 *Ibid.*

37 *Ibid.*

38 *Ibid.*

39 *Ibid.*

40 Other commentators have a markedly different perception of events in GM. A FITIM official claimed that 'in GM entire years have gone by without union meetings' (interview 25 April 1978), and Aguilar states that 'in General Motors the workers have demanded union democracy and struggled against their bureaucratic leaders' ('El sindicalismo del sector Automotríz'), p. 49.

41 D. C. Bennett and K. E. Sharpe, 'Agenda Setting and Bargaining Power: The Mexican State *versus* Transnational Automobile Corporations', *World Politics*, vol. 32, no. 1 (Oct. 1979), p. 65.

42 *Ibid.* p. 73.

43 The original union, the Sindicato de Trabajadores de la Planta Armadora de Fábricas Automex, had jurisdiction only in the Federal District. The constitution was altered to give the union national jurisdiction and in 1964 the Sindicato Nacional de Trabajadores de Fábricas Automex was formed. The name was changed again the following year to the Sindicato Nacional de Trabajadores de la Industria Automotríz Integrada, Similares y Conexos de la Republica Mexicana. Seemingly, these changes were uneventful and did not occasion any conflict or disturbance.

44 All data on union elections are drawn from the archives of the Secretaría de Trabajo y Prevision Social, department of Registro de Asociacones, and from the archives of the Junta Local de Conciliación y Arbitraje for the DF. This material is of variable quality and reliability. In this case, the

archival evidence hardly indicates an exemplary instance of democratic procedure.

45 *Solidaridad*, 31 March 1970.

46 *Expansión*, 16 May 1973, p. 38.

47 Angel Fojo, 'Estudio de un conflicto industrial: el caso Automex', mimeographed, 1973.

48 According to the documents in the Junta Local de Conciliación y Arbitraje in Mexico City, wages in the Mexico City plant in 1970 were as follows (the rates had been agreed in the collective contract of 1969):

Category	Pesos
Ayudante	57
4	82.5
3	93.25
2	102.25
1	111

Fojo's data for the Mexico City plant are not exact, and it is possible that he did not have reliable sources. If this is so, then it is necessary to be somewhat sceptical about his assertions with regard to wages in Toluca. However, since it was impossible to obtain a copy of the relevant collective contract either from the company or from the Junta Local de Conciliación y Arbitraje in Toluca, I must provisionally, and with some reservations, accept Fojo's data. It was certainly the case, and continues to be the case, that wage rates in Toluca are lower than in the DF.

49 Letter from General Secretary to Secretaría de Trabajo, archives.

50 *Solidaridad*, 31 March 1970.

51 *Ibid.* p. 38. In case this should seem implausible, it should be pointed out that I asked the person involved to confirm these facts, which he did, in an interview, though he claimed that his status had been greatly exaggerated.

52 According to a senior Chrysler executive, 'In 1970 we had to fire almost everyone and begin from scratch'. He claimed that most workers were rehired and about fifty were not (interview, 2 Aug. 1978). Antonio Juárez, *Las corporaciones transnacionales y los trabajadores mexicanos* (México, Siglo XXI, 1979), p. 229 asserts that 1400 workers were fired. In order to be rehired by the company, they had to bribe the union leader, who 'sold' them their new contracts.

53 Letter to the Executive Committee of the union, with several hundred signatures, 1 April 1972 (Registro de Asociaciones, archives).

54 Minutes, General Motors union, 12 Feb. 1972.

55 Letter to the Secretaría de Trabajo, 3 April 1972 (*Registro de Asociaciones*, archives).

56 Letter from Chrysler to Junta Central de Conciliación y Arbitraje, 23 Aug. 1973 (Junta Local de Conciliación y Arbitraje, DF, archives).

57 Aguilar, 'El sindicalismo del sector automotríz', p. 52; Juárez, *Las corporaciones transnacionales*, p. 230.

58 In 1975 the automobile industry was transferred from the jurisdiction of the local labour courts to the federal labour court, and the files of individual grievances are available from that date onwards.

59 Since Mexican labour law gives the union considerable power in hiring and firing it is not unusual for workers to cite the union as co-defendant together with the company. All but two of these twenty-one workers did so. This figure of twenty-one is very high for the Mexican auto industry.

60 The industrial relations executive of Chrysler told me, however, that it is always the company and not the union which does the firing at Chrysler. He claimed that about fifteen workers had been fired for oppositional activities (interview, 24 July 1981).

61 Similar accusations against other auto companies may be discovered in the labour court archives. Whether these accusations have any foundation in reality is beyond the competence of this book to say.

62 In a sample of one hundred individual grievances in the automobile industry, the majority were settled by compromise or in favour of the company. See chapter 8.

63 Reinstatement is a rare outcome in the sample analysed.

64 This is quite a common outcome.

65 Interview with Director, Section 9, Federación de Trabajadores del DF, 4 Sept. 1981. That the return to the CTM may not have been entirely without incident is suggested by a clause in the 1980 union contract: 'The company is obliged not to accept the representation of any other union . . . nor to encourage directly or indirectly any grouping foreign to the contracting union which is formed or attempts to form with elements in its employ.'

66 Interview, 27 Feb. 1978.

67 J. O. Quiroz Trejo, 'Proceso de trabajo en la industria automotríz', *Cuadernos Políticos*, no. 26 (Oct.–Dec. 1980), p. 67.

68 According to V. M. Villaseñor, *Memorias de un hombre de izquierda*, 2 vols. (México, Grijalbo, 1976).

69 B. Novelo and A. Urteaga, *La industria en los magueyales* (México, Nueva Imagen, 1979).

70 Letter from DINA workers to Secretaría de Trabajo, 19 Sept. 1955; letter from the Superintendent and Chief of the Department of Administration, DINA, to Secretaría de Trabajo, 14 Sept. 1955 (Secretaría de Trabajo, archives).

71 Letter from workers to Secretaría de Trabajo, 26 July 1961 (archives).

72 Letter from workers to Secretaría de Trabajo, 1 Sept. 1961 (archives).

73 Archives of Secretaría de Trabajo, report of union meeting, 8 Nov. 1961. The CROC had been formed in 1952 by some unions that had disagreements with the CTM. The CROC remained affiliated with the government. (The GM union belonged to the CROC.)

74 Archives of Secretaría de Trabajo, letter, 19. Sept. 1961.

75 *Ibid.*, letter to DINA union, 18 Dec. 1961

76 *Ibid.*, letter of 14 Dec. 1961

77 Interview with FITIM official, 23 June 1978.

78 *Nacional*, 13 Feb. 1962.

79 *Excelsior*, 14 Feb. 1962.

80 *Nacional*, 13 Feb. 1962.

81 *Ibid.*

82 On the 1948 *charrazo* and the 1958–9 railway strike, see A. Alonso, *El movimiento ferrocarrilero en México 1958–9* (Mèxico, ERA, 1972); B. Hernández, 'Del pacto de sindicatos industriales a la represión', in E. Suárez Gaona (ed.), *Memoria del Segundo Coloquio Regional de Historia Obrera*, 2 vols. (México, CEHSMO, 1979), vol. 2; O. Pellicer de Brody and J. L. Reyna, *El afianzamiento de la estabilidad política*, Historia de la revolución mexicana, vol. 22 (México, El Colegio de México, 1978); V. Campa, *Mi testimonio* (México, Cultura Popular, 1978).

83 *Universal*, 4 Feb. 1967.

84 Leaflet signed 'Grupo de Defensa Obrera', archives of Secretaría de Trabajo.

85 This is an instance of the neutral behaviour of the Ministry and should give proponents of crude analyses of government partiality pause for thought.

86 Novelo and Urteaga, *La industria en los magueyales*, pp. 156–7.

87 Interviews, industrial relations executive, 7 April 1978 and 3 April 1978.

88 Registro de Asociaciones, archives. I have also drawn heavily on Lucia Bazán, 'Sindicalismo independiente: el caso de Nissan', mimeographed, Dec. 1977.

89 *Punto Crítico*, vol. 1, no. 3 (2 March 1972), p. 29.

90 Interview, Nissan management, 13 April 1978.

91 Registro de Asociaciones, archives.

92 Schlagheck, *The Political, Economic and Labor Climate*, pp. 139–42 has an analysis of this strike. Like some other commentators he exaggerates the role of the FAT in Nissan, and also in VW and DINA.

93 *Punto Crítico*, no. 83 (Nov. 1977), p. 13; archives of Junta Federal de Conciliación y Arbitraje; L. Bazán, 'El sindicato independiente de Nissan Mexicana', in J. Woldenberg *et al.*, *Memorias del encuentro sobre historia del movimiento obrero*, vol. 3 (Puebla, Universidad Autónoma de Puebla, 1980).

94 Interview, Nissan management, 13 April 1978.

95 Interview, Nissan industrial relations executive, 22 July 1981.

96 *Punto Crítico*, no. 5 (May 1972), p. 17.

97 An ex-executive of VW suggested that the strike had been deliberately provoked by management (interview, 5 Nov. 1979). For a discussion of reasons why management might seek a strike, see H. A. Turner *et al.*, *Labour Relations in the Motor Industry* (London, Allen and Unwin, 1967). In this case, the reason appears to have been a ploy on the part of the Mexican management to hide from the head office their failure to penetrate the US market with the new Safari model.

98 Letter to union, 18 Nov. 1975, Registro de Asociaciones, archives.

99 Letter to President Echeverría, July 1975, Registro de Asociaciones, archives.

100 *Excelsior*, 11 April 1976.

101 Junta Federal de Conciliación y Arbitraje, archives, letter, VW union to company, 15 Jan. 1976.

102 *Punto Crítico*, no. 70 (Feb. 1977), p. 15. For other threats of closure, see *Proceso*, 17 July 1978, p. 32; *Punto Crítico*, no. 58 (July 1976), p. 12.
103 *Oposición*, 13–19 July 1978.
104 *Uno Más Uno*, 16 July 1978.
105 *Ibid.*, 12 Aug. 1978.
106 Hugo Vargas, 'Historia verdadera de la conquista de la clase obrera', *El Machete*, no. 14 (June 1981); *Uno Más Uno*, 18–20 March 1981.
107 *Excelsior*, 28 Oct. 1981.
108 *Latin American Weekly Report*, 29 Jan. 1982; *Uno Más Uno*, 15 April 1981.
109 An exclusion attention to national political bargaining, to the neglect of any analysis of shop-floor conflict, can be found in, *inter alia*, K. P. Erickson, *The Brazilian Corporative State and Working Class Politics* (Berkeley, University of California Press, 1977); J. Payne, *Labor and Politics in Peru* (New Haven, Yale University Press, 1965). Of course there are also works which have a more balanced focus, such as D. Kruijt and M. Vellinga, *Labor Relations and Multinational Corporations* (The Hague, Van Gorcum, 1980), and D. James, 'Rationalisation and Working Class Response: The Context and Limits of Factory Floor Activity in Argentina', *Journal of Latin American Studies*, vol. 13, no. 2 (Nov. 1981).
110 This is the image presented by Aguilar, 'El sindicalismo del sector auto-motríz' and Juárez, *Las corporaciones transnacionales*.

5 The unions: power and organization

1 Until 1977, Mexican union contracts were usually negotiated every two years. Since then, in addition to the two-yearly negotiation of the complete contract, there is a yearly salary revision.
2 F. Zapata, 'Afiliación y organización sindical en México' in J. L. Reyna *et al.*, *Tres estudios sobre el movimiento obrero en México* (México, El Colegio de México, 1976).
3 J. Payne, *Labor and Politics in Peru* (New Haven, Yale University Press, 1965).
4 On Mexican unions' economic power, see H. Garcia Muñoz, 'Occupational and Earnings Inequalities in Mexico City', unpublished Ph.D. thesis, University of Texas, 1975.
5 F. Remolina Roqueñi, *Evolución de las instituciones y del derecho del trabajo en México* (México, Junta Federal de Conciliación y Arbitraje, 1976).
6 On the importance of custom and practice, see H. Clegg, *The Changing System of Industrial Relations in Great Britain* (London, Blackwell, 1979).
7 Because it is a section of a state-wide metallurgical union, the GM union in Toluca continues to operate in the local labour courts.
8 The evidence from the Brazilian automobile industry, where job tenure is much less secure, suggests that widespread dismissals are quite frequent and are often directed at union militants. See Vera Lucia B. Ferrante, *FGTS: idologia e repressão* (São Paulo, Atica, 1978); J. Humphrey, *Capitalist Control and Workers' Struggle in the Brazilian Auto Industry* (Princeton, Princeton University Press, 1982).

9 The only available data for the VAM factory branch in Toluca are for 1968. Given the inability of the Mexico City factory branch to have a full-time member by 1980, it is improbable that the Toluca branch had a full-time union officer in the period 1976–8. The number of part-time officers may, however, have increased.

10 *Punto Crítico*, no. 28 (May 1974), p. 13.

11 Under-the-table payments are not included in this discussion. Given the widespread occurrence of corruption in Mexico, they are probably an important, though imponderable, factor.

12 It was felt that an attempt to investigate union finances directly during the period of fieldwork in Mexico would have been an inefficient use of resources for two reasons. In the first place, it was assumed that there would be a general reticence to discuss union finances. In the second place, it was felt that the resources (in terms of time) were not available to develop the kind of rapport which would permit lengthy and detailed scrutiny and questioning of union accounts. Given the widespread insinuations of union dishonesty in Mexico, it was felt that questions about union finances were likely to provoke vague and defensive answers. This assumption may well have been wrong, and there can be no doubt that a study of union finances in Mexico is sorely needed.

13 J. Schlagheck, *The Political, Economic and Labor Climate in Mexico*, Wharton School Multinational Industrial Relations Series (Philadelphia, University of Pennsylvania, 1977), p. 106.

14 *Ibid.* p. 107.

6 Control over work processes

1 H. Braverman, *Labor and Monopoly Capital* (New York, Monthly Review, 1974); A. L. Friedman, *Industry and Labour* (London, Macmillan, 1977); D. Roy, 'Quota Restriction and Goldbricking in a Machine Shop', *America Journal of Sociology*, vol. 57 (1952).

2 Quite what the effects of this policy are on overall employment is not entirely clear.

3 This is standard practice in the Ford Motor Company, for example.

4 The preferential hiring of kin is discussed in, *inter alia*, Peter Lloyd, *A Third World Proletariat?* (London, Allen and Unwin, 1982); Julian Laite, *Industrial Development and Migrant Labour* (Manchester, Manchester University Press, 1981).

5 Charles Ford, 'Past Developments and Future Trends in Mexican Automotive Policy' in Jan Herd (ed.), *The Automotive Industry in Latin America*, Northwestern Pennsylvania Institute for Latin American Studies, monograph no. 12 (Sept. 1980), p. 49 argues that efficient economies of scale will require a reduction in the number of automobile manufacturers operating in Mexico.

6 See, *inter alia*, C. Tello, *La política económica en México, 1970–76* (México, Siglo XXI, 1979).

7 *Business Week*, 11 Oct. 1976, p. 48.

8 The research for this book was completed before the recession induced by

the 1982 devaluation had affected the auto industry. With a general slump in auto sales, all companies were severely hit and there were considerable redundancies. Unfortunately, it was impossible to ascertain if there was any correlation between the severity of conflict over redundancies and the percentage of the workforce on *planta* contracts.

9 On the health hazards of DINA workers see M. Echeverría *et al.*, 'El problema de la salud in DINA', *Cuadernos Políticos*, no. 26 (Oct.–Dec. 1980).

7 Union government

1 A. Alonso, *El movimiento ferrocarrilero en México 1958–59* (México, ERA, 1972), p. 98; cf. also *Uno Más Uno*, 23 May 1978 for a discussion of the term.

2 R. Michels, *Political Parties* (New York, Collier-Macmillan, 1962; 1st edn, 1911).

3 S. M. Lipset, M. Trow and J. Coleman, *Union Democracy* (New York, Doubleday, 1956), p. 464.

4 J. Edelstein and M. Warner, *Comparative Union Democracy* (London, Allen and Unwin, 1975).

5 M. Thompson and I. Roxborough, 'Union Elections and Democracy in Mexico', *British Journal of Industrial Relations*, vol. 20, no. 2 (July 1982); H. Handelman, 'Oligarchy and Democracy in Two Mexican Labor Unions', *International Labor Relations Review*, vol. 30, no. 2 (1977).

6 However, the absence of opposing candidates need not always indicate that leaderships are unpopular or illegitimate. See, for example, the account in P. Friedlander, *The Emergence of a UAW Local, 1936–1939* (Pittsburgh, University of Pittsburgh Press, 1975).

7 A high vote was defined as any percentage greater than the arithmetic mean of the percentage of the vote going to the winner in the elections. A low vote was defined as being less than the arithmetic mean. The arithmetic mean of the twelve elections in DINA was 51.2 per cent of the votes going to the winner. In the fourteen GM elections, the winner was elected with a mean of 62.5 per cent of the total vote.

8 Cf. the attendance figures for GM–DF presented in I. Roxborough, 'El sindicalismo en el sector automotríz', *Estudios Sociológicos*, vol. 1, no. 1 (Jan.–April 1983), and P. Arias and L. Bazán, *CIVAC: un proceso de industrialización en una zona campesina* (México, La Casa Chata, 1977), p. 88.

8 The labour courts

1 *Excelsior*, 22 Aug. 1976. Useful comparative analysis of the Brazilian labour courts is contained in K. Mericle, 'Conflict Regulation in the Brazilian Industrial Relations System', unpublished Ph.D. thesis, University of Wisconsin, 1974. Cf. also *Jornal do Brasil*, 10 Sept. 1979.

2 Claims of unjust dismissal were also frequent in the 1920s (M. R. Clark, *Organized Labor in Mexico* (Chapel Hill, University of North Carolina

Press, 1934), p. 239; E. Gruening, *Mexico and its Heritage* (New York, Century, 1928), p. 378.
3 Ley Federal de Trabajo, articles 48–50.
4 The question of whether or not the worker might have won the case cannot be settled. It is conceivable that auto companies might agree to an out-of-court settlement of less than the worker was demanding in order to minimize the costs of litigation. I am inclined to think that such an explanation is implausible. It might, however, be in the interest of the worker's lawyer to settle out of court. Apparently these lawyers, often referred to as 'coyotes', accept a percentage of the award as their fee. There might come a point when further expenditure of the lawyer's time would not be counterbalanced by a probable increase in the settlement. Cf. Clark, *Organized Labor*, pp. 253–4.
5 In 1978, after the sample of cases had been drawn, some individual grievances were initiated by workers at Nissan's Cuernavaca plant which cited the union as defendant.
6 Letter, lawyer for Nissan to Junta Federal de Conciliación y Arbitraje, 14 Jan. 1976.
7 Letter, union to Junta Federal de Conciliación y Arbitraje, 30 Sept. 1977.
8 Letter, union to Junta Federal de Conciliación y Arbitraje, 28 Sept. 1977.
9 Minutes of GM union, 15 March 1975.
10 *Uno Más Uno*, 1 Aug. 1981 asserts that this practice is common in the petroleum industry.

9 The empirical findings and the dynamics of industrial militancy

1 J. O. Quiroz Trejo, 'Proceso de trabajo en la industria automotríz', *Cuadernos Políticos*, no. 26 (Oct.–Dec. 1980), p. 67.
2 It will be noted that labelling this as an intermediate case does not alter the general pattern of correlation; it merely interprets the VW case within the overall picture.
3 That such processes may not be confined to Mexico is suggested by Huw Beynon, *Working for Ford* (London, Allen Lane, 1973). However, H. A. Turner *et al.*, *Labour Relations in the Motor Industry* (London, Allen and Unwin, 1967), p. 175 suggest that there does not exist a correlation between the newness of a plant and strike frequency.
4 Moreover, within the CROC, the GM union was allowed considerable autonomy (M. Camacho, *El futuro inmediato*, La clase obrera en la historia de México, vol. 15 (México, Siglo XXI, 1980), p. 135).

10 Unions and political stability in Mexico

1 B. Anderson and J. Cockcroft, 'Control and Cooptation in Mexican Politics' in J. Cockcroft *et al.* (eds.), *Dependence and Underdevelopment* (New York, Anchor, 1972) is perhaps a classic statement to this effect.
2 L. Whitehead, 'On "Governability" in Mexico', *Bulletin of Latin American Research*, vol. 1, no. 1 (Oct. 1981), pp. 27–8.
3 In the field of organized labour, the 1958–9 railway strike and the

electricians' movement are frequently cited as examples. (See chapter 1 for details.) An agrarian illustration is presented in D. Ronfeldt, *Atencingo: The Politics of Agrarian Struggle in a Mexican Ejido* (Stanford, Stanford University Press, 1973).

4 G. O'Donnell, *Modernization and Bureaucratic-Authoritarianism* (Berkeley, Institute of International Studies, University of California, 1973); D. Collier (ed.), *The New Authoritarianism in Latin America* (Princeton, Princeton University Press, 1979); J. Malloy (ed.), *Authoritarianism and Corporatism in Latin America* (Pittsburgh, Pittsburgh University Press, 1977); J. L. Reyna and R. S. Weinert (eds.), *Authoritarianism in Mexico* (Philadelphia, ISHI, 1971).

5 There is, however, some fragmentary evidence to suggest that consumer durables are purchased by low-income groups (J. Wells, 'Underconsumption, Market Size and Expenditure Patterns in Brazil', *Bulletin of the Society for Latin American Studies*, no. 24 (March 1976)).

6 For example, by R. R. Kaufman, 'Mexico and Latin American Authoritarianism' in Reyna and Weinert (eds.), *Authoritarianism in Mexico*. It should be noted, however, that O'Donnell's first major work specifically excluded Middle American countries from the analysis.

7 See, for example, J. Serra, 'Three Mistaken Theses Regarding the Connection between Industralization and Authoritarian Regimes', in D. Collier (ed.), *The New Authoritarianism*.

8 A. Stepan, *The State and Society* (Princeton, Princeton University Press, 1978).

9 Kaufman, 'Mexico and Latin American Authoritarianism', p. 212.

10 S. Zermeño, *México: una democracia utópica* (México, Siglo XXI, 1978).

11 This statement needs some qualification. Certainly, the recent trend toward increasing the salaries of the top union officers in Nissan–Cuernavaca must give pause for thought.

12 K. Coleman and C. Davis, 'Pre-emptive Reform and the Mexican Working Class', *Latin American Research Review*, vol. 18, no. 1 (1983).

13 Surveys in other countries suggest that there are few reasons to suppose that auto workers will hold particularly radical attitudes. Cf. W. H. Form, *Blue-Collar Stratification* (Princeton, Princeton University Press, 1976); J. H. Goldthorpe et al., *The Affluent Worker: Political Attitudes and Behaviour* (Cambridge, Cambridge University Press, 1968); J. C. Leggett, *Class, Race and Labour* (Oxford, Oxford University Press, 1968).

14 Goldthorpe et al., *Affluent Worker*.

15 V. I. Lenin, *What Is To Be Done?* (Moscow, Progress Publishers, 1964; originally published 1902).

16 Cf. S. Huntington, *Political Order in Changing Societies* (New Haven, Yale University Press, 1968).

17 Cf. K. F. Johnson, *Mexican Democracy: A Critical View* (New York, Praeger, 1978).

18 Such as the pressure groups of private enterprise.

19 On contemporary union insurgency in Mexico, in addition to works cited elsewhere in this book see *inter alia*: S. Ramos et al., *Spicer, S.A.* (México, UNAM, 1979); I. Bizberg, *La acción obrera* (México, El Colegio de

México, 1982); R. Trejo, *Tres huelgas telefonistas* (México, Uno Más Uno, 1980); I. Roxborough and I. Bizberg, 'Union locals in Mexico', *Journal of Latin American Studies*, vol. 15, no. 1 (May 1983).

20 H. Garcia Muñoz *et al.*, *Migración y desigualdad social en la Ciudad de México* (México, El Colegio de México, 1977).

21 J. Nun, 'La industria automotríz argentina', *Revista Mexicana de Sociología*, vol. 40, no. 1 (1979); J. Humphrey, 'Operários da industria automovilística no Brasil', *Estudos CEBRAP*, no. 23 (1979).

22 On the destabilizing effects of inflation, see T. Skidmore, 'The Politics of Economic Stabilization in Postwar Latin America' in Malloy (ed.), *Authoritarianism and Corporatism*; I. Roxborough, 'Perspectivas del sistema político mexicano' in A. Muñoz (ed.), *Perspectivas del sistema político mexicano* (México, PRI, 1982).

23 J. L. Reyna, 'Redefining the Authoritarian Regime' in Reyna and Weinert (eds.), *Authoritarianism in Mexico*, p. 168a

24 On the political reform, see O. Bayoumi, 'State, Society and Development: Theoretical Considerations and a Mexican Case Study Focussing on the Current Political Reform', unpublished Ph.D. thesis, London School of Economics, 1981.

25 *Ibid.*, Zermeño, *México: una democracia utópica.*

Bibliography

Acevedo, B., and J. M. Ramos, 'Unidad Obrera Independiente' in E. Suárez Gaona (ed.), *Memoria del Segundo Coloquio Regional de Historia Obrera*, 2 vols. (México, CEHSMO, 1979), vol. 2.

Aguilar, F. J. 'El Sindicalismo del sector automotríz', *Cuadernos Políticos*, no. 16 (April–June 1978).

'Historia sindical de General Motors y la huelga de 1980', *Azcapotzalco*, vol. 1, no. 1 (1980).

La política sindical en México: industria del automóvil (Mexico, ERA, 1982).

Alafita Méndez, L., 'Sindicalismo independiente en México: algunos indicadores, 1971–1976' in Miguel Angel Manzano *et al.*, *Memoria del Primer Coloquio Regional de Historia Mexicana* (México, CEHSMO, 1977).

Alonso, A., *El movimiento ferrocarrilero en México 1958–59* (México, ERA, 1972).

Amin, S., *Accumulation on a World Scale* (New York, Monthly Review Press, 1974).

Anderson, B., and J. Cockcroft, 'Control and Cooptation in Mexican Politics' in J. Cockcroft *et al.* (eds.), *Dependence and Underdevelopment* (New York, Anchor, 1972).

Anderson, R., *Outcasts in their Own Land* (De Kalb, Northern Illinois University Press, 1976).

Anguiano, A., *El estado y la política obrera del Cardenismo* (México, ERA, 1975).

Araiza, L., *Historia del movimiento obrero mexicano*, 2nd edn, 4 vols. (México, Ediciones Casa del Obrero Mundial, 1975), vol. 4.

Arias, P., and L. Bazán, *CIVAC: un proceso de industrialización en una zona campesina* (México, La Casa Chata, 1977).

Ashby, J. *Organized Labor and the Mexican Revolution under Lazaro Cardenas* (Chapel Hill, University of North Carolina Press, 1963).

Baena Paz, G., 'La Confederación General de Trabajadores (1921–31)', *Revista Mexicana de Ciencias Políticas y Sociales*, no. 83 (Jan.–March 1976).

Balan, J., *et al.*, *Men in a Developing Society* (Austin, University of Texas Press, 1973).

Barbosa Cano, F., *La CROM, de Luís Morones a Antonio J. Hernández* (Puebla, Universidad Autónoma de Puebla, 1980).

'El charrazo contra el STPRM', in J. Woldenberg *et al.*, *Memorias del encuentro sobre historia del movimiento obrero*, *q.v.*, vol. 2.

Barrios, E., *El escuadrón de hierro* (México, Cultura Popular, 1978).

Basurto, J., *El proletariado industrial en México (1850–1930)* (México, Universidad Nacional Autónoma de Mexico, 1975).

Bayoumi, O., 'State, Society and Development: Theoretical Considerations and a Mexican Case Study Focussing on the Current Political Reform' (unpublished Ph.D. thesis, London School of Economics, 1981).

Bazán, L., 'Sindicalismo independiente: el caso de Nissan' (mimeographed, Dec. 1977).

'El sindicato independiente de Nissan Mexicana' in J. Woldenberg *et al.*, *Memorias del encuentro sobre historia del movimiento obrero*, *q.v.*, vol. 3.

Bennett, D. C., and K. E. Sharpe, 'Agenda Setting and Bargaining Power: The Mexican State *versus* Transnational Automobile Corporations', *World Politics*, vol. 32, no. 1 (Oct. 1979).

Beynon, H., *Working for Ford* (London, Allen Lane, 1973).

Bizberg, I., *La acción obrera* (México, El Colegio de México, 1982).

Bizberg, I., and L. Barraza, 'La acción obrera en las truchas', *Revista Mexicana de Sociología*, vol. 42, no. 4 (Oct.–Dec. 1980).

Bortz, J. 'El salario obrero en el Distrito Federal, 1939–1975', *Investigación Económica*, no. 4 (Oct.–Dec. 1977).

Brading, D. (ed.), *Caudillo and Peasant in the Mexican Revolution* (Cambridge, Cambridge University Press, 1980).

Braverman, H., *Labor and Monopoly Capital* (New York, Monthly Review, 1974).

Camacho, M., *El futuro inmediato*, La clase obrera en la historia de México, vol. 15 (México, Siglo XXI, 1980).

Campa, V., *Mi testimonio* (México, Cultura Popular, 1978).

Campero, G., *et al.*, *La incorporación obrera en un medio de industrialización reciente* (México, Instituto Nacional de Estudios del Trabajo, 1977).

Cardoso, C. F. S. *et al.*, *De la dictadura porfirista a los tiempos libertarios*, La clase obrera en la historia de México, vol. 3 (México, Siglo XXI, 1980).

Carr, B., *El movimiento obrero y la política en México 1910–1929*, 2 vols. (México, Sepsetentas, 1976).

Chassen de López, F., *Lombardo Toledano y el movimiento obrero mexicano, 1917–1940* (México, Extemporáneos, 1977).

Clark, M. R., *Organized Labor in Mexico* (Chapel Hill, University of North Carolina Press, 1934).

Clegg, H., *The Changing System of Industrial Relations in Great Britain* (London, Blackwell, 1979).

Cockcroft, J., *Intellectual Precursors of the Mexican Revolution* (Austin, University of Texas Press, 1968).

Coleman, K., and C. Davis, 'Pre-emptive Reform and the Mexican Working Class', *Latin American Research Review*, vol. 18, no. 1 (1983).

Collier, D. (ed.), *The New Authoritarianism in Latin America* (Princeton, Princeton University Press, 1979).

Collier, R. B., and D. Collier, 'Inducements *versus* Constraints: Disaggregating Corporatism', *American Political Science Review*, vol. 73, no. 4 (Dec. 1979).

Contreras, A. J., *México 1940* (México, Siglo XXI, 1977).

Contreras, E., and G. Silva, 'Los recientes movimientos mexicanos pro independencia sindical y el reformismo obrero', *Revista Mexicana de Sociología*, vol. 34, nos. 3–4 (1972).

Contreras Suárez, E., *Estratificación y movilidad social en la Ciudad de México* (Mexico, UNAM, 1978).

Córdova, A., *La política de masas del Cardenismo* (México, ERA, 1974).

'El movimiento obrero mexicano en los albores de la crisis de 1929', *Estudios Políticos*, vol. 4, nos. 13–14 (Jan.–June 1978).

En una época de crisis, La clase obrera en la historia de México, vol. 9 (México, Siglo XXI, 1980).

Cornelius, W., 'Nation-Building, Participation, and Distribution: The Politics of Social Reform under Cardenas' in G. Almond *et al.* (eds.), *Crisis, Choice and Change* (Boston, Little Brown, 1973).

Crossick, G., *An Artisan Elite in Victorian Society* (London, Croom Helm, 1978).

Crouch, C., *The Politics of Industrial Relations* (London, Fontana, 1979).

de Neymet, M., *Cronología del Partido Comunista Mexicano* (México, Cultura Popular, 1981).

de Oliveira, O., 'Industrialization, Migration and Entry Labor Force Changes in Mexico City, 1930–1970' (unpublished Ph.D. thesis, University of Texas, 1975).

Migración y absorción de mano de obra en la Cuidad de México, 1930–1970, Cuardernos del CES, no. 14 (México, El Colegio de México, 1976).

de Schweinitz, K., *Industrialization and Democracy* (London, Collier-Macmillan, 1964).

di Tella, T., 'Populism and Reform in Latin America' in C. Veliz (ed.), *Obstacles to Change in Latin America* (Oxford, Oxford University Press, 1965).

Echeverría, M., *et al.*, 'El problema de la salud in DINA', *Cuadernos Políticos*, no. 26 (Oct.–Dec. 1980).

Edelstein, J., and M. Warner, *Comparative Union Democracy* (London, Allen and Unwin, 1975).

Erickson, K. P., *The Brazilian Corporative State and Working Class Politics* (Berkeley, University of California Press, 1977).

Estatutos de la CROC (México, Cuadernos Obreros, 1976).

Everett, M., 'La evolución de la estructura salarial en México: 1939–63', *Revista Mexicana de Sociología*, vol. 42, no. 1 (Jan.–March 1980).

Faba, G., 'Características del mercado de trabajo industrial: dos estudios realizados en México, *Revista Mexicana del Trabajo*, vol. 3, no. 1 (Jan.–March 1980).

Ferrante, V. L. B., *FGTS: ideologia e repressão* (São Paulo, Atica, 1978).

Fojo, A., 'Estudio de un conflicto industrial: el caso Automex' (mimeographed, 1973).

Ford, C., 'Past Developments and Future Trends in Mexican Automotive Policy', in Jan Herd (ed.), *The Automotive Industry in Latin America*, Northwestern Pennsylvania Institute for Latin American Studies, monograph no. 12 (Sept. 1980).

Form, W. H., *Blue-Collar Stratification* (Princeton, Princeton University Press, 1976).

Foster, J., *Class Struggle and the Industrial Revolution* (London, Weidenfeld and Nicolson, 1974).

Friedlander, P., *The Emergence of a UAW Local, 1936–1939* (Pittsburgh, University of Pittsburgh Press, 1975).

Friedman, A. L., *Industry and Labour* (London, Macmillan, 1977).

Gadian, D. S., 'Class Consciousness in Oldham and Other North-West Industrial Towns', *Historical Journal*, vol. 21, no. 1 (March 1978).

Galindo, M., 'El movimiento obrero en el sexenio echeverrista', *Investigación Económica*, no. 4 (1977).

Garcia Muñoz, H., 'Occupational and Earnings Inequalities in Mexico City' (unpublished Ph.D. thesis, University of Texas, 1975).

Garcia Muñoz, H., *et al.*, *Migración y desigualdad social en la Ciudad de México* (México, El Colegio de México, 1977).

Goldthorpe, J. H., *et al.*, *The Affluent Worker: Political Attitudes and Behaviour* (Cambridge, Cambridge University Press, 1968).

Gómez Tagle, S., *Insurgencia y democracia en los sindicatos electricistas* (México, El Colegio de México, 1980).

González Casanova, P., *En el primer gobierno constitucional*, La clase obrera en la historia de México, vol. 6 (México, Siglo XXI, 1980).

González Ramírez, M. (ed.), *La huelga de Cananea* (México, Fondo de Cultura, Económica, 1956).

Gray, R. Q., *The Labour Aristocracy in Victorian Edinburgh* (Oxford, Oxford University Press, 1976).

Grayson, G. *The Politics of Mexican Oil* (Pittsburgh, Pittsburgh University Press, 1980).

Gruening, E., *Mexico and its Heritage* (New York, Century, 1928).

Guadarrama, R., *Los sindicatos y la política en México: la CROM* (México, ERA, 1981).

Gudger, W., 'The Regulation of Multinational Corporations in the Mexican Automotive Industry' (unpublished Ph.D. thesis, University of Wisconsin, 1975).

Hamilton, N., *The Limits of State Autonomy* (Princeton, Princeton University Press, 1982).

Hamilton, R., *Affluence and the French Worker in the Fourth Republic* (Princeton, Princeton University Press, 1967).

Class and Politics in the United States (New York, Wiley, 1972).

Handelman, H., 'Oligarchy and Democracy in Two Mexican Labor Unions', *International Labor Relations Review*, vol. 30, no. 2 (1977).

Harding, T., 'The Political History of Organized Labor in Brazil' (unpublished Ph.D. thesis, Stanford University, 1973).

Harris, N., *Competition and the Corporate Society* (London, Methuen, 1972).

Hart, J., *Anarchists and the Mexican Working Class 1860–1931* (Austin, University of Texas Press, 1978).

'The Urban Working Class and the Mexican Revolution: The Case of the Casa del Obrero Mundial', *Hispanic American Historical Review*, vol. 58, no. 1 (1978).

Hennessy, A., 'Latin America' in G. Ionescu and E. Gellner (eds.), *Populism* (London, Weidenfeld and Nicolson, 1969).

Hernández, B., 'Del pacto de sindicatos industriales a la represión' in E. Suárez Gaona (ed.), *Memoria del Segundo Coloquio Regional de Historia Obrera*, 2 vols. (México, CEHSMO, 1979), vol. 2.

Hernández, S., 'Tiempos libertarios: el magonismo en México: Cananea, Rio Blanco y Baja California' in C. F. S. Cardoso *et al.*, *De la dictadura porfirista a los tiempos libertarios*, *q.v.*

Hernández Chávez, A., *La mecánica cardenista*, Historia de la revolución mexicana, vol. 16 (México, El Colegio de México, 1979).

Hildebrand, G., *American Unionism* (Reading, Mass., Addison-Wesley, 1979).

Humphrey, J., 'Operários da indústria automovilística no Brasil', *Estudos CEBRAP*, no. 23 (1979)
  Capitalist Control and Workers' Struggle in the Brazilian Auto Industry (Princeton, Princeton University Press, 1982).

Huntington, S., *Political Order in Changing Societies* (New Haven, Yale University Press, 1968).

Hyman, R., *Industrial Relations* (London, Macmillan, 1975).

James, D., 'Rationalisation and Working Class Response: The Context and Limits of Factory Floor Activity in Argentina', *Journal of Latin American Studies*, vol. 13, no. 2 (Nov. 1981).

Jenkins, R. O., *Dependent Industrialization in Latin America* (New York, Praeger, 1977).

Johnson, K. F., *Mexican Democracy: A Critical View* (New York, Praeger, 1978).

Juárez, A., *Las corporaciones transnacionales y los trabajadores mexicanos* (México, Siglo XXI, 1979).

Kaufman, R. R., 'Mexico and Latin American Authoritarianism' in Reyna and Weinert (eds.), *Authoritarianism in Mexico*, *q.v.*

Kruijt, D., and M. Vellinga, *Labor Relations and Multinational Corporations* (The Hague, Van Gorcum, 1980).

Laite, J., *Industrial Development and Migrant Labour* (Manchester, Manchester University Press, 1981).

Leal, J. F., *México: estado, burocracia y sindicatos* (México, El Caballito, 1975).

Leal, J. F., and J. Woldenberg, *Del estado liberal a los inicios de la dictadura porfirista*, La clase obrera en la historia de México, vol. 2 (México, Siglo XXI, 1980).

Leggett, J. C., *Class, Race and Labour* (Oxford, Oxford University Press, 1968).

Lenin, V. I., *What Is To Be Done?* (Moscow, Progress Publishers, 1964; originally published 1902).

León, S., 'El Comité Nacional de Defensa Proletaria', *Revista Mexicana de Sociología*, vol. 40, no. 2 (April–June 1978).

Levenstein, H., 'Leninists Undone by Leninism: Communism and Unionism in the United States and Mexico 1935–1939', *Labor History*, vol. 22, no. 2 (Spring 1981).

Lipset, S. M., M. Trow and J. Coleman, *Union Democracy* (New York, Doubleday, 1956).

Little, W., 'Popular Origins of Peronism' in D. Rock (ed.), *Argentina in the Twentieth Century* (London, Duckworth, 1975).

Lloyd, P., *A Third World Proletariat?* (London, Allen and Unwin, 1982).

Loyo, A., 'El movimiento obrero y la Segunda Guerra Mundial' in J. Woldenberg *et al.*, *Memorias de encuentro sobre historia del movimiento obrero*, *q.v.*, vol. 2.

Loyola Díaz, R., *La crisis Obregón–Calles y el estado mexicano* (México, Siglo XXI, 1980).

Malloy, J., 'Authoritarianism and Corporatism in Latin America: The Modal Pattern' in Malloy (ed.), *Authoritarianism and Corporatism in Latin America*, *q.v.*

Malloy, J. (ed.), *Authoritarianism and Corporatism in Latin America* (Pittsburgh, Pittsburgh University Press, 1977).

Márquez, M., and O. Rodríguez, *El Partido Comunista Mexicano* (México, El Caballito, 1973).

Martins Rodrigues, L., *Trabalhadores, sindicatos e industrialização* (São Paulo, Brasiliense, 1974).

Medina, L. *Del Cardenismo al Avilacamachismo*, Historia de la revolución mexicana, vol. 18 (México, El Colegio de México, 1978).
  Civilismo y modernización del autoritarismo, Historia de la revolución mexicana, vol. 20 (México, El Colegio de México, 1979).

Mericle, K., 'Conflict Regulation in the Brazilian Industrial Relations System' (unpublished Ph.D. thesis, University of Wisconsin, 1974).
  'Corporatist Control of the Working Class: Authoritarian Brazil since 1964' in Malloy (ed.), *Authoritarianism and Corporatism in Latin America*, *q.v.*

Meyer, J., 'Los obreros en la revolución mexicana: los batallones rojos', *Historia Mexicana*, July–Sept. 1971.
  La Cristiada, 3 vols. (México, Siglo XXI, 1973).

Michels, R., *Political Parties* (New York, Collier-Macmillan, 1962; originally published 1911).

Middlebrook, K., 'International Implications of Labor Change: The Automobile Industry' in J. Dominguez (ed.), *Mexico's Political Economy* (Beverly Hills, Sage, 1982).

Miller, R. U., 'The Role of Labor Organization in a Developing Country: The Case of Mexico' (unpublished Ph.D. thesis, Cornell University, 1966).

Miller, R. U., *et al.*, 'Modern Sector Internal Labor Market Structure and Urban Occupational Mobility' (mimeographed, 1976).

Moises, J., *Greve de massa e crise política* (São Paulo, Polis, 1978).

Molina, D., 'La política laboral y el movimiento obrero, 1970–76', *Cuadernos Políticos*, no. 12 (1977).

Moorehouse, H. F., 'The Marxist Theory of the Labour Aristocracy', *Social History*, vol. 3, no. 1 (Jan. 1978).

Murmis, M., and J. C. Portantiero, *Estudios sobre los orígines del peronismo*, vol. 1 (Buenos Aires, Siglo XXI, 1971).

Newman, O., *The Challenge of Corporatism* (London, Macmillan, 1981).

Novelo, V., and A. Urteaga, *La industria en los magueyales* (México, Nueva Imagen, 1979).

Nun, J., 'La industria automotríz argentina', *Revista Mexicana de Sociología*, vol. 40, no. 1 (1978).

O'Donnell, G., *Modernization and Bureaucratic-Authoritarianism* (Berkeley, Institute of International Studies, University of California, 1973).

'Reflections on the Pattern of Change in the Bureaucratic-Authoritarian State', *Latin American Research Review*, vol. 13, no. 1 (1978).

'Tensions in the Bureaucratic-Authoritarian State and the Question of Democracy' in Collier (ed.), *The New Authoritarianism in Latin America*, *q.v.*

'Reply to Remmer and Merkx', *Latin American Research Review*, vol. 17, no. 2 (1982).

Payne, J., *Labor and Politics in Peru* (New Haven, Yale University Press, 1965).

Peláez, G., *Partido Comunista Mexicano: 60 años de historia* (Culiacán, Universidad Autónoma de Sinaloa, 1980).

Pellicer de Brody, O., and J. L. Reyna, *El afianzamiento de la estabilidad política*, Historia de la revolución mexicana, vol. 22 (México, El Colegio de México, 1978).

Poniatowska, E., *La noche de Tlatelolco* (México, ERA, 1971).

Quijano, A., 'The Marginal Pole of the Economy and the Marginalized Labour Force', *Economy and Society*, vol. 3, no. 4 (1974).

Quiroz,Trejo, J. O. 'Proletariado e industria automotríz' in E. Suárez Gaona (ed.), *Memoria del Segundo Coloquio Regional de Historia Obrera*, 2 vols. (México, CEHSMO, 1979), vol. 2.

'Proceso de trabajo en la industria automotríz', *Cuadernos Políticos*, no. 26 (Oct.–Dec, 1980).

Ramos, S., *et al.*, *Spicer, S.A.* (México, UNAM, 1979).

Reid, A., 'Politics and Economics in the Formation of the British Working Class', *Social History*, vol. 3, no. 3 (Oct. 1978).

Remmer, K. L. and G. W. Merkx, 'Bureaucratic-Authoritarianism Revisited', *Latin American Research Review*, vol. 17, no. 2 (1982).

Remolina Roqueñi, F., *Evolución de las instituciones y del derecho del trabajo en México* (México, Junta Federal de Conciliación y Arbitraje, 1976).

Reyna, J. L., 'Redefining the Authoritarian Regime' in Reyna and Weinert (eds.), *Authoritarianism in Mexico, q.v.*

Reyna, J. L., and R. S. Weinert (eds.), *Authoritarianism in Mexico* (Philadelphia, ISHI, 1971).

Reyna, J. L., *et al.*, *Tres estudios sobre el movimiento obrero en México* (México, El Colegio de México, 1976).

Rivera Flores, A., 'UGOCM, 1946–52' in J. Woldenberg *et al.*, *Memorias del encuentro sobre historia del movimiento obrero, q.v.*, vol. 2.

Roberts, B., *Cities of Peasants* (London, Edward Arnold, 1978).

Rodríguez, M., *Los tranviarios y el anarquismo en México* (Puebla, Universidad Autónoma de Puebla, 1980).

Ronfeldt, D., *Atencingo: The Politics of Agrarian Struggle in a Mexican Ejido* (Stanford, Stanford University Press, 1973).

Roxborough, I., 'Perspectivas del sistema político mexicano' in A. Muñoz (ed.), *Perspectivas del sistema político mexicano* (México, PRI, 1982).

'El sindicalismo en el sector automotríz', *Estudios Sociológicos*, vol. 1, no. 1 (Jan.–April 1983).

Roxborough, I., and Bizberg, I., 'Union Locals in Mexico', *Journal of Latin American Studies*, vol. 15, no. 1 (May 1983).

Ruiz, R., *Labor and the Ambivalent Revolutionaries: Mexico 1911–1923* (Baltimore, Johns Hopkins University Press, 1976).

The Great Rebellion (New York, Norton, 1980).

Salamini, H. F., *Agrarian Radicalism in Veracruz, 1920–1938* (London, University of Nebraska Press, 1971).

Sánchez, V. M., *El surgimiento del sindicalismo electricista* (México, Universidad Nacional Autónoma de Mexico, 1978).

Sánchez Díaz, S. G., 'Sobre la Unidad Obrera Independiente' in J. Woldenberg et al., *Memorias del encuentro sobre historia del movimiento obrero*, q.v., vol. 3.

Schlagheck, J., *The Political, Economic and Labor Climate in Mexico*, Wharton School Multinational Industrial Relations Series (Philadelphia, University of Pennsylvania, 1977).

Schmitter, P., *Interest Conflict and Political Change in Brazil* (Stanford, Stanford University Press, 1971).

Schonfield, A., *Modern Capitalism* (Oxford, Oxford University Press, 1965).

Secretaría de Programación Presupuesto, *La industria automotríz en México* (México, Secretaría de Programación y Presupuesto, 1981).

Serra, J., 'Three Mistaken Theses Regarding the Connection between Industrialization and Authoritarian Regimes' in D. Collier (ed.), *The New Authoritarianism in Latin America*, q.v.

Shulgovski, A., *México en la encrucijada de su historia* (México, Cultura Popular, 1968).

Skidmore, T., 'The Politics of Economic Stabilization in Postwar Latin America' in J. Malloy (ed.), *Authoritarianism and Corporatism in Latin America*, q.v.

'Workers and Soldiers: Urban Labor Movements and Elite Responses in Twentieth Century Latin America' in V. Bernhard (ed.), *Elites, Masses and Modernization in Latin America 1850–1930* (Austin, University of Texas Press, 1979).

Solís, L., *La realidad económica mexicana* (México, Siglo XXI, 1970).

Stepan, A., *The State and Society* (Princeton, Princeton University Press, 1978).

Stevens, E., *Protest and Response in Mexico* (Cambridge, Mass., MIT Press, 1974).

Tello, C., *La política económica en México, 1970–76* (México, Siglo XXI, 1979).

Thompson, M., and I. Roxborough, 'Union Elections and Democracy in Mexico', *British Journal of Industrial Relations*, vol. 20, no. 2 (July 1982).

Torre, J. C., 'Sobre as origens do Peronismo', *Estudos CEBRAP*, no. 16 (April–June 1976).

Trejo, R., 'The Mexican Labor Movement', *Latin American Perspectives*, vol. 3, no. 1 (1976).

Tres huelgas telefonistas (México, Uno Más Uno, 1980).

'Notas sobre la insurgencia obrera y la burocracia sindical' in J. Woldenberg et al., *Memorias del encuentro sobre historia del movimiento obrero*, q.v., vol. 3.

Trejo, R., and J. Woldenberg, 'Los trabajadores y la crisis' in R. Cordero (ed.), *Desarrollo y crisis de la economía mexicana* (México, Fondo de Cultura Económica, 1981).

Turner, H. A., *et al.*, *Labour Relations in the Motor Industry* (London, Allen and Unwin, 1967).

van Ginneken, W., *Socio-Economic Groups and Income Distribution in Mexico* (London, Croom Helm, 1980).

Vargas, H., 'Historia verdadera de la conquista de la clase obrera', *El Machete*, no. 14 (June 1981).

Vázquez Trejo, H., *Una década de política sobre industria automotríz* (México, Tecnos, 1975).

Vellinga, M., *Economic Development and the Dynamics of Class* (The Hague, Van Gorcum, 1979).

Villaseñor, V. M., *Memorias de un hombre de izquierda*, 2 vols. (México, Grijalbo, 1976).

Wells, J., 'Underconsumption, Market Size and Expenditure Patterns in Brazil', *Bulletin of the Society for Latin American Studies*, no. 24 (March 1976).

Whitehead, L., 'On "Governability" in Mexico', *Bulletin of Latin American Research*, vol. 1, no. 1 (Oct. 1981).

Wiarda, H., 'Corporative Origins of the Iberian and Latin American Labor Relations Systems', *Studies in Comparative International Development*, vol. 13, no. 1 (Spring 1978).

Woldenberg, J., *et al.*, *Memorias del encuentro sobre historia del movimiento obrero*, 3 vols. (Puebla, Universidad Autónoma de Puebla, 1980–1).

Würtele, W., 'International Trade Union Solidarity and the Internationalization of Capital' (unpublished paper, 1977).

Zapata, F., 'Afiliación y organización sindical en México' in J. L. Reyna *et al.*, *Tres estudios sobre el movimiento obrero en México, q.v.*

Zapata, F. (ed.), *Las Truchas* (México, El Colegio de México, 1978).

Zazueta, C., and S. Geluda, *Población, planta industrial y sindicatos* (México, Centro Nacional de Información y Estadísticas del Trabajo, 1981).

Zazueta, C., and R. de la Peña, *Estructura dual y piramidal de sindicalismo mexicano* (México, CENIET, 1981).

Zermeño, S., *México: una democracia utópica* (México, Siglo XXI, 1978).

Index

CAMBRIDGE LATIN AMERICAN STUDIES

* Published in paperback only.